EDUCATIONAL FREEDOM

FREEDOM

IN URBAN AMERICA

EDUCATIONAL FREEDOM

IN URBAN AMERICA

Brown v. Board after Half a Century

•

Edited by

David Salisbury and Casey Lartigue Jr.

CATO INSTITUTE
Washington, D.C.

Library of Congress Cataloging-in-Publication Data

Educational freedom in urban America : Brown v. Board after
half a century / edited by David Salisbury and Casey Lartigue Jr.
   p. cm.
Includes bibliographical references and index.
ISBN 1-930865-56-2 (cloth : alk. paper)
1. Education, Urban—United States. 2. Educational equalization—
United States. 3. Educational vouchers—United States. 4. School
choice—United States. I. Salisbury, David F., 1951– II. Lartigue,
Casey. III. Title.

LC5131.E364 2004
379.2'6'0973—dc22

                                                                2004045478

Cover design by Elise Rivera.

Printed in the United States of America.

CATO INSTITUTE
1000 Massachusetts Ave., N.W.
Washington, D.C. 20001
www.cato.org

Contents

Preface

Fifty years ago the U.S. Supreme Court issued its landmark ruling known as *Brown v. Board of Education*. The ruling struck down segregated public schooling. As the court wrote, "We conclude that in the field of public education the doctrine of 'separate but equal' has no place. Separate educational facilities are inherently unequal." But almost five decades later, public education remains unequal. Forty-five percent of black and 47 percent of Hispanic students drop out of public high schools (compared with 24 percent of whites). Only 5 percent of black and 10 percent of Hispanic fourth-graders reach the proficient level on the math portion of the National Assessment of Educational Progress (compared with 33 percent of whites). Minority children living in America's inner cities suffer disproportionately from a failing education system.

After 50 years of reforms, urban public school leaders still battle problems with horrendous drop-out rates, abysmal test scores, and school safety. The 2003 report titled "Status and Trends in the Education of Blacks," released by the National Center for Education Statistics, showed that performance gaps between black and white students ages 13 to 17 have widened in the last decade.

The continuing failure of public schools to provide a quality educational experience to inner-city children led the Cato Institute to convene a conference last year. The purpose of the conference was to examine the state of urban education half a century after *Brown v. Board of Education*. Conference participants were also asked to answer this question: How can inner-city students achieve the goal of educational freedom and equality? Most of the chapters in this volume were selected from the papers presented at that conference. Taken together, the chapters paint a dismal picture of educational quality in America's urban centers. The situation could be described as a sea of failure dotted by a few exceptional success stories.

To start off the volume, Howard Fuller, director of Marquette University's Institute for the Transformation of Learning, places the fight for school choice at the forefront of the ongoing struggle for social justice. "We must give poor parents the power to choose schools—public or private, nonsectarian or religious—where their children will succeed," he says.

Floyd Flake, pastor and former congressman, argues that *Brown* has failed to bring educational equality to minority youth. As we work to enlarge choice, we also need to look for ways to improve the public schools. Flake, a member of the President's Commission on Special Education, leveled heavy criticism at the special education system, which he said is too often used as a dumping ground for children with behavioral problems or who have simply fallen behind in school.

Gerard Robinson contrasts the post-*Brown* private school tuition grant movement that arose in several Southern states as a way to circumvent *Brown* with the school choice movement of the 1990s. Both of these movements involved vouchers and both used the term *freedom of choice* in their rhetoric. But their goals and ideology were diametrically opposed.

Next, Paul Peterson provides an analysis of the historic 2002 Supreme Court decision, *Zelman v. Simmons-Harris*, which held that school choice programs, if properly constructed, do not violate constitutional prohibitions against church and state entanglements. Peterson also highlights the differences between *Zelman* and *Brown*. The main difference, of course, is that *Brown* was "self-enacting"— that is, states were required to abide by it. *Zelman*, however, merely *allows* states to enact school choice measures if they wish to do so; and the political struggle for vouchers still requires substantial political muscle.

Casey Lartigue's chapter documents the history of educational failure in the nation's capital city, despite relatively high per pupil expenditures. Since that chapter was written, the U.S. Congress passed a measure that will provide vouchers to low-income children in the district's worse schools, allowing them to escape to better private schools.

Chaim Karczag of the National Council on Teacher Quality discusses the impact that teacher certification has on school quality and argues for greater flexibility in teacher certification requirements. Rather than simply ensuring the qualifications of all educators, Karczag shows how U.S. teacher certification laws have the unintended consequence of depressing teacher quality. Urban school districts are the ones that are most often left in the lurch by the smaller-than-necessary supply of excellent teachers.

Eric Wearne reports on a survey of Atlanta's private and public schools and reveals that many children in Atlanta are still forced to attend highly segregated public schools. Atlanta's private schools on the other hand, are significantly more racially integrated showing that educational quality now takes precedence over race when parents choose their children's schools. School choice, Wearne concludes, would not only improve school quality but would foster racial integration as well.

Private scholarships are another solution that have helped thousands of inner-city children gain access to quality schools. Tracey Johnson, executive director of the Washington Scholarship Fund, describes the success of the private voucher movement and its role in helping inner-city children attend better schools.

The challenges faced by enterprising and idealistic educators in founding an inner-city charter school is described by Irasema Salcido in her chapter on the Cesar Chavez Public Charter High School. Although the challenges have been great, the Cesar Chavez school is without question an island of success in the ocean of D.C.'s failing public-school system.

David Bositis of the Joint Center for Political and Economic Studies examines public attitudes toward school choice on the basis of national surveys conducted by the Center over the past six years. Although support for vouchers has increased among both white and black populations, these increases have not resulted in strong political support for school vouchers because the increase has been primarily among younger families. Older voters tend to oppose vouchers and they still hold a solid majority at the polls.

David Salisbury's chapter reports the results of a survey of private school costs in six major U.S. cities. Contrary to what many people think, private schools are not too pricey to be within reach of kids who are helped by a voucher or tax credit.

Frederick Hess of the American Enterprise Institute describes how competition can bring dramatic and positive change to urban schooling. He also describes the complementary reforms that will be needed to foster a productive market environment, such as freeing urban public school leaders from constraints that hamper their ability to respond constructively to competition. Hess also cautions against half measures: A small number of charter schools or school vouchers will not be sufficient to force systemic improvement on public schools. Only a full-fledged competitive market environment can do that.

Andrew Coulson's contribution is a comprehensive scholarly review of the literature on private versus public schooling in less developed countries. His analysis is enlightening because it reveals the features associated with superior school performance: choice and direct financial responsibility for parents and freedom, competition, and the profit motive for schools. On the basis of this analysis, Coulson concludes that a program of tuition tax credits is the most desirable policy for promoting educational excellence. The constituency poised to benefit most from education tax credits would be students in large cities. Therefore, Coulson proposes an "urban-first" phase-in of education tax credits.

As children reach school age, middle-class families regularly flee America's inner cities and escape to the suburbs, largely because of inferior and unsafe urban schools. As long as this is true, lower-income Americans will be left with inner-city schools that are, in practice, separate and unequal. As we look for ways to reform urban education, the Cato Institute is proud to offer this collection of essays. We think that they make a valuable contribution to the debate about how to achieve the dream of *Brown v. Board of Education*.

David Salisbury
Casey Lartigue Jr.

Acknowledgments

The Cato Institute expresses its appreciation to Ronald B. Rankin for his contribution to the production of this book and the Kern Family Foundation for its support of the Center for Educational Freedom.

1. The Continuing Struggle for School Choice

Howard Fuller

Martin Luther King Jr. wrote that the central quality in black people's lives is pain—"pain so old and so deep that it shows in almost every moment of [our] existence."[1] The pain was deep when we were told to move to the back of the bus. Our hearts and minds were scarred when we were told, "Niggers ain't allowed to eat here!" These dehumanizing acts caused pain and left scars. But there is nothing more painful than watching our children drop (or be pushed) out of school uneducated.

Black Americans are at a strange point in our history. Because of the gains made in the 1960s, 1970s, and 1980s—and some in the 1990s—more opportunities have opened up for us. The "talented tenth" W. E. B. Du Bois described—business leaders, scientists, celebrities, intellectuals, and political leaders who pull along the other members of a cultural group—has never been more in evidence in the black community. We have black people at all levels of the political structure of this country. We have black millionaires. We influence the cultural direction of this country with our music and the way we dress. We have young men making millions of dollars for bouncing a ball or tackling somebody who has a ball—and then getting millions more hawking T-shirts and sweatshirts and athletic shoes. At the same time, we have young men killing each other for those shoes.

These examples show the dichotomy between black folks who have made it and the masses of our people who know another kind of reality. When I travel around the country and see what is happening to our children, I know that far too many of them are dying physically and mentally. It's clear to me that we have got to have a multifaceted strategy to save our children. We know that education alone cannot do it. But what is equally clear is that education will be the cornerstone of any broad strategy that we develop and pursue.

In many areas of this country, including the District of Columbia, our failure to educate poor African-American children precludes them from becoming effective participants in our democracy. The message that teachers and schools send to our children is that "my paycheck is going to come whether you learn or not."

I believe that Mortimer Adler was right when he said there are no unteachable children. What we have are adults who have not figured out how to teach them.[2] Too many of our children are forced to stay in schools that do not work for them and, frankly, didn't work for their parents. They and their families lack the power to influence the educational institutions that continue not to serve them well.

Let me be clear about the philosophical context of my argument. I take my view of education from Paulo Freire's book, *Pedagogy of the Oppressed.* In the foreword, Richard Shaull writes—

> There is no such thing as a neutral educational process. Education functions as either an instrument which is used to facilitate the integration of the younger generation into the logic of the present order and bring about conformity to it, or it becomes 'the practice of freedom.'[3]

When education is "the practice of freedom" it enables men and women to participate in the transformation of their world. I want our children to have that power, so that they can create the 21st century rather than just live in it.

Freedom, Martin Luther King Jr. wrote, is first "the capacity to deliberate or to weigh alternatives. 'Shall I be a doctor or a lawyer?' Freedom then demands making a decision and accepting responsibility for it."[4]

Democracy, according to Dr. Kenneth Clark, "depends upon our ability to extend and deepen the insights of the people. Only an educated people can be expected to make the type of choices which assert their freedoms and reinforce their sense of social responsibility."[5] Thus education is essential to freedom and democracy.

Our mission at the Black Alliance for Educational Options is to actively support parental choice, empower families, and increase educational options for black children. We support means-tested vouchers, homeschooling, charter schools, contract schools, black independent schools, and other public and private choices. We do not support the destruction of public education. One of the reasons that people continue to run that bogus line is that they do not make a distinction between public education, which is a concept, and the system that *delivers* public education. The system that *delivers* public education, as we've structured it in America, is not public education. Public education is the concept that it is in our interest to educate all our children. What makes public education public is that it serves the public's interests. Is it available to everyone? Is it something we can all access? I would humbly argue that a school district that continues to push children out, that continues for whatever reason to be unable to teach our children to read and write, that graduates children who can't read and write, is not in the public's interest. What we therefore have to do is to commit to a *purpose*, not institutional arrangements.

You can have a lot of different delivery systems; that's clear in higher education. People have no problem with students taking Pell Grants to religious schools. People have no problems with G.I. Bill money being taken to private schools. Nobody said that was destroying public education.

Say that you have on the corner a school that everyone knows has never educated anybody's kids, but it's a "public" school. You've got another school four blocks away that is able, for whatever reason, to educate the children that can't be educated at the other one, but that school is, oh my God, a religious school. I would argue that it is in the public's interest to put the children where they can be educated.

There was a time when it was "progressive" to fight the bureaucracy. There was a time when some of us carried signs that said, "Power to the people." What is interesting is that some of the folks who used to rail against the bureaucracy now *are* the bureaucracy. The discussion is no longer about empowering the people to fight the bureaucracy. Now we're supposed to believe that magically, because they're in charge, the people's interests are going to be met. I believe the people's interests are going to be met only when the people are empowered to fight for their interests.

We have to ask why people do not want low-income parents to have choice. The hypocrisy on this point is phenomenal. We have teachers teaching in schools that they would never put their own children in and then demanding that somebody else's children stay there. We have public school teachers putting their own children in private schools. We have leaders in Congress pontificating against choice who have their own children in private schools. The argument always comes down to "If we let these poor parents out, it will destroy the system." I have a question: Is it about the system, or is it about the parents and the children?

In *Exit, Voice, and Loyalty*, Albert O. Hirschman argues that if you lack the capacity to exit an organization, your voice is diminished; when you have the power to leave, your voice is enhanced.[6] If you have the power to leave and decide to stay, you develop a deeper form of loyalty to that organization. There are excellent public schools, and terrible public schools. There are excellent private schools, and terrible private schools. We want our parents to decide which are which.

Over the last 14 years, I've heard all of the objections. One that I find interesting is that we don't know about choice because it's new. There's nothing new about choice. People with money in America have always had choice. If you have money and the public schools do not work for your children, you're going to do one of two things. You're going to move to a community where the public schools do work, or you're going to put your kids in a private school.

I understand that our position is controversial. But social change is always controversial. It transfers power to people who have never had it and takes power from those who have had it. How can that not be controversial? But you know what? We think it is the right thing to do, and we are willing to fight forever on this point. We understand that the race goes, not to the swift, but to those who can endure until the end. We intend to endure to the end.

Notes

1. Martin Luther King Jr., *Where Do We Go From Here: Chaos or Community?* (Boston: Beacon Press, 1968), pp. 102–103.

2. Mortimer Adler, *Paideia Proposal* (New York: Touchstone Books, 1998).

3. Paulo Freire, *Pedagogy of the Oppressed* (New York: Continuum, 2000).

4. King, p. 98.

5. Kenneth B. Clark, "Educational Stimulation of Racially Disadvantaged Children" in *Education in Depressed Areas*, ed. A. Harry Passow (New York: Teachers College Columbia Press, 1963), p. 145.

6. Albert O. Hirchman, *Exit, Voice, and Loyalty* (Cambridge, Mass.: Harvard University Press, 1972).

2. Fulfilling the Legacy of *Brown v. Board of Education*

Floyd Flake

I truly believe in the importance of having alternative educational sources. That's why I am so pleased that we recently followed through on our decision to increase the size of our school, Allen Christian School in Jamaica, New York, from 538 to more than 800. Annually we have between 200 and 250 people on our waiting list. We hope that the education we are providing will enable more families to benefit from what we are trying to accomplish.

Breaking ground in an effort to bring educational opportunity to another 250 children might not seem like a major achievement to some. But it is important. Expanding and opening new schools is the direction we're going to have to go in the future if we're serious about improving the quality of education for children, especially those who are not well served.

The reality of providing enough spaces for children is a challenge. But we have faced many challenges before and we've been able to overcome them. My first challenge became clear in 1970 when I started as dean of Lincoln University and later moved on to become dean of Boston University. Over those six years, I was able to see a transition that was taking place in education. It became clear that we were not getting enough young people from urban communities who had the tools to compete academically. We had to develop alternative programs within the structure of the university to accommodate them.

The discussions in the last few years about remedial education have provided me with a sense of déjà vu. The reality is that we started remedial education programs long before the last two or three years. It hasn't been a recent phenomenon for many of the urban kids not to be getting access to the kind of quality education that would lead them into higher education. There has been a lot of change that looks the same. As pastor of a church that has run

5

its own school for 20 years, as dean at two universities in the 1970s, and now as president of Wilberforce University in Xenia, Ohio, I see that we have come full circle.

We still are not doing a quality job in K–12 education. We are challenged by urban kids coming out of environments that haven't prepared them for college. We must have the necessary support system put in place to get them to focus on the value of an education. That is key because we must give them the sense that ultimately the quality of their education will make the difference between whether or not they will be at the high or low end of the pole as it relates to wealth building and prosperity.

The challenge we face is trying to get young people to understand that there is a possibility, and there are creative means by which we can teach these young people, if we would only open up the door and dare to believe that we can raise levels of expectations. We can challenge them to the point that they honestly believe within themselves that they have the capability to succeed.

On top of that, the recent census data suggest that current population shifts are going to have a serious impact on those young people who are already in severe educational circumstances. African-Americans will not be the largest minority class at the next census. That means that these youngsters, who often lack a command of English, will be competing in a test-based culture in which they must have the skills to pass the test.

These young people are not being prepared to even get to first base because they can't pass the tests at the lower levels. The ACT and SAT will be an incredible barrier for them. If you look at where they've failed, even if they're relatively good in math, they fail in basic reading comprehension. I believe that we have the ability to change that, and a part of that process of change means that we have to look at all of the alternatives that are available to us. Most urban systems are not ready to make the kind of radical changes that are essential to ensuring that every child has what *Brown v. Board of Education* guaranteed. *Brown v. Board* in my opinion guaranteed that every child would have access to a quality education that is of equal value, regardless of where that child happens to be educated, whether it is a suburban, a rural, or an inner-city community. We know that is not happening. We know that even in many suburban communities, those families that moved there in the hopes of being able to educate their young people are finding that African-American young people are still, generally, behind whites academically. How do we change this? Let me suggest a couple of things that I think may help us. One is vouchers, the other is charter schools.

Now, there are many people who obviously find the idea of vouchers to be somewhat difficult to swallow. While I think vouchers are important, I realize that small voucher programs cannot be the total answer. One reason they cannot be the total answer is that they will never be big enough to bring all of the struggling young people along. Also, legislatures will control the dynamics of the voucher process by imposing regulations on private schools. Even if you set up private vouchers, as the Children's Scholarship Fund did, the reality is you will only be able to educate a limited number of students. The question becomes, what do you do with the rest of them?

Another reason the voucher process is a problem is that many of the institutions in which vouchers can be traded are already oversubscribed. In most urban communities, vouchers go to Catholic schools or other religious schools like the one I run and, in most instances, those schools cannot absorb any more students than they already have. In addition, thus far, vouchers do not represent enough of an income source to justify expanding properties or capital base so that those institutions can grow. Yet, vouchers are still a major player. They bring a level of attention to the problems of education that forces us to deal with the reality that parents are desperate to get education for their children. They cause us to have to deal with the reality that in spite of the fact that there are those who would suggest that those are poor parents and they really don't know, the reality is they do know. They know what they want for their children, they're willing to make sacrifices to try to give them the best education possible and, in many instances, what they discover is that there is nothing they can do about the situation. Even the No Child Left Behind legislation is limited in dealing with this problem. Children supposedly are able to transfer from one school to another, but the reality is that most of the schools they could transfer to are already oversubscribed and there are still barriers in the districts against such transfers.

Our reality then is that we have to look at other alternatives. Charter schools represent probably one of the greatest possibilities but, again, we're in a position in which legislative control will never let charters settle on a solid foundation. Legislators are not going to allow charters to be able to get the running start that they would need to be in a position in which they would be as competitive as possible. Right now charters are limited in the amount of funding they receive, which is generally two-thirds or less of what is given to traditional schools. They lack access to the capital necessary to acquire adequate facilities. The probability is that this model, as good as it might be, won't reach its potential. The other problem is that, in many instances, the charter school process did not do a great job of screening persons who were coming into the business. What has happened in many of these charter schools is that people who have never been in the education business or have been in the business of teaching but never as an administrator are now running schools. What they're discovering is what I learned 20 years ago. In my situation, if our church had not put up a $40,000-a-month subsidy into the program, our school would not be able to operate. Charter school operators don't have a place to go to be able to get that subsidy to make their schools operative and to make them as competitive as they can possibly be.

So those two models may not have enough capacity to be able to solve the problem. What are we left with? The reality is we're still left with the traditional public system. The changes must be made within; the challenges are great, but the opportunities are many. The question is, what do we do within the public structure then to be able to change public education in a way in which every child receives the fullness of the promise and the guarantee that *Brown v. Board of Education* intended? I would suggest to you that several things must happen.

First of all, we probably need a whole new training modality as it relates to teachers who are going to function in public schools. I think there is a sense that when a teacher comes into that environment, they generally take on the culture of the environment, believing that these kids cannot learn. The reality is that most of the kids *can* learn but too many people have taken the position that they cannot.

Many of us would not be where we are today if such judgments had been made about us early on. I was a behavior problem, and I will confess to that. Decades later, I can afford to confess to many things. By definition, if you're going around and turning on water faucets because you want to see how much water will flood the school on weekends, and unplugging ice cream machines to see whether or not the ice cream would melt by Monday morning, that's a behavior problem. It did not mean that I was sick or disabled. It's just that I had some behavioral issues. That's what many of these young people are going through. The nuclear family structure as we know it is gone. Mothers and fathers are younger, many kids are being raised by grandparents or by anybody who happens to have the luxury of being able to take them in. They don't have the time, the talent, or the energy to be able to invest in the child in the same way we have traditionally seen those investments made. And so we have seen a paradigm shift, and in that paradigm shift many of these young people find themselves struggling, trying to find themselves, and their hope is that ultimately—either by athletic skills, entertainment capabilities, or some other means—they will be able to rise above and come out of their ghetto experiences. In reality, most of them will not have the talent to go to the pros as an athlete or to make it in entertainment.

Every once in a while someone will succeed that way, meaning, sadly, that a number of other young people will believe they can be the next "50 Cent." The new sensation is 50 Cent. He's from my neighborhood. He doesn't have an education, but he's been writing music, selling his CDs on the corner for years, and he's finally made it. Such success stories will be few and far between, so we have to make sure that we give the other young people the best possible education. It is still education that provides the key that unlocks the door to the possibility of being able to compete in a society that is always demanding and always requiring so much more of individuals who are part of this landscape. And with that in mind, it becomes incumbent upon educators and legislators to open the doors to allow educational options to flourish.

First, we need to get away from traditions that have locked out so many people who have the potential to become much greater than they are now. And they could be greater if we would just give them the opportunity to do so.

Second, we probably need to diminish, if not eliminate, special education. As a member of the President's Commission on Special Education, I can tell you that in too many cases special education has become the dumping bin for children whose teachers cannot or do not know how to educate. What teachers do is merely dump those children into this bin, sit them on the side, and take them outside of the classroom without the sense of a reality that those kids will never be able to get back into a traditional track. For the most part, a large percentage of them will later wind up being incarcerated. If they are taken out of the classroom at the fourth grade, for instance, they're not coming back into a regular class four years later. By then they've gotten to a place where they know that coming back into the classroom means that they are scarred and marked. What they do is drift into the streets. By the time they get into the streets, they are lost. There is no reversal in the process and there is no rehabilitative process once they become a part of the incarcerated population. Special education was intended to address the problems of the most severely damaged young people. Now we take behavioral problems and treat them as if they are, in fact, disabilities. And in most instances, the problems are not about disabilities. Problems proliferate because many teachers lack the ability to maintain the kind of discipline that is necessary to train young people. Too many teachers think the antics of the students are funny. I've been in classrooms with teachers sitting there laughing at the antics that I would never tolerate, and I suspect many of you would never tolerate, and certainly the teachers I grew up with would never tolerate. Of course, those were the days of corporal punishment. Parents did not call lawyers. If anything, parents exacerbated your condition by letting you know that they agreed with the teacher by punishing you all over again. But the reality is that those days are long gone. We may not all wish for those days again, but certainly we would hope for the kind of discipline that allows for an environment in which education can take place.

Third, we need to resist the temptation to lower expectations for those young people. When we lower the level of expectations, what we in fact do is lower their ability to compete. No matter where that level of expectation is, the children are going to try, if they try at all, to reach that level of expectation. If it is low, it means they will end up below where others with high expectations will be. That is because those who they're competing against will have outperformed them. When those young people graduate and enter the marketplace, they will discover that they've been handed a bogus piece of paper. And in spite of the fact that we would argue that social promotions have come to an end, the reality is they have not. Because every child represents a dollar value within the system, most schools are not prepared to lose those students. That is true, even if it means pushing them along and not giving them the kind of tools they need to survive.

Lastly, let me suggest the other need that is lacking for most of those young people. A tremendous difference exists between what is available in the average urban school and what is available in the average suburban school. In many instances, what is available in one part of a district is not available in another part of the same district even though the same state dollars are going into that school system. We have long thought that integration would mean the integration of all resources. We must deal with the reality that those resources have not been allocated equitably. Those young people need access to the kind of tools that they will have to work with when they go directly into higher education or the marketplace, and so we need to make sure that public school districts allocate resources fairly.

Much work still needs to be done before we can say that every child has access to a quality education. We need to give parents more options through vouchers, through charter schools, and through more choice. We also need to make sure that those who teach our young people in the public schools actually believe that they can learn. Finally, we need to make sure that young people, particularly those in urban areas, are not shortchanged through the inequitable allocation of resources. Only when these needs are fulfilled and when parents have options, can we say that we have fulfilled the legacy of *Brown v. Board.*

3. Freedom of Choice: *Brown*, Vouchers, and the Philosophy of Language

Gerard Robinson

Freedom of Choice: Introduction

I suppose you mean to say, Cratylus, that as the name is, so also is the thing, and that he who knows the one will also know the other, because they are similars, and all similars fall under the same art or science, and therefore you would say that he who knows names will also know things.[1]

— Socrates

Freedom and *choice* are concepts deeply embedded into the American political psyche. Each idea embodies the founding spirit of the Republic, as well as the ambition of our 18th century "Charters of Freedom"—the Declaration of Independence, the Constitution, and the Bill of Rights.[2] Government officials have for more than 200 years struggled with the responsibility to incorporate freedom and choice into American society. The advancement or curtailment of freedom and choice will remain an energetic battle as long as these terms are used by organized interests seeking to advance their own particular ideology or goals.

The 20th century is replete with examples of organized interests advancing their own agenda by capturing the terms *freedom* and *choice* and using them to their own ends. Advocates of policies such as free housing for the poor, reproductive rights for women, and union membership all used *freedom* and *choice* to advance their particular political causes. But few policy topics reveal the schizophrenic nature of American politics when it comes to freedom and choice as well as education. It is here where modern anxiety about freedom and choice fuels two competing philosophies regarding the role of schooling in a democratic society.

Differing definitions of freedom and choice in education have competed for acceptance during the 20th century. The same battle continues today. This is why organized interests remain in perpetual competition to define freedom and choice for our nation's schools. Although the meaning of these terms sounds seemingly straightforward, implementation of freedom and choice in American education has had a strange career. "Freedom of choice" in the 20th century gave birth to two private choice movements: one was fear-based, the other freedom-based. Each movement shares the identical "freedom of choice" name, but the latter movement suffers from mistaken identity.

The fear-based choice movement began in the South during the 1950s as a backlash against the Supreme Court's decision in *Brown v. Board of Education*, which required states to desegregate all public schools.[3] Southern states abused the rhetoric of "freedom" and "choice" to circumvent integration efforts by using sham "school choice" programs and threats of violence to preserve Jim Crow. Fear-based choice might have succeeded if it had not been for several federal court decisions between 1959 and 1969. In those cases, judges concluded that this type of "freedom of choice" was blatantly inconsistent with the U.S. Constitution and the American way of life.

The freedom-based choice movement began in the Midwest during the 1990s in opposition to academic mediocrity. Unlike programs created during the fear-based choice era, freedom-based choice sought to remedy the disparities between rich and poor students by providing vouchers to children from low-income families of all races to attend better schools. The U.S. Supreme Court in 2002 upheld this type of "freedom of choice" in *Zelman v. Simmons-Harris*.[4] The Court has thus recognized, if only indirectly, the ideological dissimilarity between these two freedom-of-choice movements.

Anti-voucher groups, however, do not acknowledge the important historical distinctions between the fear-based choice movement of the 1950s and the modern freedom-based choice movement. Instead, they lump the movements together to support their thesis that school choice is socially harmful, proclaiming that the 1990s voucher is nothing more than the 1950s tuition grant clothed in a corporate blue suit rather than a pearly white sheet. To opponents, the only private choice beneficiaries are conservative white (male) elites, and black schoolchildren and their parents are choice victims once again.[5] Anti-voucher groups promote these conclusions through the symbolic use of language. This is very important to know because, as

14

Elmer E. Schattschneider has pointed out, at the root of all politics is the universal language of conflict.[6]

The use of language to affect public perceptions of vouchers will be exceptionally energetic in 2004. Unlike previous election cycles, political aspirants for the White House, Congress, or school board will have to discuss the merits of vouchers in the year *Brown* celebrates its golden anniversary. *Brown* has multiple meanings in our education lexicon, as do freedom of choice and vouchers. Therefore, the strategic use of language will remain a very important vehicle in this debate both for those who want to discredit private choice and for choice proponents who must explain to scholars and taxpayers alike how vouchers will not circumvent *Brown*.

This chapter focuses on the fear-based school choice movement of the 1950s and on the subsequent freedom-based movement of the 1990s, probing the similarities and differences between the two movements. It also describes direct-aid statutes in the form of tuition grants or vouchers enacted in Virginia, Louisiana, Arkansas, Alabama, South Carolina, Mississippi, Wisconsin, and Ohio, and reviews the modern voucher programs in Wisconsin and Ohio. [7]

Brown, Policy Image and Massive Resistance, 1954–1956

The nation's first private school freedom-of-choice movement occurred during one of the most controversial periods in the history of American education. What began initially as a symbolic legislative protest by southern policymakers against *Brown* evolved into a decade-plus political confrontation for the soul of public and private education. At the heart of the battle to reconstruct education in the South was a constitutional issue central to a Civil War fought less than a century earlier: States rights vs. federalism. The U.S. Supreme Court drew first blood in this battle on May 17, 1954.

The Court declared in *Brown v. Board of Education* that maintaining two public school systems—one white, one Negro—violated the federal equal-protection clause and deprived Negro students of equal educational opportunity.[8] This decision overturned in public education the "separate but equal" doctrine affirmed by the same judicial body in *Plessy v. Ferguson* (1896). *Brown* not only freed the Court from "the burden of its history" of support for segregation, *Brown* also marked the beginning of a new chapter in the American civil rights crusade for quality schooling. [9]

However, centuries of institutional norms that had kept Jim Crow at the head of his class do not crumble overnight with one defiant bang of a judicial gavel. *Brown* has had its fair share of victories and losses, and its legacy remains at the center of race relations and educational politics 50 years later. This is true because so much remains undone. The principles of *Brown* remain illusive at worst, or unfulfilled at best.[10] To appreciate *Brown*'s significance to public education in 2004, one cannot overlook its relationship to private education.[11] In an ironic twist of fate, the meaning and scope of *Brown* was shaped early on by federal court decisions striking down public funding of racially discriminatory private schools during the fear-based choice movement of the 1950s and 1960s.

It is no accident that the period of noncompliance with *Brown* in public education coincided with the rise in private school freedom of choice. From 1954 to 1964, very little desegregation occurred in public schools. For example, Negro student enrollment in desegregated public schools located in 11 states was only 2.14 percent by 1964. Executive and congressional assistance to full-scale desegregation during this period was sparse.[12] As for the judiciary, the U.S. Supreme Court's declaration of war in *Brown* was followed by an early withdrawal from the battle.[13] Southern resistance to *Brown* also slowed the movement to dismantle a dual system of education. Tuition grants were one of the South's most powerful tools of resistance. In fact, the tuition grant was used to shape the policy image of *Brown* between 1956 and 1964.

According to professors Frank R. Baumgartner and Bryan D. Jones, a policy image is created by the transformation of a private issue into a public concern.[14] Southern policymakers appalled by *Brown* quickly identified an important private issue that was not explicitly about race: *parental choice*. The concept of parental choice has enjoyed strong support throughout the history of Western Civilization.[15] The U.S. Supreme Court first recognized the constitutional significance of parental choice in education in the 1923 *Meyer v. Nebraska* decision.[16] Two years later, the Supreme Court in *Pierce v. Society of Sisters* said that schoolchildren were not merely "creatures of the state." Rather, a parent has a constitutional right to decide whether a public or private school is best for a particular child.[17] Southern policymakers knew that parental choice was usually protected by the Constitution. So they had to transform it into a public concern if they were to succeed in using its rhetoric to preserve racial segregation.

The primary public concern was *federal encroachment* into public education. Public opposition to *Brown* thus focused on preserving a state's traditional right to control its school system. Even the Supreme Court declared in *Brown* that education "is perhaps the most important function of state and local governments."[18] Southern policymakers used this language to create a dilemma for its citizens to consider: If the Supreme Court recognized a parent's right to choose where to send a child to school, and at the same time respected education as an important state function, then how could the court use *Brown* to prevent the creation of private school-choice programs, even if they effectively maintained racial segregation? With the private issue turned into a public concern, southern policymakers had to market the plan to its citizens. Before desegregation could begin in earnest, southern policymakers began using the popular protest language of massive resistance to foment opposition to *Brown*.

Virginia Sen. Harry F. Byrd was the symbolic pinnacle of massive resistance to desegregation in the Capitol Rotunda.[19] Byrd opposed *Brown*, and he knew millions of citizens did also, but without a strategy to transform a private issue into a public concern, no action could be taken. So Byrd came up with a strategy and put it into motion. By March 12, 1956, Byrd had successfully encouraged 101 of 128 congressmen from the South to sign the Declaration of Constitutional Principles. This document was commonly known as the "Southern Manifesto."[20]

The Southern Manifesto claimed that the Supreme Court's *Brown* decision was the product of naked power and abuse contrary to established principles of federal law. The Manifesto also warned, "Outside agitators are threatening immediate and revolutionary changes in our public-school systems." If such social engineering proceeded unchecked, the Manifesto argued, it was "certain to destroy the system of public education in some of the States."[21] Ironically, the destruction of public education in some southern states did occur, but not through the efforts of *outside* agitators. Rather, it was accomplished by southern state legislators determined to implement Southern Manifesto-type public policies.

Eight of the 11 former Confederate States of America enacted versions of the Southern Manifesto. It was called an "interposition resolution." It purported to interpose a state's reading of the law between itself and an unfavorable Supreme Court decision. Alabama, Arkansas, Florida, Georgia, Louisiana, Mississippi, South Carolina, and Virginia each passed an interposition resolution between 1956 and 1958.[22]

This was not the first time in American history that a state had ever produced an interposition resolution. James Madison authored an interposition resolution for Virginia, and Thomas Jefferson did the same for Kentucky, to protest the passage of the Alien and Sedition Act of 1798.[23] During the 1950s, the interposition resolutions were written in response to a supposedly "seditious" decision from the U.S. Supreme Court. The core of each interposition resolution defined the state's right to "interpose" against the "deliberate, palpable and dangerous" abuse of powers by the federal government that are not granted by the U.S. Constitution.[24] All of the states borrowed parts of the Virginia interposition resolution, which was based a great deal on the original Virginia Resolution written by James Madison in 1798.[25]

With the exception of Florida, every state that passed an interposition resolution also enacted a tuition grant statute. North Carolina enacted a tuition grant statute even though it did not pass an interposition resolution. Arkansas, Georgia, North Carolina, and Virginia all enacted tuition grant statutes as a constitutional amendment approved by voters.[26] Alabama, Louisiana, Mississippi, and South Carolina enacted tuition grant statutes without a voter referendum. Interestingly, not every state with a tuition grant law used it to its full capacity. Georgia and North Carolina are two examples.

Georgia voters ratified a "private school amendment" in 1954. Seven years later Georgia legislators enacted a tuition grant statute. It was on the books as late as 1967, but it was inactive.[27] The North Carolina tuition grant statute was a paper tiger as well. Legal historian Davison Douglas has noted that by the time the first student applied for an education expense grant to attend a private school in North Carolina, the statute had already been deemed unconstitutional.[28]

The name of each school-aid statute varied, though "tuition grant" is a commonly accepted name for this direct-aid program.[29] In Louisiana it was called an education expense grant. South Carolina called its school-aid plan a state scholarship grant. Virginia had multiple names for its school-aid plan: tuition grant, state scholarship, and local scholarship. Despite these various euphemisms, each tuition grant spelled racial discrimination. Tuition grants during the 1950s and 1960s were part of larger movement maturing in the South that made the rhetoric of "freedom of choice" popular during this period of massive resistance.[30] Virginia, Louisiana, Arkansas, Alabama, South Carolina, and Mississippi all used the phrase, to varying degrees, to rally support for their goal of preserving Jim Crow education.

Fear-Based Choice: 1956–1969

If we can organize the Southern States for massive resistance to this order [Brown], I think that in time the rest of the country will realize that racial integration is not going to be accepted in the South.[31]

— Sen. Harry F. Byrd (D-Va.)

Virginia

The Virginia General Assembly in 1956 approved its first tuition grant statute. Its purpose was to circumvent *Brown*. Similar statutes were enacted between 1958 and 1960.[32] Private, nonsectarian schools were the original recipients of the tuition grant.[33] Virginia legislators extended tuition grants to public schools in 1959 in response to state and federal court decisions that prohibited Virginia officials from simply abolishing public schools while making public money available for private education.[34] Some Virginia counties complied with the law. Prince Edward County was not one of them.[35]

Prince Edward County instead closed all public school doors to both white and Negro students from 1959 to 1964. White-only private academies founded by the Prince Edward County Foundation opened during that period, and the tuition grant became a source of revenue to the academies. Not all eligible white schoolchildren enrolled in a Foundation academy. Some white schoolchildren received no formal education at all during the five-year school closure. Nearly two-thirds of Negro schoolchildren did not.[36] The U.S. Supreme Court eventually decided to intervene directly because Prince Edward County repeatedly ignored court orders to open its public schools.

In 1964, the U.S. Supreme Court decided in *Griffin v. County School Board of Prince Edward County* that the closing of public schools,

19

combined with providing public funds to racially segregated private schools, violated the equal protection clause.[37] Public schools in Prince Edward County finally had to open their doors to all students. The Supreme Court, however, did not say that Virginia's tuition grant statute was itself unconstitutional. Therefore, Virginia parents continued to use tuition grants to pay for private education.

By 1964, Virginia had spent more than $10 million to fund tuition grants.[38] The vast majority of this money supported private schools that denied admission to Negro students. But in 1969, a federal district court in *Griffen v. State Board of Education* said Virginia's entire tuition grant scheme violated the equal protection clause. Therefore, "the entire law must go."[39] This decision put to rest a 13-year battle by Virginia to use a tuition grant to circumvent *Brown*.

Louisiana

Louisiana enacted four education expense grant statutes between 1958 and 1967.[40] The 1958 statute authorized grants "for children attending non-sectarian non-public schools where no racially separate public school is provided."[41] In no other state did the tuition grant play such a significant role in the development of private education than in Louisiana. Sixteen private schools were in operation in Louisiana before the 1954 *Brown* decision. The New Orleans metropolitan area was home to 15 of the 16 schools. In 1962, 33 private schools were in operation. The number rose to 60 by 1967.[42]

The State Board of Education and the local parish board initially administered the grants.[43] In 1960, policymakers created the Education Expense Grant Fund. The sole purpose of the Fund was to divert public money from the Louisiana Public Welfare Fund to discriminatory private schools. In 1961, the legislature transferred $2.5 million from the Public Welfare Fund to the Education Expense Grant Fund.[44] Eligibility for a grant was often triggered by a school closing. Voters in St. Helena Parish, for example, voted to close its public schools in favor of education expense grants to pay for private education.

In 1961, a federal district court in *Hall v. St. Helena Parish School Board* invalidated the use of tuition grants in St. Helena Parish. The court said, "Grants-in-aid, no matter how generous, are not an adequate substitute for public schools."[45] The U.S. Supreme Court affirmed this decision in 1962.[46] Public aid to private schools in general, however, was not ruled unconstitutional. Louisiana legislators responded to the *Hall* decision by enacting a third tuition grant statute.

This third statute, Act 147, was passed in 1962. It shifted grant management responsibility to the Louisiana Financial Assistance Commission. During the 1962–63 school year, the Commission issued 7,093 tuition grants. Four years later the number increased to 15,177 tuition grants.[47] By 1967, Louisiana had spent more than $15 million on children attending private schools.[48] But 1967 was also the beginning of the end for the Louisiana tuition grant program.

In 1967, a federal district court said in *Poindexter v. Louisiana Financial Assistance Commission* that the 1962 tuition grant statute violated the equal protection clause. The court also concluded that the tuition grant was a fruit of Louisiana's desire to use public money to maintain the operation of schools exclusively for white children. The U.S. Supreme Court affirmed this decision.[49] In 1968, a federal district court in *Poindexter v. Louisiana Financial Assistance Commission* invalidated Act 99: Louisiana's fourth grant statute. The purpose of Act 99, according to the federal court, was discrimination. The U.S. Supreme Court affirmed this decision in 1968.[50] The *Poindexter* decisions put an end to Louisiana's 10-year endeavor to use private school aid to circumvent *Brown*.

Arkansas

The Arkansas General Assembly in 1958 passed two acts in response to *Brown*. Act 4 empowered the governor to close public schools anywhere in Arkansas to avoid racial integration. Act 5 authorized the Arkansas Commission of Education to use a state tuition grant to pay for education at a public school located outside of a student's district, or at a private school when the governor closed a student's public school.[51] Governor Orval Faubus used his authority on September 12, 1958, to close all senior high schools in the capital city of Little Rock.[52]

In 1959, a federal district court in *Aaron v. McKinley* said that Act 4 and Act 5 were unconstitutional. Act 4 violated the equal protection and the due process clauses of the Fourteenth Amendment. The court also said Governor Faubus's school closing proclamation of September 12, 1958, denied Negro and white students the right to attend a public senior high school within Little Rock. The U.S. Supreme Court affirmed this decision in 1959.[53]

Alabama

"Segregation Now! Segregation Tomorrow! Segregation Forever!" is a slogan popularized by Governor George Wallace during his 1963 inaugural speech.[54] Governor Wallace used this slogan to define Alabama-style resistance to school integration. Higher education was the first test case. On June 11, 1963, Governor Wallace physically blocked two Negro students from entering the doors of a University of Alabama administration building. President John F. Kennedy federalized the Alabama National Guard later that day in preparation for a possible confrontation with the governor. Federal authorities returned to the University of Alabama the next day and asked Governor Wallace to move aside. Governor Wallace acquiesced.[55] This symbolized the beginning of a new era for higher education in Alabama and the South. However, Governor Wallace's promise to keep segregation alive remained intact. With the higher education battle lost, Governor Wallace turned his attention to secondary education.

On September 2, 1963, Governor Wallace sent Alabama state troopers to surround Tuskegee High School to avoid school integration. Ultimately, Tuskegee High closed its doors to both Negro and white students. Some white students transferred to segregated public high schools elsewhere in Alabama, and others enrolled in the private, white-only Macon Academy.[56] Financial support for the Macon Academy was obtained under a statute enacted by the Alabama legislature in 1957. This statute authorized payment of tuition grants to parents with children in any city where the public schools were closed.[57] Governor Wallace lobbied state employees for money to fund a "private school foundation" for white students.[58] Governor Wallace's plan for secondary education was put to rest by a 1964 federal court decision.

In *Lee v. Macon County Board of Education*, a federal district court in Alabama invalidated the 1957 statute. The court said that grant-in-aid payments to a segregated private school were unconstitutional for two reasons. First, the statute's illegitimate purpose was to further segregation in the public schools. Second, tuition grants were only available to students in a city where public schools were closed. The court, however, did not say that Alabama's grant-in-aid statute was unconstitutional on its face.[59] This left the door open for future use of tuition grants.

In 1965, Alabama legislators approved a new tuition grant statute. However, it met the same fate as the first statute. In 1967, a district court stated in *Lee v. Macon County Board* that the 1965 statute was no different from the 1957 statute. It was another attempt by Alabama officials "to circumvent the principles of *Brown*."[60] The court also said the 1965 statute was "born of the same effort to discriminate against Negroes,"[61] and was simply designed to "assist private discrimination." The U.S. Supreme Court affirmed this decision in 1968.[62] Federal courts relied on the *Lee* decision(s) when they invalidated tuition grant programs in Virginia, Louisiana, and South Carolina.

South Carolina

South Carolina began its formal protest to *Brown* in 1952, the year voters supported a constitutional amendment to abolish the state's public school system.[63] In response to the *Brown* decision, South Carolina legislators adopted a segregation policy in every session from 1954 through 1961.[64] In 1963, policymakers enacted a state scholarship grant statute. Act 297 made a state scholarship grant available to any student between six and 20 years of age. Various groups in South Carolina voiced concern about the constitutionality of the statute, and a district court placed a temporary restraining order on Act 297 in 1965.

Three years later a court finally held the scholarship grant statute unconstitutional. After reviewing historical records associated with the enactment of the statute, a federal court in *Brown v. South Carolina State Board of Education* said Act 297 was unconstitutional. The judges concluded that the state scholarship grant had at its core the "purpose, motive and effect . . . to unconstitutionally circumvent the requirement first enunciated in *Brown v. Board of Education*." The U.S. Supreme Court affirmed this decision in 1968.[65]

Mississippi

Mississippi enacted its tuition grant statute in 1964. It authorized cities, towns, and counties to levy taxes on their residents to provide

23

public money to current *and* future nonsectarian private school students in Mississippi.[66] Responsibility for tuition grant administration was given to the Mississippi Educational Finance Commission. Many grassroots organizations supported the law. The White Citizens' Council was one of them.

The White Citizens' Council was formed in Indianola, Mississippi, in 1954.[67] One aim of the Council was to resist the public-school integration mandate announced on "Black Monday"—a euphemism for the May 17, 1954, *Brown* decision.[68] Years later, some Council chapters expanded their mission to include preserving racial segregation in private schools. This decision helped to influence the rise of white segregated private academies during the late 1960s, although the exact level of involvement is vague.[69] Nonetheless, it is well known that this movement did not mature without assistance from Mississippi law.

For example, white students attended 24 of the 25 private schools in Mississippi during the 1965–66 school year. Sixty-seven percent of those white private schools refused to admit any black students. During the 1967–68 school year, no black students were enrolled in 48 of the 49 Mississippi state-tuition grant-supported private schools. Saints Academy was the only private school in Mississippi with a black population.[70]

A group of black parents filed a suit in 1966 against the Mississippi Educational Finance Commission. The U.S. government intervened in the case on behalf of the parents under the Civil Rights Act of 1964.[71] After examining the records related to the statute, a federal district court in the 1969 *Coffey v. State Educational Finance Commission* decision said that the program was unconstitutional, observing that Mississippi's "tuition grants have fostered the creation of private schools" that catered to white students eager to "avoid desegregated public schools."[72] The district court also said that Mississippi's tuition grant program "will significantly encourage and involve the State in private discriminations."[73] Mississippi had spent more than $3.2 million on private school education at that time.[74]

The fear-based freedom-of-choice movement came to an end in 1969. Federal courts said that tuition grants could no longer serve as a conduit to circumvent *Brown*, or to promote racial discrimination in public or private education. Private school freedom of choice, in the form of direct aid, remained dormant for many years, except

24

for a few small-scale experiments. System-wide private choice in urban education did not again become a reality until the 1990s.

Freedom-Based Choice: 1990–2003

> *What hinges on this decision [Zelman] is whether the promise of*
> Brown v. Board of Education *of an equal educational opportunity*
> *is going to be realized. If we have to go outside the public sector,*
> *then that's what we have to do.*[75]

— Constitutional Attorney Clint Bolick

The 1990s breathed new life into American education. Private school freedom of choice became vogue again, but this time it came without the ugly ideology of racial separatism and hatred.[76] True to the organic meaning of freedom of choice, the 1990s movement made parental decisionmaking and academic uplift its two most essential components. The Midwest is home to this private choice movement. Milwaukee and Cleveland, each with a unique history of experimentation with freedom of choice in public education, are the primary big-city school districts now experimenting with freedom-based private choice.[77]

Wisconsin

Governor Tommy Thompson signed into law the Milwaukee Parental Choice Program on April 27, 1990.[78] This was a crowning achievement for a legislative battle shepherded by state representative Polly Williams (D-Milwaukee) and black leaders in the Milwaukee community.[79] The goal of MPCP is to provide a voucher to lower-income public and private school parents in search of a quality education for their child. Parental eligibility for a voucher is means tested. Only households with an income at, or below, 1.75 times poverty-level guidelines established by the federal Office of Management and Budget are eligible to participate in MPCP.[80]

Legal battles against MPCP were common during the 1990s. One contentious issue was the use of public funds to pay for private education. MPCP's breach between the separation of church and state was another issue. From 1990 to 1998, only private, nonsectarian schools were eligible for participation in MPCP. Wisconsin legislators amended MPCP in 1995 to include religious schools, but court

25

Table 3-1
STUDENT ENROLLMENT IN MILWAUKEE PARENTAL CHOICE
PROGRAM: 1990–2003

Academic School Year	Private Schools	Student Enrollment
1990–91	7	300
1991–92	6	512
1992–93	11	594
1993–94	12	704
1994–95	12	771
1995–96	17	1,288
1996–97	20	1,616
1997–98	23	1,497
1998–99*	83	5,761
1999–00	90	7,575
2000–01	100	9,238
2001–02	102	10,497
2002–03 (est.)	103	11,350

* Inclusion of religious schools after 1998 decision.

SOURCE: Milwaukee Parental Choice Program, Informational Paper 29, Wisconsin Legislative Fiscal Bureau, January 2003, p. 3.

decisions blocked religious school participation. In 1998, the state's highest court put this issue to rest.

In *Jackson v. Benson*, the Wisconsin Supreme Court said MPCP was constitutional, and participation of religious schools in it did not violate the religious establishment provision of the Wisconsin constitution.[81] The U.S. Supreme Court declined to address the decision. Since 1998, both student enrollment and the number of private schools participating in MPCP increased dramatically (see Table 3-1).

The largest single-year student-enrollment increase occurred during the 1998–99 school year. Student enrollment jumped 4,264 students from the 1997–98 school year total. This increase was larger than the total number of students enrolled in MPCP from 1990 to 1996. As of January 2003, an estimated 102 private schools served approximately 11,621 Milwaukee students in grades K–12.[82] The maximum voucher amount for 2003–04 is estimated to be $6,020.00 per student. [83]

Ohio

Governor George Voinovich signed into law the Cleveland Project Scholarship Program on June 30, 1995.[84] This effort was championed by city council member Fannie Lewis (D-Cleveland).[85] Like MPCP, the Cleveland voucher program is means tested. Households with an income at, or near, 200 percent of the federal poverty level are eligible for the state to pay 90 percent of a school's tuition, and up to the voucher maximum of $2,250 per year. Families in this income bracket are responsible for paying no more than $250 toward payment of private school tuition.[86] Households with an income above 200 percent of the federal poverty level are eligible for the state to pay 75 percent of a school's tuition cost, and up to the voucher maximum of $1,875 per year. Parents with incomes below the 200 percent threshold are given first consideration for a voucher.[87]

Legal battles against the Cleveland voucher program were common. Cleveland, unlike Milwaukee, allowed religious schools to participate in its choice program right away. This made involvement between church and state a central legal issue. The first challenge to the law began in a state court in 1996, and then it moved to the federal judiciary. On December 11, 2000, the U.S. Court of Appeals for the Sixth Circuit said Cleveland's voucher program was unconstitutional.[88] The U.S. Supreme Court reversed this decision. In *Zelman* (2002), the Supreme Court said Cleveland's voucher program did not violate the federal establishment clause.[89]

In the 2002–03 school year, 5,147 students in 50 private schools participated in the Cleveland program—up significantly from the student enrollment of 1,994 during the 1996–97 school year.[90] The average income for Cleveland choice participants is $18,750 a year. And according to 1999 data, racial minorities accounted for approximately 74 percent of all voucher students. African-Americans were 60 percent of choice students. Hispanics and others were 13.4 percent of choice students. Whites were 26.6 percent of choice students, and their participation is increasing.[91]

Two Freedom-of-Choice Movements: Similarities and Differences

Laws are not abstract propositions. They are expressions of policy arising out of specific situations and addressed to the attainment

27

of particular needs . . . And the bottom problem is: What is below
the surface of the words and yet fairly a part of them.[92]
— Justice Felix Frankfurter

Private school freedom-of-choice movements of the 1950s and 1990s have similarities and differences. The decision to focus solely on choice similarities, or choice differences, is at the heart of today's debate about vouchers in American education. Little attention is given to comparing and contrasting choice similarities and differences. Below are some results from such a comparison.

Religion

During the fear-based choice era, the states of Virginia, Louisiana, Arkansas, Alabama, South Carolina, and Mississippi enacted tuition grant statutes that forbade religious school participation.[93] In contrast, all of the freedom-based choice programs allow students to attend religious or nonreligious schools. Therefore, church-state battles that arose during the 1990s were practically nonexistent during the fear-based choice movement of the 1950s and 1960s.

Schools

During the fear-based choice era, Virginia, Louisiana, and Arkansas allowed a student to use a tuition grant at public *or* private schools. Alabama, South Carolina, and Mississippi tuition grants were redeemable only at private schools. Today, Ohio vouchers are redeemable at public *and* private schools. In Wisconsin, only private schools are eligible for vouchers.

In 1962, Louisiana became the only state to waive a requirement that a private school must be a nonprofit organization to qualify for a tuition grant. This statute provided a way for entrepreneurs to open new schools with public funds.[94] No other early tuition grant legislation enacted in Virginia, Arkansas, Alabama, South Carolina, or Mississippi made for-profit organizations eligible for a tuition grant.

Students and Parents

During the fear-based choice era, public school students were eligible for tuition grants in Virginia, Arkansas, Alabama, and South Carolina. The rationale for this policy was simple. Parents with children in a public school likely to be integrated by a federal court order needed an escape. The tuition grant was the passport. White parents used this option more often than black parents. In certain locales in Virginia and Louisiana, only white parents were eligible for a tuition grant. In Mississippi, however, students who attended a private school, or planned to attend a private school, were eligible for tuition grants. Today, both private and public school students are eligible for vouchers in Wisconsin and Ohio (see Tables 3-2 and 3-3).

The fear-based and freedom-based choice movements share similarities. These similarities, however, pale compared with the ideologically differences between them. Ideology is at the heart of America's choice debate, and it is ideology that segregates fear-based choice from freedom-based choice.

Still, anti-voucher groups choose to focus solely on private choice similarities. Their goal is to prove that a voucher is a step backward in the direction of state-sponsored racism and private school discrimination. Philosophy of language is their tool of choice.

Freedom of Choice: Interest Groups and the Philosophy of Language

> [T]he most universal and effectual way of discovering the true meaning of a law, when the words are dubious, is by considering the reason and spirit of it; or the cause which moved the legislator to enact it.[95]
>
> — Sir William Blackstone

David B. Truman observes in *The Governmental Process* that special-interest groups tend to form around one or more shared attitudes. They achieve their political goals, Truman writes, by using these shared attitudes to influence public opinion in their favor.[96] In the field of education policy, anti-voucher interest groups such as teacher unions actively seek to influence public opinion against vouchers. There are also interest groups such as the Black Alliance for Educational Options that work to influence public opinion in favor of vouchers.[97]

The National Association for the Advancement of Colored People and People for the American Way are both leading voucher opponents.[98] In 1997, the two groups jointly created the Partnership for

Table 3-2
ELIGIBILITY FOR PUBLIC AID DURING FEAR-BASED CHOICE MOVEMENT: 1956–1969

State	For Use at a Nonsectarian Private School Only	For Use at a Public School or Nonsectarian Private School	For Public School Students Only	For Private School Students Only	For Public and Private School Students
Virginia	*	X	X		
Louisiana	*	X			X
Arkansas		X	X		
Alabama	X		X		
South Carolina	X		X		
Mississippi	X			X	

*Original statute included private schools only.

SOURCES: Virginia (public schools): *Race Relations Law Reporter* 1 (1956): 1094. Virginia (tuition grants): *Race Relations Law Reporter* 4 (1959): 191 ("grants for children in public schools outside of the locality"). Louisiana (tuition grants): *Race Relations Law Reporter* 3 (1958): 1062–63 (a student with no public school available due to closing, or assigned to a public school attended by members of another race, or assigned to a school against parental wishes was eligible for an education expense grant in 1958). Louisiana (tuition grants): *Race Relations Law Reporter* 7 (1962): 922 (for student in private school, or student "eligible" for admission into a public school). Arkansas: *Aaron v. McKinley*, 173 F.Supp 944, 951 n. 2 (1959). Alabama: See generally *Lee v. Macon County Board of Education*, 231 F.Supp. 743 (1964). South Carolina (tuition grants): *Race Relations Law Reporter* 8 (1963): 711. Mississippi (tuition grants): *Race Relations Law Reporter* 9 (1964): 1499, 1501.

Table 3-3
ELIGIBILITY FOR PUBLIC AID DURING FREEDOM-BASED CHOICE MOVEMENT: 1990–2003

State	For Use at a Nonsectarian or Sectarian Private School	For Use at a Public School or Private School	For Public School Students Only	For Private School Students Only	For Public and Private School Students
Wisconsin	X				X
Ohio	X	X*			X

*Cleveland parents can use a voucher to attend alternative public schools.

SOURCES: Wisconsin Statutes Annotated §119.23(2)(a) (2001), and Ohio Revenue Code Annotated §3313.97.5 and §3313.977.

Public Education to promote an anti-voucher, pro-public school message.[99] The American Civil Liberties Union also opposes vouchers for reasons similar to those voiced by the NAACP.

For example, groups like the NAACP and the ACLU are concerned about the possible segregative effects of voucher programs, both inside private school classrooms and in the public school systems that voucher recipients "leave behind." This concern is not limited to Milwaukee or Cleveland. It is a national concern. In 1997, ACLU legislative representative Terri Schroeder recalled the history of the old, fear-based choice movement to predict that voucher programs, if widely implemented, would produce segregative effects nationwide. "These [white, segregation] academies [of the 1950s and 1960s], which discriminated in admission based on race, allowed communities to continue de facto segregation." Taking this analogy to its logical conclusion, Schroeder said, "The same could easily reoccur around the county if modern voucher plans are adopted."[100]

Such concerns about private school aid, racial politics, and choice are not wholly unwarranted.[101] Private choice was once used to support racial discrimination in schools, and vouchers could be used for the identical purpose. So our collective determination not to resurrect Jim Crow-inspired education choice with public money is important, and most voucher enthusiasts support this objective. But voucher enthusiasts part ways with the anti-voucher camp when it grossly misappropriates fear-based choice ideology across space and time, wedding two very different sociopolitical eras, and two equally divergent educational agendas, through the careful misuse of language.

Philosophy of language is the study of relationships between words, ideas, and intentions. The discipline dates back to antiquity. Plato was an early student of language,[102] as was Aristotle. Enlightenment thinkers, including Thomas Hobbes, René Descartes, and John Locke were interested in the conceptual framework of language. But philosophy of language did not emerge as a major preoccupation within the field of philosophy until the 20th century.[103]

Philosophy of language is important to the study of the private school freedom of choice movement because the symbolic use of language has become an extremely important part of public discourse on this issue.[104] Philosophy of language reveals that anti-private choice groups use at least two strategies to discredit vouchers. The first is an iconographic reference I refer to as the "tuition grant-voucher quandary." The second is of a type that philosophers call semiotics, which I will refer to as the "segregation academy" metaphor.

Iconographic Reference: The Tuition Grant-Voucher Quandary

An iconographic reference is a communicative technique used to identify and link familiar cultural images in society. The goal of an iconographic reference is to establish a conceptual link between a referent (a specific thing) and a positive or negative value judgment.[105] In the case of the voucher debate, choice opponents create an iconographic reference between school choice *referents*—fear-based freedom of choice, tuition grants, and vouchers—and a *value judgment*—racism is wrong. Their goal is to use this iconography to convince the public that a voucher, or a "private school tuition voucher,"[106] is a racist freedom-of-choice scheme that is as harmful to black schoolchildren today as it was during the 1950s and 1960s.

Freedom-of-choice opponents use voucher-specific iconographic references to incite suspicion against private choice among the general public, and in the black community in particular. Examples of voucher-specific iconographic references vary. Some link race and education, such as NAACP president Kweisi Mfume's statement, "vouchers don't educate, they segregate." Linking religious themes to education is also common. Reverend Wendell Armstrong said at a 1999 anti-voucher rally in Detroit, "The wolves are coming in the shape of vouchers, dressed in sheep's clothing."[107]

Brown and the history of segregation are popular items for creating voucher-specific iconographic references. In 2003, Rep. Elijah E. Cummings (D-Md.) and Rep. Robert C. "Bobby" Scott (D-Va.) in honor of the 49th anniversary of *Brown* said, "Vouchers were the very scheme used in Virginia to fund segregated academies."[108] In 2002, Barry Lynn, executive director of Americans United for Separation of Church and State, said, "It's sad to say this, but the history of vouchers didn't begin yesterday. . . . It began after the *Brown v. Board of Education* decision."[109]

Choice opponents use voucher-specific iconographic references in an attempt to establish guilt by association—to ensure, symbolically, that the sins of the fear-based choice movement of the 1950s haunt its modern offspring: vouchers. In addition to the extravagant misuse of simile, these references are flawed because they treat a 1950s tuition grant and a modern voucher as synonymous. This is incorrect. A tuition grant is not a voucher, in name or ideology. Neither is the administration of private choice in Milwaukee or Cleveland today identical to the administration of private choice in Prince Edward County, Virginia, decades ago. Federal courts, which interest groups often call upon to determine the constitutionality of direct-aid programs in education, have rarely if ever treated tuition grants and vouchers interchangeably during either choice movement.

A survey of federal court decisions delivered between 1954 and 1969 shows multiple uses for the term "voucher."[110] For example, the word "voucher" was used in relation to jury duty, reimbursement, and payment for travel expenses. Most often a voucher was referenced in cases dealing with voting.[111] When the U.S. Supreme Court referenced vouchers and schools, it was related to payment of an educational expense, or a state appropriation of money to a college.[112] Throughout the history of the fear-based choice movement, no federal court invalidated a voucher program because of racial discrimination in education. Extension of this survey produced similar results.

At least 35 U.S. Supreme Court decisions delivered between 1970 and 2003 referenced the term "voucher." Financial transactions were the most referenced use for the term. One voucher reference was made to food stamps.[113] References between vouchers and schools were mostly for educational payments. During this 33-year period, no federal court invalidated a voucher program because of racial discrimination. The federal courts have never found that a voucher served as a financial incentive to maintain racial discrimination in private education during, and after, the fear-based freedom-of-choice movement. This was not the case for early tuition grants.

A survey of federal court decisions delivered between 1954 and 1969 indicates less legal dexterity for the term "tuition grant." Its use was overwhelmingly synonymous with discrimination in education. Virginia, Louisiana, Arkansas, Alabama, South Carolina, and Mississippi provide examples of this. A similar result occurred from a survey of U.S. Supreme Court decisions delivered between 1970 and 2003.

For example, the U.S. Supreme Court in *Committee for Public Education & Religious Liberty v. Nyquist* (1973) invalidated a New York tuition grant statute, because parents with children not enrolled in

34

private schools were ineligible for a tuition grant. Racial discrimination was not a factor in this tuition grant case.[114] Racial discrimination and tuition grants were a topic of interest in *Norwood v. Harrison* (1973).[115] In *Norwood*, the U.S. Supreme Court said that a Mississippi statute that permitted state officials to loan textbooks to schoolchildren in attendance at a racially segregated private school was unconstitutional.

In conclusion, although the tuition grant versus voucher analysis may seem trivial at first glance, it is not. Such distinctions are important when, as here, the practical-political goal of a speaker is to entice endorsement rather than to merely inform.[116] An awareness of common voucher-specific iconographic references is important to our understanding how interest groups define—or misrepresent—freedom-of-choice ideology in American education.

Semiotics and the "Segregation Academy" Metaphor

In *The Politics of Misinformation*, Murray Edelman writes that images dominate human communication and thinking. This is why images ultimately become the means by which we negotiate change in our world.[117] "Segregation academy" is an emotionally powerful slogan that not only conjures bad feelings in the heart but also invokes vulgar images in the mind. Voucher opponents know this, and they misuse the "segregation academy" cliché to generate feelings of fear and racial mistrust. For example, the Reverend Jesse Jackson said, "The same ideology that supported *Plessy*, opposed *Brown*, and inspired the formation of all-White academies, is now behind the school voucher issue."[118]

Education activist Jonathan Kozol is another voucher opponent who uses emotionally charged language to instill fear. While on his mission to discover and reveal to the world the "savage inequalities" that persist in American education, Kozol touches on the voucher issue. Kozol dislikes vouchers. He considers them dangerous, particularly because voucher money, could "be used for a David Duke school or a right-wing militia school or a Louis Farrakhan school."[119] Statements like this demonstrate that Kozol is more interested in the rhetoric of hate than the rhetoric of hope. No such academy is actually operating in Milwaukee or Cleveland with support of a voucher. In fact, the probability that a "segregation academy" will ever open in either city is very unlikely because anti-discrimination provisions in the voucher law prohibit spending public money at such schools. In any event, such schools could not accept vouchers under the anti-discrimination provisions of the voucher laws. Nevertheless, the "segregation academy" imagery, despite Kozol's predatory sensationalism, is not without historical resonance.

A report published by the U.S. Commission on Civil Rights documented the rise of the "segregation academy" in the South during the mid-1960s. The Commission estimated that 200 segregated private schools were open in six southern states by 1967. Louisiana had 65 all-white schools. Beginning in 1963, South Carolina had 44 segregated private schools. In Mississippi, 30 of the 35 segregated private schools were created between 1965 and 1967. Alabama had 13 private schools for whites only, and Virginia had 30.[120] So examples do exist of state officials assisting a "segregation academy" during its early years. However, today's voucher-redeeming private "academy" is nothing like the "segregation academy" of the past. Only by using semiotics and the "segregation academy" metaphor can anti-voucher groups support this conclusion.

Semiotics is a philosophical study more than a technical one.[121] It is concerned with the way humans use written and spoken language to represent our worldview to each other, as well as with signs coded in everyday messages.[122] Semiotics is equally interested in the social and political significance of "word-signs."[123] Symbols also play a role in semiotics. A symbol, according to Charles D. Elder and Roger W. Cobb, is a human invention by which an object receives meaning through discourse.[124] In this example, a voucher is the object to which human language gives meaning—both good and bad.

At the root of semiotics is metaphor. Metaphors, according to Deborah Stone, are prevalent in policy language. Metaphors serve as devices we use to draw comparisons between objects.[125] The symbolic power a metaphor gives to language is supported by two concepts. The first concept is *transfer*. Two components of *transfer* are "replacement" and "substitution." The second concept is *similarity*. Two components of *similarity* are "likeness" and "analogy."[126]

A statement made by Rep. Jesse Jackson Jr. (D-Ill.) in response to the U.S. Supreme Court's decision to uphold school vouchers in *Zelman* is an example of the "segregation academy" metaphor in action. "After the 1954 *Brown* desegregation decision, which was directed mainly at Southern Jim Crow public schools, white protestant private religious academies sprung into existence to avoid integration."[127] Jackson made a metaphorical link between the rise of the "segregation academy" in the South as a result of *Brown*, and voucher-redeeming private religious "academies" in Ohio.

Thus, the rise of "white protestant . . . private religious academies" is a potent *metaphor* for private schools operating in Cleveland (or Milwaukee): religious and sectarian. A voucher is a "replacement" for tuition grant. Cleveland (or Milwaukee) is a "substitute" for Prince Edward County, Virginia. And "like" the "segregation academy" of the South, vouchers are financed by state money. The "analogy" being "segregation" academies in both eras would not likely exist without financial backing from the state. Therefore, today's freedom-based choice movement is identical to yesteryear's fear-based choice movement.

Jackson's use of semiotics to support the uniform private-choice thesis finds support from law professor Steven K. Green. Green was a lawyer for the groups that opposed the Cleveland voucher program, so it is not surprising that Green holds dear the conviction that vouchers are incapable of promoting equality for disadvantaged city schoolchildren. Green also believes that it is manipulative for anyone to build a bridge to connect vouchers, equality, and *Brown* because it promotes an illusion about private schools. The history of fear-based choice in America is a guide to what could happen today. Green concludes, "Choice will lead to self-segregation and inequality of opportunity."[128] Green, like Jackson, relies on metaphors to support a uniform private-choice thesis.

Donald A. Schön and Martin Rein have said that when naming and framing a policy issue, a metaphor is the process by which ideas are transported across time. The goal of this metaphor process is to make the "familiar and the unfamiliar come to be seen in a new way."[129] Green uses the metaphorical phrases "like" and "similar" to carry fear-based choice ideology across time. For example, Green said, "*Like* current voucher programs, the freedom of choice plans commonly. . . ." "*Similar* to the current debate [about parental choice]." "*Similar* to the current voucher plan, the 'freedom of choice' programs [of old]."[130] Not everyone agrees that the metaphorical comparison is valid. Professor John Eastman, in a reply to Green's article, made note of Green's attempt to compare the choice movements in order "to tarnish the voucher movement with the brush of racial segregation."[131]

Green and Jackson use similar techniques to build a symbolic bridge of segregation to connect the old, fear-based choice to the modern, freedom-based choice. To test the uniform private-choice thesis, it is necessary to compare and contrast the history of each choice movement from five perspectives.

First, Jackson is correct that private schools served as a safe-haven for white parents eager to avoid integration after the *Brown* decision. Green is correct that federal courts neutralized tuition grants in South Carolina, Louisiana, Virginia, Mississippi, and Alabama. Green, however, credits the tuition grants' benefits to private schools rather than to racial discrimination itself as the reason for their demise.[132] He thus wrongly focuses on a symptom rather than on the underlying disease of fear-based choice.

Private education was merely a symptom. State financing of racial discrimination was the disease federal courts sought to remove root and branch. This is why public funding of private education is not necessarily the evil of fear-based choice. For some reason, voucher opponents fail to acknowledge two U.S. Supreme Court decisions in effect during the fear-based choice movement. Each decision upheld the use of public money to pay for educational services at private religious schools.

In *Cochran v. Board of Education*, the U.S. Supreme Court upheld a Louisiana statute that provided for the purchase of textbooks for students in religious schools.[133] Circuit Judge John Minor Wisdom noted this distinction in his 1967 decision invalidating Louisiana's tuition grant program: "The free lunches and textbooks Louisiana provides for all its schoolchildren are the fruits of racially neutral benevolence. Tuition grants are not the products of the same policy."[134] Therefore, racial discrimination, not public support of private schools per se, was the culprit. In fact, federal courts invalidated public support for the "segregation academy" in Virginia, Louisiana, Arkansas, and Mississippi under the equal protection clause.

During the 14-year history of the Milwaukee voucher program, no federal court said a voucher violated the federal equal protection clause or otherwise circumvented *Brown*. The same is true for the 9-year history of the Cleveland voucher program. By contrast, federal courts invalidated tuition grants in Arkansas, Alabama, South Carolina, and Mississippi within one to five years of operation. Ten and 13 years, respectively, passed before Louisiana and Virginia tuition grant programs met the same fate. Therefore, the history of fear-based choice is not identical to the history of freedom-based choice (see Table 3-4).

Second, race is not a factor in voucher eligibility. White, black, Hispanic, and other parents can enroll their children into a racially diverse private school if they choose—and without fear that the state will close a public school, and city or church officials will pass a "white-only" voucher resolution to protest their decisions. Such responses were common during the 1950s and 1960s. Therefore, the history of fear-based choice is not identical to the history of freedom-based choice.

Third, tuition grant statutes in Virginia, Louisiana, Arkansas, Alabama, and South Carolina were enacted before 1964. Mississippi is the exception. The passage by Congress of the Civil Rights Act of 1964 provided the government with a way to deal head-on with racial segregation in private education.[135] In 1967, for example, two federal courts relied upon the Civil Rights Act of 1964 as part of their rationale for invalidating tuition grants in Alabama and Louisiana. The U.S. Supreme Court affirmed both decisions.[136]

By contrast, the Ohio voucher statute requires its private schools "not to discriminate on the basis of race, religion, or ethnic background." The Wisconsin voucher statute requires its private schools to comply with guidelines of the Civil Rights Act of 1964.[137] Thus far, no federal court has said that the Ohio or Wisconsin voucher statute violates the Civil Rights Act of 1964. Therefore, the history of fear-based choice is not identical to the history of freedom-based choice.

Fourth, eligibility for a tuition grant in Virginia, Louisiana, Arkansas, and Alabama was triggered by a school closing.[138] In Virginia, Chapter 68 of 1956 called for the closing of any public school that became integrated, either "voluntarily or under compulsion of any court order."[139] Section 6 authorized the governor to assign a student to another public school, especially when "mixing of white and colored children constitutes a clear and present danger" to the welfare of the Virginia.[140] In Arkansas, Act 4 of 1958 gave Governor Faubus the authority to close any public school in the state. Factors

Table 3-4

FEDERAL COURT TREATMENT OF TUITION GRANTS (1954–1969) AND VOUCHERS (1990–2003)

State	Tuition Grant Use/Statute Violated Equal Protection Clause[1]	Tuition Grant Use/Statute Circumvented Brown[2]	Closing of Public School (can or did) Trigger Tuition Grant Use[3]	Voucher Use/Statute Did Not Violate Equal Protection Clause[4]	Voucher Use/Statute Did Not Circumvent Brown[5]
Virginia	X	X	X		
Louisiana	X	X	X		
Arkansas	X		X		
Alabama		X	X		
South Carolina		X			
Mississippi	X				
Wisconsin				X	X
Ohio				X	X

(continued next page)

Table 3-4

FEDERAL COURT TREATMENT OF TUITION GRANTS (1954–1969) AND VOUCHERS (1990–2003) (*Continued*)

[1] Virginia: *Griffin v. County School Board of Prince Edward County*, 377 U.S. 218, 225 (1964); *Griffin v. State Board of Education*, 239 F.Supp. 560, 565 (1965); and *Griffin v. State Board of Education*, 296 F.Supp. 1178, 1180 (1969). Louisiana: *Hall v. St. Helena Parish School Board*, 197 F.Supp. 649, 651 (1961), *aff'd mem.*; *St. Helena Parish School Board v. Hall*, 368 U.S. 515 (1962); *Poindexter v. Louisiana Financial Assistance Commission*, 275 F.Supp. 833, 835 (1967), *aff'd mem.*; and *Louisiana Financial Assistance Commission v. Poindexter*, 389 U.S. 571 (1968). Arkansas: *Aaron v. McKinley*, 173 F.Supp. 944, 945 (1959), *aff'd mem. sub nom.*; and *Faubus v. Aaron*, 361 U.S. 197 (1959). Mississippi: *Coffey v. State Educational Finance Commission*, 296 F.Supp. 1389, 1392 (1969).

[2] Virginia: *Allen v. County School Board of Prince Edward County*, 198 F.Supp. 497, 502–03 (1961); and *Griffin v. Board of Supervisors of Prince Edward County*, 339 F.2d. 486, 492 (1964). Louisiana: *Hall v. St. Helena Parish School Board*, 197 F.Supp. 649, 656 (1961), *aff'd mem.*; and *St. Helena Parish School Board v. Hall*, 368 U.S. 515 (1962). Alabama: *Lee v. Macon County Board of Education*, 267 F.Supp. 458, 476 (1967), *aff'd mem. sub nom.*; and *Wallace v. United States*, 389 U.S. 215 (1967). South Carolina: *Brown v. South Carolina State Department of Education*, 296 F.Supp. 199, 202–03 (1968), *aff'd per curiam*; and *South Carolina State Department of Education v. Brown*, 393 U.S. 222, (1968).

[3] Virginia: *Griffin v. County School Board of Prince Edward County*, 377 U.S. 218, 233 (1964). Louisiana: *Hall v. St. Helena Parish School Board*, 197 F.Supp. 649, 651 (1961), *aff'd mem.*; and *St. Helena Parish School Board v. Hall*, 368 U.S. 515 (1962). Arkansas: *Aaron v. McKinley*, 173 F.Supp. 944, 945 (1959), *aff'd mem. sub nom.*; and *Faubus v. Aaron*, 361 U.S. 197 (1959).

[4] The NAACP filed an equal protection clause challenge to MPCP in 1998. The Wisconsin Supreme Court did not "assume as true the legal conclusions pled by the NAACP." *Jackson v. Benson*, 578 N.W.2d 602, 631–32. No federal court said the Cleveland voucher program violated the equal protection clause.

[5] No federal court said Milwaukee or Cleveland vouchers circumvented *Brown*.

41

that could result in a school closing included (1) threats of potential violence to humans or property from school integration, (2) the presence of federal troops in or around Arkansas public schools, and (3) the demise of educational standards due to desegregation.[141] This is the type of fear-based ideology that opened the door to tuition grants in the South.

By contrast, neither the governor of Wisconsin nor Ohio had to shut public school doors to trigger the voucher statutes. Neither did Wisconsin and Ohio legislators disregard their states' obligation to provide public education to Milwaukee and Cleveland students in favor of private school vouchers. Justice Sandra Day O'Connor noted this fact in her concurring opinion in *Zelman*. During the 1999–2000 school year, Ohio spent $114.8 million on magnet schools, $9.2 million on community schools, and $8.2 million on private school vouchers.[142] Therefore, the history of fear-based choice is not identical to the history of freedom-based choice (see Table 3-4).

Fifth, the U.S. Supreme Court's support of voucher-redeeming religious schools in Cleveland is not analogous to support for the "segregation academy" model. In *The Politics of Massive Resistance*, Francis M. Wilhoit said the Supreme Court resolved this issue when it affirmed *Green v. Connally*. In *Green*, a district court said that racially segregated private schools in Mississippi could not receive the same tax benefit afforded to other educational or charitable organizations.[143] The Supreme Court did not stop there. In *Runyon v. McCrary*, the Supreme Court struck down federal funding of discriminatory private schools.[144] In *Bob Jones University v. United States*, the Supreme Court said that a private school could lose its tax-exempt status for practicing discrimination.[145] By contrast, no federal court has invalidated Wisconsin or Ohio voucher programs for supporting a "segregation academy" with public money.

Voucher opponents' use of semiotics and the "segregated academy" metaphor to support a uniform private-choice thesis fails to hold up to historical analysis. Fear-based choice is ideologically dissimilar to freedom-based choice, but this fact does not eliminate the possibility that private choice can produce the type of segregation that *Brown* sought to end forever. Private choice has this potential, but it also has the propensity not to do so. Interest groups genuinely interested in education can achieve the latter goal by identifying—and avoiding—past private-choice mistakes. Freedom-based private choice is not perfect, nor is it a panacea. But focusing solely on similarities, real and manufactured, between it and the old fear-based choice, while failing to acknowledge the blatant dissimilarities between these two movements, is counterproductive to our nation's aim: to provide quality education to all students.

Freedom of Choice: Conclusion

Then a name is an instrument of teaching and distinguishing natures as the shuttle is of distinguishing the threads of a web.[146]

— Socrates

In conclusion, a comparative analysis of private school freedom-of-choice movements in America proves the 1950s version is ideologically dissimilar to the 1990s version. Fear-based private choice was nurtured by the "Southern Manifesto," while freedom-based private choice has its ambition rooted in our "Charters of Freedom." It is also worth noting that the horrors associated with the misuse of public money for private discrimination—in 1959 or in 2004—is not a problem endemic to freedom of choice in education. Rather, it is a painful commentary about the human heart. James Madison reminds us in *Federalist 51* that "if men were angels, no government would be necessary."[147] Men used tuition grants irresponsibly during the fear-based choice movement, and government institutions stepped in to correct hateful policies created by the spirit of an unreconstructed heart. The same governmental responses are available to us today.

This comparative analysis also shows the black community as a beneficiary of freedom-based choice, unlike its counterpart during fear-based choice. To consciously turn a blind-eye to this dissimilarity in choice outcome for the black community does a great disservice to the civil rights movement. It also overlooks the wonderful gains made in education during the last 50 years. In fact, hanging a scarlet letter R (for racism) around the neck of a voucher to cheapen its appeal to the black community is unproductive for two reasons.

First, it arrests our nation's ability to fully comprehend what was happening in America during the 1950s. Second, it devalues our

43

appreciation for what was *not* happening in America during the 1990s when private choice gained popularity again. Therefore, it is more productive to look at private choice similarities and differences across time. If we do so, our nation and its educators can approach this controversial policy issue in a way that will support, rather than corrupt, honest dialogue about how best to use vouchers to deliver educational services to *Brown's* grandchildren in big city America.

Notes

1. Edith Hamilton and Huntington Cairns, eds., *The Collected Dialogues of Plato* (Princeton, N.J.: Princeton University Press, 1961). See *Cratylus* 435(d-6 to e-3), p. 469.

2. Pauline Maier, *American Scripture: Making the Declaration of Independence* (New York: Alfred Knopf, Inc., 1997), p. ix.

3. *Brown v. Board of Education*, 347 U.S. 483 (1954) [herein *Brown I*]. *Brown v. Board of Education*, 349 U.S. 294 (1955) [herein *Brown II*].

4. 536 U.S. 639 (2002).

5. See generally Commentary, *"Black Spinelessness in High Places: D.C. Mayor Sells Out on Vouchers—For Nothing!"* BlackCommentator.com at http://www.blackcommentator.com/41/41_commentary.html. And Makani N. Themba, *"School 'Choice' and Other White Lies,"* SeeingBlack.com at http://www.seeingblack.com/x051701/vouchers.shtml.

6. Elmer E. Schattschneider, *The Semisovereign People: A Realist's View of Democracy in America* (New York: Holt, Rinehart and Winston, 1960), p. 2.

7. This chapter does not address public school freedom-of-choice movements in either era nor does it deal with modern indirect-aid statutes such as tax credits or tax deductions.

8. *Brown I* at 493.

9. J. Harvie Wilkinson III, *From Brown to Bakke: The Supreme Court and School Integration: 1954–1978* (New York: Oxford University Press, 1979), p. 23. *Plessy v. Ferguson*, 163 U.S. 537 (1896).

10. See Jack M. Balkin, ed., *What Brown Should Have Said: The Nation's Top Legal Experts Rewrite America's Landmark Civil Rights Decision* (New York: New York University Press, 2002); James T. Patterson, *Brown v. Board of Education: A Civil Rights Milestone and Its Troubled Past* (New York: Oxford University Press, 2001); Mark Whitman, *The Irony of Desegregation Law 1955–1995: Essays and Documents* (Princeton, N.J.: Markus Wiener Publishers, 1998); Derrick Bell, ed., *Shades of Brown: New Perspectives on School Desegregation* (New York: Teachers College Press, 1980); and Richard Kluger, *Simple Justice* (New York: Vintage Books, 1975). But also see Gerald N. Rosenberg, *The Hollow Hope: Can Courts Bring About Social Change?* (Chicago: University of Chicago Press, 1993).

11. Modern-day school-choice advocates rarely give consideration to the relationship between *Brown* and nondiscrimination policies it helped to establish for private schools that receive public money. Failure to acknowledge this relationship underestimates the importance of *Brown's* legacy to American public *and* private education.

12. Mark G. Yudof, David L. Kirp, and Besty Levin, *Education Policy and the Law* (3d ed.) (New York: West Publishing Company, 1992), pp. 479–482. See page 479 for 2.14 percent reference. Cited from Harrell R. Rodgers and Charles S. Bullock, *Law*

and Social Change: Civil Rights Laws and Their Consequences (New York: McGraw-Hill, 1972), p. 18. See generally Gary Orfield, *The Reconstruction of Southern Education: The Schools and the 1964 Civil Rights Act* (New York: Wiley-Interscience, 1969).

13. Lino A. Graglia, *Disaster by Decree: The Supreme Court Decisions on Race and the Schools* (Ithaca, N.Y.: Cornell University Press, 1976), p. 37.

14. Frank R. Baumgartner and Bryan D. Jones, *Agendas and Instability in American Politics* (Chicago: University of Chicago Press, 1993), p. 26.

15. *Wisconsin v. Yoder*, 406 U.S. 205, 232 (1972); and *Parham v. J.R.*, 442 U.S. 584, 602 (1979).

16. 262 U.S. 390, 401(1923).

17. 268 U.S. 510, 535 (1925).

18. *Brown I* at 493.

19. Ira M. Lechner, "Massive Resistance: Virginia's Great Leap Backward," *Virginia Quarterly Review* 74 (1998): 632 n. 4; Numan V. Bartley, *The Rise of Massive Resistance: Race and Politics in the South during the 1950s* (Baton Rouge, La.: Louisiana State University Press, 1997), p. 111; and Francis M. Wilhoit, *The Politics of Massive Resistance* (New York: George Braziller, 1973), p. 77.

20. Bartley, *The Rise of Massive Resistance*, p. 116.

21. *Congressional Record—Senate*, Vol. 102, part 4, March 8, 1956, to March 27, 1956, p. 4460.

22. Davison M. Douglas, *Reading, Writing & Race: The Desegregation of Charlotte Schools* (Chapel Hill, N.C.: University of North Carolina Press, 1995), p. 33.

23. Paul Clark, *"Reviving the Doctrine of Interposition,"* 1998 Marks the Bicentennial of Madison and Jefferson's Call for States to Resist the Federal Government. Available at http://www.localsov.com/cls/reviving.htm. See also Ralph Ketcham, *James Madison: A Biography* (Charlottesville, Va.: University of Virginia Press, 1990), pp. 394–397.

24. Irving Bryant, "Madison and Interposition," *New South* 11 (1956): 6.

25. Bartley, *The Rise of Massive Resistance*, p. 131. The U.S. Supreme Court in *Cooper v. Aaron*, 358 U.S. 1 (1958) denied the constitutional validity of any interposition resolution to thwart federal law.

26. Wilhoit, *The Politics of Massive Resistance*, p. 77 (Virginia), and p. 139 (North Carolina). Florence B. Irving, "Segregation Legislation by Southern States," *New South* 12 (1957): 3 (Arkansas).

27. Irving, "Segregation Legislation by Southern States," p. 3, and Jim Leeson, "Private Schools for Whites Face Some Hurdles," *Southern Education Report* 3 (1967): 14.

28. Davison M. Douglas, "The Rhetoric of Moderation: Desegregating the South during the Decade after *Brown*," *Northwestern University Law Review* 89 (1994): 94, n. 6.

29. "Tuition grant" is a name used often, though not solely, in the subheading of *Race Relations Law Reporter* to describe private-school aid statutes of the 1950s and 1960s. Most of those statutes were racially discriminatory.

30. Scholars of massive resistance agree that it began in 1956 with Senator Byrd. Sen. Strom Thurmond from South Carolina played a key role as well. The demise of massive resistance, however, is open for debate. One view is that the fall began where it was born: Virginia. Governor Almond's January 28, 1959, speech to the Virginia General Assembly calling for moderation marked the end of massive resistance in that state, setting in motion the slow death of massive resistance in the South. And the slow death continued until the signing of the 1964 Civil Rights Act. See Wilhoit, *The Politics of Massive Resistance*, pp. 213–230. Numan V. Bartley believes

massive resistance first lost initiative in the upper South from 1958–59 and later in the Deep South during the 1960s. Reasons other than passage of the 1964 Civil Rights Act played a roll as well. See Bartley, *The Rise of Massive Resistance: Race and Politics in the South during the 1950s*, pp. 320–322, 341.

31. Ira M. Lechner, "Massive Resistance: Virginia's Great Leap Backward," *Virginia Quarterly Review* 74 (1998): 632.

32. *Race Relations Law Reporter* 3 (1958): 1241; *Race Relations Law Reporter* 4 (1959): 191; and Chapter 448, *Race Relations Law Reporter* 5 (1960): 521.

33. Chapter 58, *Race Relations Law Reporter* 1 (1956): 1094–1096; and Chapter 62, *Race Relations Law Reporter* 1 (1956): 1097–1098.

34. See generally *Harrison v. Day*, 200 Va. 439 (1959), and *James v. Almond*, 170 F.Supp. 331 (1959).

35. Scholarly books about the subject include Matthew D. Lassiter and Andrew B. Lewis, eds., *The Moderates' Dilemma: Massive Resistance to School Desegregation in Virginia* (Charlottesville, Va.: University of Virginia Press, 1998); Alexander Leidholdt, *Standing Before the Shouting Mob: Lenoir Chambers and Virginia's Massive Resistance to Public-School Integration* (Tuscaloosa, Ala.: University of Alabama Press, 1997); James W. Ely Jr., *The Crisis of Conservative Virginia: The Byrd Organization and the Politics of Massive Resistance* (Knoxville, Tenn.: University of Tennessee Press, 1978); Robert Collins Smith, *They Closed Their Schools; Prince Edward County, Virginia, 1951–1964* (Chapel Hill, N.C.: University of North Carolina Press, 1965); Benjamin Muse, *Virginia's Massive Resistance* (Bloomington, Ind.: University of Indiana Press, 1961).

36. *Allen v. County School Board of Prince Edward County*, 198 F.Supp. 497 (1961), pp. 501–502; and Wilkinson II, *From* Brown *to* Bakke, p. 99.

37. 377 U.S. 218, 225 (1964).

38. Jerome C. Hafter and Peter M. Hoffman, "Segregation Academies and State Action," *Yale Law Review* 82 (1973): 1445 n. 58.

39. *Griffin v. State Board of Education*, 296 F.Supp. 1178, 1180, 1182 (1969).

40. The Louisiana legislature enacted hundreds of bills to circumvent *Brown*. For this chapter, the focus is on four private-school aid statutes only. See Act 258, *Race Relations Law Reporter* 3 (1958): 1062 (first statute); *Poindexter v. Louisiana Financial Assistance Commission*, 275 F.Supp. 833, 842 (1967) for Act 3 of 1960, *aff'd mem.*, 389 U.S. 571 (1968) [herein *Poindexter* (1967)] (second statute); *Poindexter* (1967), p. 843 for Act 147 of 1962 (third statute); and *Race Relations Law Reporter* 12 (1967): 1604 (Act 99 was the fourth statute).

41. *Race Relations Law Reporter* 3 (1958): 1062.

42. *Poindexter* (1967) at 846.

43. *Poindexter* (1967) at 841, and Liva Baker, *The Second Battle of New Orleans: The Hundred-Year Struggle to Integrate the Schools* (New York: Harper Collins, 1996), p. 297.

44. *Poindexter* (1967) at 843.

45. *Hall v. St. Helena Parish School Board*, 197 F.Supp. 649, 659 (1961).

46. *St. Helena Parish School Board v. Hall*, 368 U.S. 515 (1962).

47. *Poindexter* (1967) at 848.

48. Hafter and Hoffman, "Segregation Academies and State Action," p. 1445 n. 58

49. *Poindexter* (1967) at 835, *aff'd mem.*, 389 U.S. 571 (1968). The establishment of a three-judge district court to hear tuition grant cases was a requirement pursuant to 28 U.S.C. §2281 and §2284 with respect to injunctions of state statutes.

50. *Poindexter v. Louisiana Financial Assistance Commission*, 296 F.Supp. 686 (1968) [herein *Poindexter 1968*], *aff'd per curiam sub nom. Louisiana Educ. Comm'n for Needy*

Children v. Poindexter, 393 U.S. 17 (1968). The court ruled the purpose and motive of Act 99 was discriminatory, even though the program had not yet begun operation. The court relied on *Gomillion v. Lightfoot*, 364 U.S. 339 (1960) to invalidate a statute even before it goes into effect based on predications of what could happen.

51. *Frithugh v. Ford*, 230 Ark. 531, 532 (1959).

52. It is worth noting that on September 1, 1958 (the same day Governor Faubus closed Little Rock senior high schools), the U.S. Supreme Court ruled in *Cooper v. Aaron*, 358 U.S. 1, 17 (1958) that the constitutional right of Negro students not to be discriminated against by the governor or state legislature on the grounds of race is a principle stated in *Brown*.

53. *Aaron v. McKinley*, 173 F.Supp 944, 945 (1959), *aff'd mem. sub non. Faubus v. Aaron*, 361 U.S. 197 (1959).

54. Wilhoit, *The Politics of Massive Resistance*, pp. 86, 88.

55. David J. Garrow, *Bearing the Cross: Martin Luther King, Jr., and the Southern Christian Leadership Conference* (New York: Vintage Books, 1988), p. 269.

56. *Lee v. Macon County Board of Education*, 231 F.Supp. 743 (1964), p. 747 [herein *Lee I*].

57. *Lee v. Macon County Board of Education*, 267 F.Supp. 458 (1967), p. 476, *aff'd mem. sub. nom. Wallace v. United States*, 389 U.S. 215 (1967) [herein *Lee II*].

58. *Lee I* at 748.

59. *Lee I* at 754.

60. *Lee II* at 476.

61. *Lee II* at 476–477.

62. *Aff'd per curiam sub nom* in *Wallace v. United States*, 389 U.S. 215 (1967).

63. John A. Allen, "The Tax-Exempt Status of Segregated Schools," *Tax Law Review* 24 (1969): 411.

64. Jim Lesson, "The Crumbling Legal Barriers to School Desegregation," *Southern Education Report* 2 (1966): 12.

65. *Brown v. South Carolina State Board of Education*, 296 F.Supp. 202 (1968), *aff'd per curiam*, 393 U.S. 222, (1968).

66. Tuition Grants—Mississippi: *Race Relations Law Reporter* 9 (1964): 1500. Also see *Coffey v. State Educational Finance Commission*, 296 F.Supp. 1389 (1969), p. 1390. Language in the statute leaves open for debate its applicability to public school students.

67. Wilhoit, *The Politics of Massive Resistance*, p. 49. See also Hafter and Hoffman, "Segregation Academies and State Action," p. 1448 n. 69.

68. Kenneth T. Andrews, "Movement—Countermovement Dynamics and the Emergence of New Institutions: The Case of 'White Flight' Schools in Mississippi," *Social Forces* 80 (March 2002): 916.

69. Ibid., pp. 922–923.

70. *Coffey* at 1392.

71. 42 U.S.C. 2000c-6. Civil actions by the Attorney General.

72. *Coffey* at 1392.

73. Citing *Reitman v. Mulkey*, 387 U.S. 369, 381, (1967), found in *Coffey* at 1392.

74. Hafter and Hoffman, "Segregation Academies and State Action," p. 1445 n. 58. Student enrollment in white academies ballooned to more than 40,000 one year after the *Coffey* decision. Reasons for the increase are beyond the scope of this chapter. See generally Andrews, "Movement—Countermovement Dynamics and the Emergence of New Institutions: The Case of 'White Flight' Schools in Mississippi" (2002).

75. NewsHour with Jim Lehrer, available at http://www.pbs.org/newshour/bb/law/jan-june02/vouchers_2-20a.html. For a good history of the voucher movement, see Clint Bolick, *Voucher Wars: Waging the Legal Battle over School Choice* (Washington: Cato Institute, 2003).

76. Private school aid programs were operating for decades in Vermont and Maine before vouchers arrived in Milwaukee and Cleveland. However, the introduction of vouchers in Milwaukee and Cleveland put the topic of private school aid on the forefront of policy debate in ways Vermont and Maine did not. For information about Vermont and Maine (and Florida), see http://www.schoolchoiceinfo.org/facts/index.cfm.

77. A great deal of scholarly treatment is available dealing with the good, bad, and ugly aspects of school vouchers in Milwaukee and Cleveland. Consensus within academia is mixed about the success or failure of these programs. See generally R. Kenneth Godwin and Frank R. Kemerer, *School Choice Tradeoffs: Liberty, Equity, and Diversity* (Austin, Tex.: University of Texas Press, 2002); David L. Brennan, *Victory for Kids: The Cleveland School Voucher Case* (Beverly Hills, Calif.: New Millennium Press, 2002); Frederick Hess, *Revolution at the Margins: The Impact of Competition on Urban School Systems* (Washington: Brookings Institution, 2002); Terry M. Moe, *Schools, Vouchers, and the American Public* (Washington: Brookings Institution, 2001); Mikel Holt, *Not Yet "Free At Last": The Unfinished Business of the Civil Rights Movement* (Oakland, Calif.: Institute for Contemporary Studies, 2000); John F. Witte, *The Market Approach to Education: An Analysis of America's First Voucher Program* (Princeton, N.J.: Princeton University Press, 2000); Elchanan Cohn, ed., *Market Approaches to Education: Vouchers and School Choice* (Tarrytown, N.Y.: Pergamon, 1997); Jeffrey R. Henig, *Rethinking School Choice: Limits of the Market Metaphor* (Princeton, N.J.: Princeton University Press, 1994); and Peter W. Cookson Jr., *School Choice: The Struggle for the Soul of American Education* (New Haven, Conn.: Yale University Press, 1994).

78. Wisconsin Statutes Annotated §119.23 (2001).

79. Moe, *Schools, Vouchers, and the American Public*, pp. 32–34; and Holt, *Not Yet "Free At Last,"* pp. 59–78.

80. Wisconsin Statutes Annotated §119.23(2)(a)(1) (2001).

81. 578 N.W. 2d 206, 620 (1998), *cert. denied*, 525 U.S. 997 (1998).

82. Department of Public Instruction, Milwaukee Parental Choice Program—Facts and Figures as of February 2003. See http://www.dpi.state.wi.us/dfm/sms/choice.html.

83. Department of Public Instruction, Milwaukee Parental Choice Program—Frequently Asked Questions—2003–04 School Year. See http://www.dpi.state.wi.us/dfm/sms/choice.html. The per student amount paid to each MPCP private school is not $6,020 automatically. Only the actual tuition amount is paid to the school. For example, if tuition at private school A is $3,000, then MPCP will pay only $3,000.

84. Nina Shokraii Rees, *School Choice: What's Happening in the States* (Washington: Heritage Foundation, 2000), p. 130. To maintain consistency, I refer to the Cleveland Project Scholarship Program as the Cleveland voucher program.

85. Moe, *Schools, Vouchers, and the American Public*, pp. 37–38.

86. Ohio Revenue Code Annotated §3313.978(A) and (C)(1).

87. Ohio Revenue Code Annotated §3313.978(A), and Kaleem Caire, "Cleveland (OH) Scholarship and Tutorial Program" (2002). Copy in author's files.

88. *Simmons-Harris v. Zelman*, 234 F.3d 945 (6th Cir. 2000).

89. 536 U.S. 639 (2002). On April 16, 2003, Colorado Governor Bill Owens signed into law a statewide voucher program.

90. SchoolChoiceInfo.org, "School Voucher Enrollment Growth" available at http://www.schoolchoiceinfo.org/facts/index.cfm?fpt_id=5&fl_id=2.

91. SchoolChoiceInfo.org available at http://www.schoolchoiceinfo.org/facts/index.cfm?fpt_id=6&fl_id=2, citing Kim Metcalf, "Evaluation of the Cleveland Scholarship Program and Tutoring Grant Program, 1996–99," Indiana Center for Evaluation, September 1999.

92. Justice Felix Frankfurter, "Some Reflections on the Reading of Statutes," *Columbia Law Review* 47 (1947): 533. Quote found in *Poindexter* (1967) at 837 n. 16.

93. This does not mean that no religious school in the six southern states ever received a tuition grant. The point is simply to indicate the intent of the statute.

94. *Poindexter* (1967) at 843.

95. Blackstone, Commentaries 61 (8th ed. 1778). Heydon's Case, 3 Co. Rep. 7a, 7b, 76 *Eng. Rep.* 637 (1584). Quote found in *Poindexter* (1967) at 837 n. 15.

96. David B. Truman, *The Governmental Process: Political Interests and Public Opinion* (Berkeley, Calif.: Institute of Governmental Studies, 1993), pp. 33–34, 216–217. For additional study of interest groups, see Mark P. Petracca, *The Politics of Interests: Interest Groups Transformed* (San Francisco: Westview Press, 1992).

97. Black Alliance for Educational Options Web site http://www.baeo.org/home/index.php. For varying perspectives on school vouchers in the black community, see David A. Bositis, *Education: 2002 National Opinion Poll*, pp. 7–8 available at http://www.jointcenter.org/publications/details/opinion-poll/n-NOP-education-2002.html.

98. Moe, *Schools, Vouchers, and the American Public*, p. 27, and People for the American Way, "Why Vouchers Won't Work," available at http://www.everychild-counts.org/. See also "Myths and Facts About School Vouchers" at http://www.pfaw.org/pfaw/general/default.aspx?oid=1427.

99. People for the American Way, "Partners for Public Education," available at http://www.everychildcounts.org/. See also "Myths and Facts About School Vouchers," available at http://www.pfaw.org/pfaw/general/default.aspx?oid=1427.

100. American Civil Liberties Union, Press Release, October 9, 1997. "House Narrowly OKs Discriminatory Voucher Scheme; Defying Senate, President, and American Public." Available at http://archive.aclu.org/news/n100997a.html.

101. See generally Molly Townes O'Brien, "Private School Tuition Vouchers and the Realities of Racial Politics," *Tennessee Law Review* 64 (1997): 359; and Helen Hershkoff and Adam S. Cohen, "School Choice and the Lessons of Choctaw County," *Yale Law & Policy Review* 10 (1992): 1.

102. Maria Baghramian, ed., *Modern Philosophy of Language* (London: J. M. Dent, 1998); pp. xix–xxx.

103. Ibid., p. xxx.

104. See generally Murray J. Edelman, *The Symbolic Uses of Language in Politics* (Urbana, Ill.: University of Illinois Press, 1985).

105. Bruce Hawkins, "Ideology, Metaphor, and Iconographic Reference," in *Language and Ideology: Volume III: Descriptive Cognitive Approaches*, ed. René Dirven, Roslyn Frank, and Corlelia Ilie (Philadelphia: John Benjamins Publishing Company, 2001), p. 32.

106. Molly Townes O'Brien, "Private School Tuition Vouchers and the Realities of Racial Politics," p. 406.

107. Evan Thomas and Lynette Clemetson, "A New War Over Vouchers," *Newsweek*, November, 22, 1999, p. 46.

108. Rep. Elijah E. Cummings (D-Md.), "CBC [Congressional Black Caucus] Special Order Commemorating the 49th Anniversary of *Brown v. Board of Education*," House of Representatives—May 14, 2003. See http://www.house.gov/cummings/cbc/cbcspeech/sp051403.htm; and Rep. Robert C. "Bobby" Scott (D-Va.), "Remarks of Congressman Robert C. 'Bobby' Scott on Behalf of the 49th Anniversary of the *Brown v. Board of Education* Supreme Court Decision." See http://www.house.gov/scott/press/remarks_Brown_vs_Board_of_Education.htm.

109. *NewsHour with Gwen Ifill*, http://www.pbs.org/newshour/bb/law/jan-june02/vouchers_2-20a.html.

110. Survey conducted on Lexus-Nexus search engine. Searches from 1954–1969 for "voucher" and "school" and "tuition grant" were done for district, appellant, and Supreme Court decisions. Searches from 1970–2003 for "voucher" and "school" and "tuition grant" focused on Supreme Court decisions.

111. Examples include, but are not limited to, *Darcy v. Handy*, 130 F.Supp. 270 (1955) (jury); *Wirtz v. Healy*, 227 F. Supp. 123 (1964) (travel expense); and *South Carolina v. Katzenbach*, 383 U.S. 301 (1966) (voting).

112. *USA v. Beacon Musical Instruments Co.*, 135 F.Supp. 220 (1955) (educational payment); and *Powe v. Miles*, 407 F.2d. 73 (1968).

113. Examples of voucher used in U.S. Supreme Court decisions between 1970–2003. *Hubbard v. U.S.*, 514 U.S. 695 (1995) (transaction); *Presley v. Etowah County Comm'n*, 502 U.S. 491 (1992) (voting); and *Blum v. Bacon*, 457 U.S. 132 (1982) (food stamps). Here are four references for voucher and education made between 1970 and 2003. *Committee for Public Education & Religious Liberty v. Regan*, 444 U.S. 646 (1980) (audit voucher); *U.S. v. Lopez* 514 U.S. 549 (1995); *Board of Trustees of the University of Alabama v. Garrett*, 531 U.S. 356 (2001) (voucher for disabled student); and *Zelman v. Simmons-Harris*, 536 U.S. 639 (2002) (Cleveland voucher).

114. 413 U.S. 756 (1973).

115. 413 U.S. 455 (1973).

116. Fred R. Dallmayr, *Language and Politics: Why Does Language Matter to Political Philosophy* (Notre Dame, Ind.: University of Notre Dame Press, 1984), p. 3.

117. Murray Edelman, *The Politics of Misinformation* (New York: Cambridge University Press, 2001), pp. 11–12.

118. "School Vouchers: Few v. All," *Rainbow/Push* VII, Issue 9 (2002). See http://www.rainbowpush.org/weeklyfax/2002/RPF_02_21_02.pdf .

119. Quote found in Jonathan Kozol, "Falling Behind: An Interview with Jonathan Kozol," *The Christian Century*, May 10, 2000, pp. 541–543. See http://www.religion-online.org/cgi-bin/relsearchd.dll/showarticle?item_id=1990.

120. Allen, "The Tax-Exempt Status of Segregated Schools," p. 412, and Note, "Federal Tax Benefits to Segregated Private Schools," *Columbia Law Review* 68 (1989): 924; David Asaki, Michael A. Jacobs, and Sharon Y. Scott, "Racial Segregation and the Tax-Exempt Status of Private Educational and Religious Institutions," *Howard Law Journal* 25 (1982): 546 n. 7; and Mark I. Silberblatt, "Denial of Tax Exempt Status to Southern Segregated Academies: *Green v. Kennedy* (D.D.C. 1970)," *Harvard Civil Rights/Civil Liberties Law Review* 6 (1970): 179.

121. David Lidov, *Elements of Semiotics* (New York: St. Martin's Press, 1999), p. 4.

122. David Sless, *In Search of Semiotics* (London: Croom Helm, 1986), pp. 1, 10.

123. Jack Solomon, *The Signs of Our Times: The Secret Meaning of Everyday Life* (New York: Harper & Row Publishers, 1988), p. 9.

124. Charles D. Elder and Roger W. Cobb, *The Political Uses of Symbols* (New York: Longman, 1983), p. 29.

125. Deborah Stone, *Policy Paradox* (New York: W. W. Norton & Company, 1997), p. 148. For a different perspective on metaphor, see Donald Davidson, *Inquires into Truth and Interpretation* (New York: Oxford University Press, 2001) (". . . metaphors mean what the words, in their most literal interpretation, mean, and nothing more."), p. 245.

126. Winfried Noth, *Handbook on Semiotics* (Bloomington, Ind.: Indiana University Press, 1990), p. 128.

127. Editorial by Rep. Jesse Jackson Jr (D-Ill.), Truthout, "Vouchers: Illegitimate Cure for Legitimate Concerns." See http://www.truthout.com/docs_02/06.28C.jjj.vouch.htm.

128. Steven K. Green, "The Illusionary Aspect of 'Private Choice' for Constitutional Analysis," *Willamette Law Review* 38 (2002): 556–557. See pp. 556–557 for Green's reference to equality and choice. For a supportive view of this position, see Joseph Vitteritti, *Choosing Equality: School Choice, the Constitution, and Civil Society* (Washington: Brookings Institution, 1999), pp. 11–15.

129. Donald A. Schön and Martin Rein, *Frame Reflection: Toward the Resolution of Intractable Policy Controversies* (New York: Basic Books, 1994), pp. 26–27.

130. Green, "The Illusionary Aspect of 'Private Choice' for Constitutional Analysis," pp. 565–566. Emphasis added.

131. John E. Eastman, "The Magic of Vouchers Is No Sleight of Hand: A Reply to Steven K. Green," *Willamette Law Review* 38 (2002): 205.

132. Green, "The Illusionary Aspect of 'Private Choice' for Constitutional Analysis," p. 565.

133. 281 U.S. 370 (1930). The other case is *Everson v. Board of Education*, 330 U.S. 1 (1947). The Court upheld a New Jersey statute to pay the cost for transporting parochial schoolchildren. Robert S. Alley, ed., *The Constitution & Religion: Leading Supreme Court Cases on Church and State* (Amherst, N.Y.: Prometheus Book, 1999), pp. 45–47.

134. *Poindexter* (1967) at 835.

135. Allen, "The Tax-Exempt Status of Segregated Schools," p. 411, and Note, "Federal Tax Benefits to Segregated Private Schools," pp. 924, 947.

136. *Lee II* (1967) at 466 (Alabama), *aff'd mem. sub. nom. Wallace v. United States*, 389 U.S. 215 (1967). *Poindexter* at 836 (Louisiana), *aff'd mem.*, 389 U.S. 571 (1968).

137. Ohio Revenue Code Annotated §3313.976(4) (West Supp. 2002); and Eastman, "The Magic of Vouchers Is No Sleight of Hand: A Reply to Steven K. Green," p. 205. See Wisconsin Statute Annotated §119.23(4)-(5)(2001), and 42 U.S.C. 2000d for 1964 Civil Rights Act.

138. Virginia, Louisiana, and Alabama later removed this requirement.

139. Public Schools—Virginia: Chapter 68 *Race Relations Law Reporter* 3 (1958): 1103.

140. *Harrison v. Day*, 200 Va. 439, 443 n. 1 (1959).

141. Ibid.

142. *Zelman* at 664.

143. 330 F.Supp. 1150 (1971), *aff'd sub. nom. Coit v. Green* 404 U.S. 997 (1971). Wilhoit, *The Politics of Massive Resistance*, p. 154.

144. 427 U.S. 160 (1976).

145. 461 U.S. 574 (1983).

146. Hamilton and Huntington, *The Collected Dialogues of Plato*, p. 426. See *Cratylus* 388 (c 1–3).

147. Clinton Rossiter, ed., *The Federalist Papers* (New York: Mentor, 1961), p. 322.

4. The Meaning of *Zelman* and the Future of School Choice

Paul E. Peterson

In the most anticipated decision of its 2002 term, the Supreme Court ruled, in the case of *Zelman v. Simmons-Harris*, that the school-voucher program in Cleveland, Ohio, did not violate the Constitution's ban on the "establishment" of religion. Opponents of vouchers—that is, the use of public funds to help low-income families pay tuition at private schools, including religious schools—were predictably disappointed, but pledged to fight on. As Sen. Edward M. Kennedy declared, "Private school vouchers may pass constitutional muster," but they "are still bad policy for public schools."[1]

The policy's sympathizers, needless to say, saw the ruling in a different light. President Bush used the occasion of the Supreme Court's decision to issue a full-throated endorsement of vouchers. *Zelman*, he told a gathering in Cleveland, did more than remove a constitutional cloud; it was a "historic" turning point in how Americans think about education. In 1954, in *Brown v. Board of Education*, the Court had ruled that the country could not have two sets of schools, "one for African-Americans and one for whites." Now, he continued, in ruling as it did in the Cleveland case, the Court was affirming a similar principle, proclaiming that "our nation will not accept one education system for those who can afford to send their children to a school of their choice and one for those who can't."[2] *Zelman*, according to the President, is *Brown* all over again.

But is it? That remains the central question as we consider the future of school choice.

Publicly funded school vouchers got their start in Milwaukee, Wisconsin, in 1990. Established at the urging of local black leaders and Wisconsin Governor Tommy Thompson (now the Secretary of Health and Human Services), the program was originally restricted to secular private schools and included fewer than a thousand needy students. To accommodate growing demand, religious schools were later allowed to participate, an arrangement declared constitutional in 1998 by the Wisconsin Supreme Court. The Milwaukee program now provides a voucher worth up to $5,785 to more than 10,000 students, amounting to more than 15 percent of the school system's eligible population.

In 1999, at the behest of Governor Jeb Bush, Florida also established a publicly funded voucher program, aimed at students attending public schools that failed to meet state standards. The failing-school program in Florida is also noteworthy because it served as a model for the voucher-like federal scholarship program advocated by George W. Bush during the 2000 presidential campaign—and which, in modified form, was incorporated into the federal No Child Left Behind Act. In 2003, only a few hundred students were participating in this, the failing-school program, but another nine thousand students were participating in a little-noticed companion program that made vouchers available for those students in need of special education.

Until the voucher law passed by the Colorado legislature in the spring of 2003, the Milwaukee and Florida voucher initiatives were the only publicly funded programs—except for the small program in Cleveland that proved more important than any other simply by reaching the writing desk of the Chief Justice. At the time the program was under Supreme Court consideration, it provided a maximum of $2,250 a year in tuition aid to each of roughly 4,000 students. Parents used the vouchers overwhelmingly for religious schools, which in recent years have matriculated more than 90 percent of the program's participants. This, according to lawyers for the teachers unions, the most powerful foe of vouchers, constituted an obvious violation of the separation between church and state. And they prevailed twice in federal court, winning decisions at the trial and appellate level against Susan Zelman, Ohio's superintendent of public instruction and the official responsible for administering the Cleveland program.

The Meaning of *Zelman*

But the five justices of the Supreme Court were not persuaded by the teachers unions' arguments. In his opinion for the majority in *Zelman*, Chief Justice William Rehnquist pointed to three well-known precedents—*Mueller* (1983), *Witters* (1986), and *Zobrest* (1993)—in which the Court had allowed government funds to flow to religious schools. What these cases had in common, he wrote, and what they shared with the Cleveland voucher program, was that public money reached the schools "only as a result of the genuine and independent choices of private individuals." Under Cleveland's program, families were in no way coerced to send their children to religious schools; they had a range of state-funded options, including secular private schools, charter schools, magnet schools, and traditional public schools. Rehnquist concluded that the voucher program was "entirely neutral with respect to religion."

The dissenters in *Zelman*, led by Justice David Souter, challenged the majority's reading of the relevant precedents—especially of *Nyquist* (1973), a ruling that struck down a New York State program giving aid to religious schools—and suggested that the choice in Cleveland between religion and nonreligion was a mere legal fiction. They saved their most pointed objections, however, for what they saw as the likely social consequences of the ruling. The Court, Souter wrote, was promoting "divisiveness" by asking secular taxpayers to support, for example, the teaching of "Muslim views on the differential treatment of the sexes," or by asking Muslim Americans to pay "for the endorsement of the religious Zionism taught in many religious Jewish schools." Justice Stephen Breyer suggested that the decision would spark "a struggle of sect against sect," and Justice John Paul Stevens wondered if the majority had considered the lessons of other nations' experience around the world, including "the impact of religious strife . . . on the decisions of neighbors in the Balkans, Northern Ireland, and the Middle East to mistrust one another."

Responding to the worries of the dissenters, Justice Sandra Day O'Connor reminded her colleagues of the wide range of ways in which government and religion in fact relate to one another within the United States. She pointed out that taxpayer dollars have long flowed to various religious institutions through Pell Grants to denominational colleges and universities; through child-care subsidies that can be used at churches, synagogues, and other religious institutions; through direct aid to parochial schools for transportation, textbooks, and other materials; and, indirectly, through the tax code, which gives special breaks to the faithful. If government aid to religious institutions were such a problem, she suggested, wouldn't American society be torn already by sectarian strife?

55

There is, of course, little in the practice of religious schools in the United States that justifies the language used by Justices Souter, Breyer, and Stevens. Several well-designed studies have shown that students who attend private schools in the United States not only are just as tolerant of others as their public school peers but also are *more* engaged in political and community life. Catholic schools have a particularly outstanding record, probably because for more than a century American Catholics have felt compelled to teach democratic values as proof of their patriotism. There are obviously extremist outliers among them, but there is no reason to doubt that most of the country's religious schools are attempting to prove that they too can create good citizens. Moreover, most of the world's democracies fund both religious and secular schools without causing undue domestic turmoil. For the most part, tensions are managed without bitter, divisive controversy.

Still, if judicial rhetoric is all that counts, the dissenters in *Zelman* had the better of it. In the majority opinion, by contrast, there is very little that rises to the level of *Brown*'s often-cited language about the demands of American equality. Even observers pleased by the ruling were disappointed that the majority's opinion did not go much beyond showing how the facts of the case fit past precedents; no ringing declarations are to be found in Chief Justice Rehnquist's stodgy prose. In fact, the decision may have been a narrow one, hardly in the same league as *Brown*. In Cleveland, vouchers were accompanied by charter schools (called community schools in Ohio) and other forms of school choice that give parents a range of secular options that accompanied the religious ones obtained through vouchers. It is not altogether clear whether voucher initiatives are unconstitutional in the absence of a significant range of secular choices.

But if the majority opinion was legalistic, and the O'Connor opinion fact-driven, in a separate concurring opinion written by Justice Clarence Thomas, one gets a sense of the wider issues at stake. Invoking *Brown* as an explicit precedent, he quotes Frederick Douglass to argue that today's inner-city public school systems "deny emancipation to urban minority students."[3] As he observed,

> The failure to provide education to poor urban children perpetuates a vicious cycle of poverty, dependence, criminality, and alienation that continues for the remainder of their lives.

> If society cannot end racial discrimination, at least it can arm
> minorities with the education to defend themselves from
> some of discrimination's effects.[4]

For Justice Thomas—as for President Bush, whose own remarks
were undoubtedly influenced by these passages—vouchers are a
civil-rights issue; they promise not to intensify religious strife, as
the Court's dissenters would have it, but to help heal the country's
most enduring social divide.

Moving Beyond *Zelman*

Whether *Zelman* can in fact meet these high expectations remains
very much to be seen. *Brown*, in principle, was self-enacting. Neither
state legislatures nor local school boards could defy the ruling without running afoul of the law. George Wallace, Bull Conner, and
many other Southern politicians were willing to do just that but, in
the end, federal authorities imposed the Supreme Court's decision
on the vested interests that opposed it. *Zelman* is different. Though
it keeps existing voucher programs intact, it does not compel the
formation of new ones. Here the barricades to change remain extraordinarily high. When *Brown* was handed down, northern public opinion was moving against segregation; on the issue of vouchers, by
contrast, public opinion is highly uncertain. Pollsters can get either
pro-voucher or anti-voucher majorities simply by tinkering with the
wording of their questions and the order in which they are asked.
And despite greater exposure for the issue, the public's views have
not evolved much in recent years; questions asked in 1995 generated
basically the same results in 2000.

Vouchers suffer from more serious problems among members of
the political class. To become law, either at the national or state
level, substantial bipartisan support is usually necessary. Only with
broad political backing can supporters of new initiatives negotiate
a bill through multiple legislative committees, get it past a vote in
two chambers, and have it signed into law. For vouchers, such
support has materialized in only four states—and even there for only
limited programs. Strong opposition among Democratic legislators is
a major obstacle. Whatever their opinions—many have sent their
own children to private school—for most it is political suicide to

support vouchers publicly. Teachers unions have long placed vouchers at the top of their legislative kill list, and they are a key Democratic constituency, providing the party with both substantial financing and election-day shock troops.

Nor can voucher proponents rely on wholehearted support from the GOP. Most Republicans, especially social conservatives and libertarians who have read their Milton Friedman, support vouchers in principle. Still, an idea whose primary appeal is to black Americans, the most faithful of all Democratic voting blocs, is a hard sell among the Republican rank and file. Vouchers simply do not have much resonance with well-heeled suburbanites who already have a range of educational choices. When vouchers came up as state ballot questions in both California and Michigan two years ago, most Republican politicians found a way to dodge the issue—and the proposals lost badly.

Even if this political situation were to change, most states have constitutional restrictions of their own that may be invoked to scuttle attempts to provide vouchers for use at religious schools. Many of these provisions are so-called Blaine amendments, dating to the 19th century, when James Blaine, a Senator from Maine and a Republican presidential candidate, sought to win the anti-immigrant vote by campaigning to deny public funds to Catholic schools. (Blaine is perhaps most famous for describing the Democrats as the party of "Rum, Romanism, and Rebellion.") In its classic version, the Blaine amendment read as follows:

> No money raised by taxation for the support of public schools, or derived from any public fund therefore, nor any public lands devoted thereto, shall ever be under the control of any religious sect; nor shall any money so raised or lands so devoted be divided between religious sects or denominations.[5]

In a number of cases, state courts have interpreted Blaine amendments to mean nothing more than what is required, according to the Supreme Court, by the establishment clause of the First Amendment. On this view, vouchers are safe, but not every state judge necessarily shares this view. Such language may prove to be a hurdle for the voucher program in Florida, for example, where a trial court has found the law in violation of the state constitution. Depending on what happens at the state level, the Supreme Court may eventually be asked to decide whether, on account of their nativist and anti-Catholic origins, the Blaine amendments and their derivatives are themselves unconstitutional.

Other Forms of School Choice

If school vouchers should falter on either political or state constitutional grounds, this would not necessarily forestall the school choice movement. Three other avenues remain under active consideration—tax credits, charter schools, and public school choice—though each contain their own set of speed bumps and potholes.

Tax credits and tax deductions, reducing taxes by a portion of the amount one pays for school tuition or one contributes toward private school scholarships, are being tried out in several states, including Minnesota, Arizona, Florida, and Pennsylvania. In some forms, private school tax credits and deductions are indistinguishable from vouchers, the only difference being the distribution of funds to parents via the tax code rather than by means of the grant-making authority of government. To many economists, this is a legal distinction without substantive meaning. But in the world of law and practice, state tax credits and deductions have an entirely different standing. For one thing, their constitutionality is much more difficult to challenge, having stood tests in both state and federal courts. For another, they are more popular with the general public, winning higher levels of support than vouchers in opinion polls. In addition, many private-school operators prefer tax credits and deductions because they are less likely to be accompanied by government strings. On the other hand, it is more difficult to target tax credits and deductions toward disadvantaged populations. Much of the equal opportunity élan that has motivated the voucher movement might be lost were this to become the sole form of school choice.

Charter schools, schools run under government charters by private entities, have gained even broader acceptability than tax credits and tax deductions. As many as 39 states have allowed the formation of charter schools, though in many states the law restricts charter-school operations in important ways, either by limiting the number of charter schools, subjecting them to restrictive controls, or placing them under the authority of potentially hostile regulatory agencies. But the idea has been popular enough that, as of 2002, more than

600,000 students, better than one percent of the school age population, were attending more than 2,700 charter schools. The period of rapid growth occurred in the mid to late 1990s; since 2000, the growth rate has tapered off in the face of strengthened union opposition, tighter regulatory controls, and a series of well-publicized scandals at a few charter schools.

Charters have one important advantage over school vouchers: they address the supply side of the school choice equation. Although vouchers may give parents resources with which they can pay for private school, that means little unless private schools increase in number or expand in size. Yet the initial costs of starting a new school and recruiting a constituency for the school can be very large. With a charter from the state in hand, charter school operators are better placed to open a new school. Also, charter schools have typically received financial support that comes close to the amount received for the operation of traditional public schools, a level of fiscal support not yet achieved by any existing voucher program. But even with these advantages, charter schools still face many practical and political problems that can be addressed only if they receive greater support for their start-up costs and if they develop their own networks of support and shared information.

Finally, there is the public school choice encouraged under the recent federal legislation, No Child Left Behind, enacted into law in January 2002. The legislation says that any failing school must allow students to attend other public schools within the school district. Yet it remains unclear whether this nationwide choice provision will open the door to a wide set of school choices. A choice among traditional public schools within the central city is not enough of an option for most of those trapped within the inner core of our large metropolitan areas. Even worse, local school districts have done little to implement the legislation in the first year that it has taken effect. But one should not rush to judgment. Perhaps groups will form to spur more effective implementation of the law. The question deserves continuing close scrutiny.

Equal Opportunity for African-Americans

Depending on the way these various courses of action evolve—new voucher initiatives, tax credits, charter schools, public school choice—the Court's famed ruling in *Zelman* could still make the decision as critical as *Brown*. Certainly, the pro-choice movement, like the desegregation movement, means much more for minority students and their families than for other Americans.

For decades, and despite a host of compensatory reforms, the sizable gap in educational performance between blacks and whites has remained roughly the same. According to the National Assessment of Educational Progress, black eighth-graders continue to score about four grade levels below their white peers on standardized tests. Nor is this gap likely to close as long as we have, in President Bush's words, "one education system for those who can afford to send their children to a school of their choice and one for those who can't."

When parents choose a neighborhood or town in which to live, they also select, often quite self-consciously, a school for their children. That is why various Internet services now provide buyers and real-estate agents with detailed test-score data and other information about school districts and even individual schools. But there is a catch: the mobility that makes these choices possible costs money. It is no accident that children lucky enough to be born into privilege also attend the nation's best schools.

African-Americans are often the losers in this arrangement. Holding less financial equity and still facing discrimination in the housing market, they choose from a limited set of housing options. As a result, their children are more likely to attend the worst public schools. Richer, whiter districts rarely extend anything more than a few token slots to low-income minority students outside of their communities.

It is thus unsurprising that blacks have benefited most when school choice has been expanded. In multi-year evaluations of private voucher programs in New York City, Washington, D.C., and Dayton, Ohio, my colleagues and I found that African-American students, when given the chance to attend private schools, scored significantly higher on standardized tests than comparable students who remained in the public schools. In New York, where the estimates are most precise, those who switched from public to private schools scored, after three years, roughly nine percentage points higher on math and reading tests than their public school peers, a difference of about two grade levels. If reproduced nationwide, this result would cut almost in half the black-white test-score gap.[6]

These findings about the especially positive effects of private schools on African-American students are hardly isolated. One review of the literature, conducted by the Princeton economist Cecilia Rouse, concludes that even though it is difficult to discern positive benefits for white students, "catholic schools generate higher test scores for African-Americans."[7] Another, done by Jeffrey Grogger and Derek Neal, economists from the University of Wisconsin and the University of Chicago, respectively, finds little in the way of detectable gains for whites, but concludes that "urban minorities in Catholic schools fare much better than similar students in public schools."[8] We do not know precisely what accounts for the gains that black students have made by switching to private schools. The answer is certainly not money because the private schools they attend are usually low-budget, no-frills operations. The most striking difference, according to the research conducted by William Howell, Patrick Wolf, David Campbell, and Paul Peterson, lies in the general educational environment: the parents of these students have reported being much more satisfied with everything from the curriculum, homework, and teacher quality to how the schools communicate with the parents themselves. The classes tend to be smaller, they say, and there is less fighting, cheating, racial conflict, or destruction of property.

That vouchers can produce such results has been known for some time. The question now is whether the ruling in *Zelman* will have any impact on what the public and politicians think about the issue. If nothing else, the Court's authoritative pronouncement on the constitutionality of vouchers has already conferred new legitimacy on them. Newspaper editors and talk-show hosts have been forced to give the idea more respect, and political opponents cannot dismiss it so easily.

No Child Left Behind

But how about those students left behind in traditional public schools? Even if students attending private schools are better off, will not those remaining in public schools be adversely affected? Do vouchers attract the best and brightest from public schools? Does public schools' performance spiral downward? Do public schools lose critically important fiscal resources?

Do Vouchers Attract the Best and the Brightest?

My own research has looked at this question in two different ways. In one study, my colleagues and I compared a random sample of all those who applied for a voucher offered nationwide by the Children's Scholarship Fund with a national cross-section of all those eligible to apply. African-American students were twice as likely to apply as others. Specifically, 49 percent of the applicants were African-American, even though they constituted just 26 percent of the eligible population. Other results reveal little sign that the interest in vouchers is limited to only the most talented. On the contrary, voucher applicants were just as likely to have a child who had a learning disability as all those in the eligible population. Nor is it only the better-educated families who take an interest. Twenty-three percent of the mothers of applicants said they had graduated from college, as compared with 20 percent of the mothers in the eligible population.

In a second study, this time of vouchers in New York, Washington, D.C., and Dayton, my colleagues and I looked at those who actually made use of a voucher when it was offered to them. We did not find any evidence that private schools discriminated on the basis of a young student's test-score performance at the time they received an application from a voucher recipient. Among young applicants in New York City and Washington, D.C., there was no significant difference in the test scores at the time of application between vouchers users and those who turned down the voucher and remained in public school. In Dayton, those using the voucher actually had lower math scores at the time of application, showing even more clearly that private schools were willing to take the educationally challenged student. Only among older students (grades 6–8) in Washington, D.C., did we see some signs that private schools expected students to meet a minimum educational standard before admission.

Other researchers find much the same pattern. In Milwaukee, the Wisconsin Legislative Audit Bureau found that the ethnic composition of the participants in Milwaukee's voucher program during the 1998–1999 school year did not differ materially from that of students remaining in public schools. Similarly, a University of Wisconsin evaluation of an earlier, smaller voucher program in Milwaukee found few consistent test-score or family-background differences between those who took vouchers and those who remained in public schools. Also, in Cleveland, Indiana University analysts said that voucher "students, like their families, are very similar to their public school counterparts."[9] In short, vouchers tend to recruit a cross-section of the families and students eligible for participation.

Upon reflection, these findings are not particularly surprising. Families are more likely to want to opt out of a school if their child is doing badly than if that child is doing well. A number of families, moreover, select a private school because they like the religious education it provides, or because it is safe, or because they like the discipline. When all of these factors operate simultaneously, the types of students who take a voucher usually look little different from those who pass up the opportunity.

Public School Performance

If vouchers do not simply pick off the top students within the public schools but attract instead a cross-section of students, then there is no obvious educational reason why public schools should suffer as a result of the initiative. On the contrary, public schools, confronted by the possibility that they could lose substantial numbers of students to competing schools within the community, might well pull up their socks and reach out more effectively to those they are serving. Interestingly enough, there is already some evidence that public schools do exactly that.

Harvard economist Caroline Minter Hoxby has shown, for example, that since the Milwaukee voucher program was established on a larger scale in 1998, it has had a positive impact on public school test scores. The public schools in the low-income neighborhoods most intensely affected by the voucher program increased their performance by a larger amount than scores in areas of Milwaukee and elsewhere in Wisconsin not affected by the voucher program. She also found a similar positive impact of charter school competition on public school test scores in Michigan and Arizona, the two states in the country with the largest number of students attending charter schools. In other words, when substantial numbers of students are using vouchers or going to charter schools, public schools in the vicinity apparently respond by improving their educational offerings and, as a result, public school performance is enhanced.

Even the threat of a voucher can have a positive effect on test scores. Research by Manhattan Institute scholar Jay Greene shows that when public schools were in danger of failing twice on the statewide Florida exam, making their students eligible for vouchers, these public schools made special efforts to avoid failure. Their test scores climbed more than did almost equally bad schools (which had D-minus test scores) that were not threatened by vouchers. Greene was able to rule out the possibility that the improvements were the result of the additional resources made available to the F schools. In other words, competition—even the threat of competition—had positive effects in Florida.

One can look at the impact of choice on public schools over the long run by comparing student performance across metropolitan areas with varying numbers of private schools—the more private schools, the more the competition, and the greater the impact on public schools. If the presence of private schools undermines public schools, then one expects to find lower public school performance in those metropolitan areas where private schools abound. But a Harvard study has shown exactly the opposite: public school students do better in those parts of the country where there is more ready access to private school. Similarly, some metropolitan areas have more school districts than others, giving parents the option to choose among different public school systems by moving to the neighborhood of choice. Knowing that these kind of parental choices can affect community property values, school boards may respond by providing parents better quality education. Research shows that this in fact happens, that in those metropolitan areas with more school districts, students are given more demanding academic courses, school sports are given less emphasis, costs are reigned in, and students learn more.

Fiscal Impacts on Public School Children

To see how school vouchers affect the fiscal resources available to public school children, the structure of public school financing needs to be briefly considered. Although the financial arrangements vary from one state to the next, on average, nationwide, 49 percent of the revenue for public elementary and secondary schools comes from state governments, while 44 percent is collected from local sources; the balance is received in grants from the federal government. Most of the revenue school districts get from state governments is distributed on a "follow the child" principle. The more

65

students in a district, the more money it receives from the state. If a child moves to another district, the state money follows the child. Local revenue, most of which comes from the local property tax, stays at home, no matter where the child goes. As a result, the amount of money the district has per pupil actually increases if a district suffers a net loss of students simply because local revenues can now be spread over fewer pupils.

The voucher programs in Milwaukee, Cleveland, and Florida have been designed along similar lines. The state money follows the child, but the local revenue stays behind in local public schools, which means that more money is available per pupil. In Milwaukee, per pupil expenditures for public school children increased by 22 percent between 1990 and 1999, rising from $7,559 to $9,036. Not all of the increase was a direct result of the voucher program, but the case disproves any claim that public schools necessarily suffer financially when voucher programs are put into effect.

Though voucher programs have been designed in such a way as to be fiscally advantageous to public school children, a central-city pilot program should do even more. It should be designed in such a way as to enhance resources available to public and private schools alike. If funds for public schools are greatly enhanced, they will be given every opportunity to respond effectively to the competition private schools pose. And given the competition, public schools will have strong incentives to make effective—and efficient—use of the extra monies. At the same time, vouchers that are much larger than those currently available will attract new entrepreneurs to education, both nonprofits and for-profits. Existing private schools will be as challenged as public schools by new, energetic educators.

Conclusions: The Future of School Choice

Despite their potential, vouchers may not win the necessary political support in the foreseeable future. If so, the school choice movement will gain substantial ground only if tax credits and tax deductions are combined with charter schools and assiduous efforts to implement the choice provisions of No Child Left Behind. Still, there is hope that a substantial new voucher initiative will be considered, namely, a citywide voucher program within a large central city. With some local officials in Washington, D.C., endorsing the idea in the wake of the *Zelman* decision, the nation's capital would provide an excellent site for such a larger scale voucher program.

Until now, all voucher programs have been limited to students from low-income families. Although this may have been appropriate for initial demonstration programs, a larger program should not encourage segregation of students by income. Instead, programs should be designed to encourage both public and private school integration, both economically and socially. For this to happen, vouchers need to be generally available.

A citywide voucher program may also attract some of the middle- and working-class families who left cities because of the low quality of the urban schools. Gentrification has restored a number of urban neighborhoods in a few parts of the country, but city life has proven mainly attractive to young people, oldsters, and tourists—folks who need not worry about school quality. Unfortunately, many young couples leave the city they enjoy simply because they cannot bear the thought of placing their child in a public school—and a private school is beyond their means. Vouchers would provide an option for such families. If enough people are enticed into remaining in the city, schools will gradually become better integrated—and central cities will be revitalized.

Still, the key to change lies within the black community, and especially with parents, who increasingly know that private schools provide a better education for their children. A 1998 poll by Public Agenda, a nonpartisan research group, found that 72 percent of African-American parents supported vouchers, as opposed to just 59 percent of white parents. A poll conducted two years later by the Joint Center for Political and Economic Studies had similar results, with just under half of the overall adult population supporting vouchers but 57 percent of African-American adults favoring the idea. Perhaps more to the point, blacks constituted nearly half of all the applicants for the 40,000 privately funded vouchers offered nationwide by the Children's Scholarship Fund in 1999, even though they comprised only about a quarter of the eligible population.

Even in the face of such numbers, it is too much to expect that those civil rights leaders who have long opposed vouchers will alter their position; their political tendencies are too well defined. But pressure to support school vouchers is building among black parents, and black leaders will have to respond. Howard Fuller, the former superintendent of Milwaukee's public school system, has formed the Black Alliance for Educational Options, a pro-voucher group that has mounted an effective public relations campaign and is making waves in civil rights circles.

Not even the Supreme Court, it should be recognized, can make educational change come quickly in America. Though *Brown* was handed down in 1954, it took more than a decade before major civil rights legislation was enacted. Southern schools were not substantially desegregated until the 1970s. Anyone writing about *Brown* 10 years after its passage might have concluded that the decision was almost meaningless outside a few border states. Yet after 50 years, few can deny that, in spite of all the educational work that yet needs to be done, the place of African-Americans in U.S. politics and society has been transformed.

The same may be said about *Zelman* on both its 10th and 50th anniversaries. Ten years of progress will be discernible, but only just. But in four or five decades, American education will have been altered dramatically in ways we cannot anticipate by the parental demand for greater choice—a demand codified in *Zelman*. Many battles will be fought and lost along the way, to be sure, but the victories will accumulate, because choice, once won, is seldom conceded.

Notes

1. Elisabeth Bumiller, "Bush Calls Ruling about Vouchers a 'Historic' Move," *New York Times*, July 2, 2002, p. A1.

2. Ibid.

3. *Zelman v. Simmons-Harris*, 536 U.S. 639, 676 (2002).

4. *Zelman*, 536 U.S. at 683.

5. Lloyd P. Jorgenson, *The State and the Non-Public School, 1825–1925* (Columbia, Mo.: University of Missouri Press, 1987), pp. 138–139.

6. Interestingly, there is no evidence that vouchers have improved the academic performance of students from other ethnic groups. In my own research, they had no impact—positive or negative—on the test scores of either whites in Dayton or Hispanics in New York City.

7. Cecilia Elena Rouse, "School Reform in the 21st Century: A Look at the Effect of Class Size and School Vouchers on the Academic Achievement of Minority Students," Working Paper 440, Princeton University, 2000, p. 19.

8. Jeffrey Grogger and Derek Neal, "Further Evidence on the Effects of Catholic Secondary Schooling," in *Brookings-Wharton Papers on Urban Affairs 2000*, ed. William G. Gale and Janet Rothenberg Pack (Washington: Brookings Institution, 2000), p. 153.

9. Kim K. Metcalf, *Evaluation of the Cleveland Scholarship and Tutoring Grant Program* (Bloomington: Indiana Center for Evaluation, Indiana University, 1999), p. 14.

5. Educational Freedom for D.C. Schools

Casey Lartigue Jr.

Let us keep our eye steadily on the whole system.

—Thomas Jefferson, February 15, 1821[1]

The year 2004 marks two anniversaries in education. In 1804, public education was founded in the nation's capital. In 1954, the Supreme Court handed down its historic *Brown v. Board of Education* ruling banning racial segregation in public schooling. Although the two anniversaries are 150 years apart, it is fitting that both anniversaries are marked during 2004.

The school system in the nation's capital was established by the city council on December 5, 1804, in an act "to establish and endow a permanent institution for the education of youth in the city of Washington." Thomas Jefferson, then president of the United States, was named one of the trustees as well as president of the board after he contributed $200 toward the endowment of the schools.[2]

A comprehensive report prepared by a select committee and adopted by the board of trustees on September 19, 1805, read, "In these schools poor children shall be taught reading, writing, grammar, arithmetic, and such branches of the mathematics as may qualify them for the professions they are intended to follow."[3]

Two centuries after public education was founded in the District, and 50 years after the *Brown v. Board of Education* decision, has the District been successful in fulfilling its mission to educate District residents? Unfortunately, it has not. There is plenty of evidence to show that public schools in the District have historically failed to educate children living in the nation's capital.

During congressional hearings, a U.S. senator concluded, "A crisis has been reached in the school system of Washington. The education of more than 60,000 children is involved." While that would accurately describe the situation in the nation's capital today, those words

69

were actually spoken by Sen. Pat Harrison (D-Miss.) in May 1920 in a select committee report investigating the D.C. public school system.[4]

Harrison's words were echoed in a report issued 76 years later. In 1995 Congress passed and President Bill Clinton signed a law creating a presidentially appointed District of Columbia Financial Responsibility and Management Board (usually referred to as the "Control Board") to rescue the District from its financial troubles. A year later in its report, the Control Board labeled the leadership of D.C.'s public school system "dysfunctional," concluded that children had been cheated out of a decent education, and stripped the D.C. Board of Education of its powers until June 2000. The Control Board noted that its assessment found that "for each additional year that students stay in DCPS, the less likely they are to succeed, not because they are unable to succeed, but because the system does not prepare them to succeed."[5]

Other reports throughout the past century have documented failures with the public school system:

- In a 1939 report to the D.C. Board of Education, the superintendent of D.C. schools decried "illiterates"[6] in the District's white schools and pointed out that principals requested police protection from "youthful hoodlums."[7]
- In 1947, seven years before the *Brown v. Board of Education* decision, Hobart M. Corning, then the new superintendent of schools, declared that Washington, D.C., had "one of the sorriest school systems in the country."[8]
- A 1949 survey of D.C. schools by Columbia University professor George F. Strayer found poor academic achievement among blacks and whites: "All white divisions were retarded in paragraph meaning and word meaning, and spelling scores were below national norms." Strayer found that "nearly all [white] junior high schools were below national norms by approximately one year," while "the median for all [black] junior schools was 2½ years below norms."[9]
- An analysis of standardized test scores in the 1950s reveals that even when one-third of the students in the District were white, public school students in the District were trailing the national average on all subjects tested.[10]

- In 1967, a comprehensive 15-month study of the government schools in the District of Columbia by Columbia University professor A. Harry Passow found a "low level of scholastic achievement as measured by performance on standardized tests."[11] A few months earlier, in an editorial titled "The Silent Disaster," the *Washington Post* said, "The collapse of public education in Washington is now evident."[12]

Unfortunately, academic underachievement of D.C. public school students has persisted to this day. Despite numerous alarming reports, superintendents being fired or forced out, and attempts to reform the system from within, public education in the nation's capital has consistently produced education trailing the national and regional average on every conceivable measure of academic achievement.

- In the late 1970s at the University of the District of Columbia, the only public institution of higher education in the District, it took one year of remediation on average to bring D.C. public school students up to speed; today, the average is about two years, according to sources at UDC and in the city government. Eighty-five percent of D.C. public school graduates who enter the University of the District of Columbia need remedial education.[13]
- A majority of D.C. public school graduates who took the U.S. Armed Forces Qualification Test—a vocational aptitude exam—got a failing grade in 1994, the most recent year for which results are available.[14]
- An estimated 40 percent of students who start the 8th grade in D.C. drop out or leave before graduating.[15] This is not a recent phenomenon—a 1976 report cited estimates from the statistical office of the D.C. schools that between 30 and 35 percent of students who entered the 7th grade would not complete high school. The same report found that 47 percent of D.C. pupils who were enrolled in the 7th grade in 1964–65 had dropped out and not finished high school by the 1969–70 year.[16]
- From 1978 to 1996, D.C. public school students routinely performed below the national average on the Comprehensive Test of Basic Skills.[17] Students in lower grades often performed at or above the national average starting in 1983. In contrast, D.C.

high school students consistently trailed the national average on CTBS.[18]

- In 2001, D.C. private school students averaged 1200 on the SAT, while D.C. public school students averaged 798.[19] D.C. public school students score 222 points below the national average (1020) on the SAT.[20]

- On the Stanford-9 achievement test in 2001, 25 percent of D.C. students read and 36 percent performed math at the "Below Basic" level, demonstrating little or no mastery of fundamental knowledge and skills at their grade level. Seventy percent of 10th- and 11th-graders performed math at the Below Basic level.[21] On the National Assessment of Educational Progress, D.C. students scored well below the national average on the scale score, with more than 85 percent of students scoring at the Basic or Below Basic level.

- Thirty-seven percent of District residents read at or below 3rd-grade level, according to the State Education Agency, Adult Education, University of the District of Columbia.[22]

As reports over the last several decades have concluded, the public schools in the District of Columbia have failed to provide children with an adequate education.

In 1940, the D.C. Board of Education adopted a statement of philosophy of education for the public schools of the District of Columbia. Developed by teachers and officers, the statement proclaimed that the child "is the center of the educational process."[23]

Has the D.C. public school system put children at "the center of the educational process"? A review of the historical record reveals that children have been herded into unsafe schools, taught by teachers that even the president of the school board derided as unqualified or incompetent,[24] and been promoted to higher grades although they had yet to master lower-level work.

Evidence that administrators have put themselves ahead of children abounds:

- In 1979, the school system had 113,000 students and 511 office positions. By 1992, the school system had lost 33,000 students, but the number of central office positions had almost doubled, to 967.[25]

- The *Washington Post* reported in 1997 that officials had misallo-cated to salaries $1.6 million intended for extra instruction for underprivileged students as required by law. The federal gov-ernment revoked $20 million of grants because the system had mismanaged grant funds.[26]
- A 1990 internal school audit and a 1995 study of census data found that the District padded enrollment totals, overreporting the number of students by 6,500 in 1990 and by more than 13,000 during the following years until 1995. "I've never seen a discrepancy like this before," said George Grier, the demogra-pher who conducted the 1995 study. "Either kids are staying in the city while their parents are leaving or something equally strange is happening." As the *Washington Post* reported, the discrepancy had been discussed by the school board, but it was not publicly disclosed for months—after the board had requested a $100 million increase in the school budget.[27]
- Year after year, the schools have employed more people than authorized in annual budgets approved by the D.C. Council and Congress.[28]
- In 1997, the *Washington Post* learned that school officials had "reprogrammed" money to pay unauthorized workers by keep-ing two sets of books.[29]
- The city and federal government spend almost $11,000 per pupil in the District, an amount well above the national average and similar to nearby regions that are performing much better, and yet the system lacks basic school supplies or facilities.
- This year, a GAO report found that the system's billion-dollar modernization program is behind schedule and already $170 million over budget.[30]
- DCPS has one employee for every six students. The system is so bureaucratically heavy that only about half of the people on the DCPS payroll are teachers.[31]

As the above facts show, the DCPS has not put children at the center of the educational process. Instead, too many people have focused on saving the system as a whole, even at the cost of students being poorly educated. Although the system has been a failure, attempts to put competitive pressure on the failing system have consistently been blocked by the District's elected officials.

As shown in Table 5-1, 13 of 19 high schools in the District of Columbia have more than 90 percent of their students reading at a basic or below-basic level. "Below Basic" indicates little or no mastery of fundamental knowledge and skills. "Basic" denotes only partial mastery of the knowledge.[32]

In addition, 14 of 19 D.C. high schools have 90 percent of students unable to perform math above the Basic level. Despite this, more than 80 percent of senior high school students at District of Columbia Public Schools get promoted to the next grade. D.C. elected officials and education representatives who continue to oppose school choice don't often discuss the outright failure of some schools, highlighted in Table 5-2. DCPS students score well below the national average on the National Assessment of Educational Progress (see Table 5-3). Even the staunchest school choice opponents decline to defend the current performance of some D.C. public schools.[33]

In 2002, D.C. public school students averaged a total score of 796 out of 1600 on the Scholastic Assessment Test. In comparison, as Table 5-4 demonstrates, the national average was 1020 and D.C. private school students averaged 1210 on the SAT (1188 for religiously affiliated schools, 1210 for independent schools). Table 5-5 shows that the D.C. Public School average was 224 points below the national average of 1020 on the SAT and about 400 points below the average of D.C.'s private school students. Instead of narrowing, the gap between the national average and D.C. public schools has increased from 203 to 224 points since 1998.[34] The gap has also widened between D.C.'s public and private schools.

On the Stanford-9 achievement test in 2002, 24 percent of D.C. students read and 36 percent performed math at the "Below Basic" level, demonstrating little or no mastery of fundamental knowledge and skills at their grade level. More than 70 percent of 10th- and 11th-graders performed math at the "Below Basic" level. On the National Assessment of Educational Progress, D.C. students scored well below the national average on the scale score, with more than 85 percent of students scoring at the "Basic" or "Below Basic" level.[35] Also, according to the state education agency, 37 percent of District residents read at or below the 3rd-grade level.[36]

In a more targeted comparison, data from six urban school districts (Washington, D.C.; Atlanta; Chicago; Houston; Los Angeles; and New York) were compiled for the NAEP 2002 Trial Urban District

Table 5-1
STANFORD-9 READING AND MATH SCORES, 2002 (IN PERCENTAGES)

High School	Reading Scores				Promoted
	Below Basic	Basic	Proficient	Advanced	
Anacostia	65	33	3	0	70.7
Ballou	61	35	4	0	70.4
Banneker	0	30	58	12	98.7
Bell	44	49	6	1	91.2
Business & Finance SWSC at Woodson	33	57	10	1	82.1
Cardozo	51	46	3	0	80.2
Coolidge	47	48	5	0	90.3
Dunbar	50	46	4	0	72.6
Eastern	53	41	5	0	88.7
Ellington	30	49	19	2	87.0
Phelps	68	31	1	0	87.3
Preengineering SWSC at Dunbar	8	67	23	2	94.8
Roosevelt	56	41	3	0	87.9
School Without Walls	2	41	40	17	96.9
Spingarn	51	43	6	0	83.3
Washington, MM	61	38	1	0	84.0
Wilson, W.	25	41	26	8	94.5
Woodson, HD	61	36	4	0	86.0
System-wide	24	46	23	7	86.5*

(continued next page)

Table 5-1
STANFORD-9 READING AND MATH SCORES, 2002 (IN PERCENTAGES) *(continued)*

High School	Math Scores				
	Below Basic	Basic	Proficient	Advanced	Promoted
Anacostia	90	10	0	0	70.7
Ballou	85	14	1	0	70.4
Banneker	12	47	37	3	98.7
Bell	54	34	11	2	91.2
Business & Finance SWSC at Woodson	56	37	7	0	82.1
Cardozo	70	27	3	0	80.2
Coolidge	82	17	1	0	90.3
Dunbar	77	21	2	0	72.6
Eastern	85	15	1	0	88.7
Ellington	69	24	6	1	87.0
Phelps	94	6	0	0	87.3
Preengineering SWSC at Dunbar	23	53	23	2	94.8
Roosevelt	78	20	3	0	87.9
School Without Walls	21	43	30	6	96.9
Spingarn	70	22	7	0	83.3

(continued)

| | Math Scores | | | | |
High School	Below Basic	Basic	Proficient	Advanced	Promoted
Washington, MM	86	13	1	0	84.0
Wilson, W.	55	26	15	5	94.5
Woodson, HD	82	17	1	0	86.0
System-wide	36	35	21	7	86.5

Terms and definitions, according to Harcourt Brace & Company.

Below Basic: The student has little or no mastery of skills needed for that subject in that grade.

Basic: The student has partially mastered skills needed for that grade level.

Proficient: The student has mastered skills needed for the grade.

Advanced: The student is above grade level.

* The system-wide percentage for students in grades 7–12 was 86.6 percent.

SOURCE: Paul L. Vance, *A Five-Year Statistical Glance at D.C. Public Schools: School Years 1997–98 through 2001–02* (Washington: Division of Educational Accountability, Student Accounting Branch, November 2002).

Table 5-2
Worst Performing Schools on Stanford-9, Reading and Math Scores, 2002

High School	Reading Scores				
	Below Basic	Basic	Proficient	Advanced	Promoted
Anacostia	65	33	3	0	70.7
Ballou	61	35	4	0	70.4
Dunbar	50	46	4	0	72.6
Eastern	53	41	5	0	88.7
Washington, MM	61	38	1	0	84.0
System-wide	24	46	23	7	86.5*

High School	Math Scores				
	Below Basic	Basic	Proficient	Advanced	Promoted
Anacostia	90	10	0	0	70.7
Ballou	85	14	1	0	70.4
Dunbar	77	21	2	0	72.6
Eastern	85	15	1	0	88.7
Washington, MM	92	8	0	0	90.2
System-wide	36	36	21	7	86.5

Terms and definitions:

Below Basic: The student has little or no mastery of skills needed for that subject in that grade.

Basic: The student has partially mastered skills needed for that grade level.

Proficient: The student has mastered skills needed for the grade level.

Advanced: The student is above grade level.

* The system-wide percentage for students in grades 7–12 was 86.6 percent.

SOURCE: Paul L. Vance, *A Five-Year Statistical Glance at D.C. Public Schools: School Years 1997–98 through 2001–02* (Washington: Division of Educational Accountability, Student Accounting Branch, November 2002).

Table 5-3
DISTRICT OF COLUMBIA, NAEP PERFORMANCE

Subject	Grade	Year	Scale Score State Avg.	Scale Score [National Avg.]	Advanced Level Percent Below Basic	Advanced Level Percent Basic	Advanced Level Percent Proficient	Advanced Level Percent Advanced
Mathematics (scale: 0–500)	4	1992	193	[219]	77	18	4	1
		1996	187	[222]	80	15	4	1
		2000	193	[226]	76	18	5	1
	8	1990	231	[262]	83	14	2	1
		1992	235	[267]	78	18	3	1
		1996	233	[271]	80	15	4	1
		2000	234	[274]	77	17	5	1
Reading (scale: 0–500)	4	1992	188	[215]	70	20	8	2
		1994	179	[212]	76	16	6	2
		1998	182	[215]	72	18	7	3
	8	1998	236	[261]	56	32	11	1
Science (scale: 0–300)	8	1996	113	[148]	81	14	5	0
Writing (scale: 0–300)	8	1998	126	[148]	37	52	10	1

SOURCE: National Center for Education Statistics, Nation's Report Card (Reading).

Table 5-4
SAT SCORES FOR PUBLIC, INDEPENDENT, AND
RELIGIOUS SCHOOLS IN WASHINGTON, D.C., 1998–2002

School	1998	1999	2000	2001	2002
Public	811	813	822	798	796
Independent	1183	1194	1184	1187	1210
Religious	1170	1177	1200	1200	1188
U.S. Average	1017	1016	1019	1020	1020

SOURCE: *A Five-Year Statistical Glance at D.C. Public Schools: Schools Years 1997–98 through 2001–02.*

Table 5-5
THE SAT GAP, IN TOTAL POINTS, BETWEEN THE
D.C. PUBLIC SCHOOLS WITH THE NATIONAL AVERAGE,
D.C. RELIGIOUS SCHOOLS, D.C. INDEPENDENT SCHOOLS,
1998–2002

School	1998	1999	2000	2001	2002
Independent	372	381	362	389	414
Religious	359	364	378	402	392
U.S. Average	206	203	197	222	224

SOURCE: *A Five-Year Statistical Glance at D.C. Public Schools: Schools Years 1997–98 through 2001–02.*

Assessment in reading and writing at grades 4 and 8 (see Tables 5-6 and 5-7).[37] All of the urban districts performed below the national average, with D.C. scoring at the bottom in most categories.[38]

The children who most suffer from a failing education system are those in the poorest areas of D.C. Adults who live in the poorest areas of the city are much less likely to be college educated. D.C. residents who live in Ward 3 of the city, perhaps the most affluent area of the nation's capital, are 10 times more likely than residents of Ward 8 to have a college diploma (see Table 5-8).

The Case for School Choice

What could be the argument against allowing children a choice to leave the worst performing schools? It certainly can't be that they'll somehow be worse off than they already are. Not every child

Table 5-6
TRIAL URBAN DISTRICT ASSESSMENT, READING ACHIEVEMENT LEVEL PERCENTAGES, 2002

Grade 4 Public Schools		
	At or Above Basic	At or Above Proficient
National (Public)	62	30
Central City (Public)	51	21
Atlanta	35	12
Chicago	34	11
Houston	48	18
Los Angeles	33	11
New York City	47	19
District of Columbia	31	10

Grade 8 Public Schools		
	At or Above Basic	At or Above Proficient
National (Public)	74	31
Central City (Public)	64	23
Atlanta	42	8
Chicago	62	15
District of Columbia	48	10
Houston	59	17
Los Angeles	44	10

NOTE: According to NCES, data are not reported for New York at the eighth-grade level because of a low response rate.
SOURCES: U.S. Department of Education, National Center for Education Statistics, National Assessment of Educational Progress, 2002 Trial Urban District Reading Assessment.

would leave, but children whose parents want to make a change should be allowed to do so.

According to D.C. school board president Peggy Cooper Cafritz, "All of our high schools—except Banneker, Walls, Ellington, and Wilson—are generally lousy, so where do we send the children?"[39] Even a school like Paul Lawrence Dunbar High School, at one time one of the leading high schools in the city regardless of race, is mediocre. (See sidebar on page 98.)

There is no reason to limit the choices of schools to those in the current system. Because of the District's long-term failure to educate

Table 5-7
NAEP 2002 TRIAL URBAN DISTRICT ASSESSMENT, WRITING
ACHIEVEMENT LEVEL PERCENTAGES

Grade 4 Public Schools		
	At or Above Basic	At or Above Proficient
National (Public)	85	27
Central City (Public)	81	21
Atlanta	77	13
Chicago	76	12
District of Columbia	73	11
Houston	81	23
Los Angeles	77	16
New York City	85	27
Grade 8 Public Schools		
	At or Above Basic	At or Above Proficient
National (Public)	84	30
Central City (Public)	77	22
Atlanta	68	10
Chicago	72	16
District of Columbia	66	10
Houston	74	19
Los Angeles	64	11

NOTE: According to NCES, data are not reported for New York at the eighth-grade level because of a low response rate.
SOURCES: U.S. Department of Education, National Center for Education Statistics, National Assessment of Educational Progress, 2002 Trial Urban District Reading Assessment.

District children, any solution limited to the D.C. public schools would have little benefit. What is needed is a system that allows parents and children to opt out of the D.C. schools and select another provider. A competitive system that used a combination of vouchers, tuition tax credits, and contracting would be the best way to increase educational quality.

The historical case for school choice in America goes back to the nation's founding. Adam Smith, whose writings greatly influenced America's founding fathers, noted that government-run education was likely to be inferior to privately run education.[40] In 1859, John

Table 5-8
2000 EDUCATIONAL LEVEL BY WARD

Ward	Persons 25 Years and Over		Percent High School Graduates		Percent College Graduates	
	1990	2000	1990	2000	1990	2000
City	409,131	384,535	73.1%	77.8%	33.3%	39.1%
1	54,614	48,695	67.6%	68.4%	35.6%	38.5%
2	52,940	45,950	81.4%	86.8%	52.3%	64.1%
3	57,808	55,796	94.1%	95.7%	70.1%	79.1%
4	56,539	53,092	73.5%	77.9%	24.8%	32.9%
5	50,657	48,031	65.6%	72.4%	19.4%	20.7%
6	50,952	49,884	71.0%	78.8%	31.8%	43.6%
7	46,839	45,309	64.3%	71.1%	11.6%	12.6%
8	38,782	37,779	61.3%	66.3%	8.0%	8.0%

NOTE: U.S. high school graduates, 25 years and over: 80.4 percent. U.S. college graduates, 25 years and over: 24.4 percent. Prepared by the D.C. Office of Planning/State Data Center.
SOURCE: U.S. Census Bureau. Wards effective January 1, 2002.

Stuart Mill argued that government should seek to make sure that every child gets educated, but he also wrote that government should not itself be in charge of that education.[41] In 1955, Milton Friedman proposed vouchers as a way to separate government financing of education from government administration of public schools.[42] More recently, a number of states have adopted school-choice plans that allow parents to choose the schools their children attend. Evidence continues to mount that those programs increase parental involvement, raise the academic performance of students in both public and private schools, and create incentives for both public and private schools to improve.[43]

For much of American history, choice and parental control played a far greater role in education than they do today. Indeed, for more than 100 years after the nation's founding, there was no public "system" of education.[44] Instead, schooling was primarily a family responsibility, which was accomplished through tutors and private schools. Even after the advent of the common school, parents had a large role in governing schools. Not until the first few decades of the 1900s did school "systems" arise under the control of political authority far removed from the local neighborhood school. Since that time, education has been treated like a government monopoly and has become increasingly resistant to change.

Bureaucratic monopolies don't work in education any more than they work in medicine, telecommunications, or manufacturing. As Cato's executive vice president David Boaz notes in *Liberating Schools: Education in the Inner City*, "Perhaps it is time to learn, as the reformers around Soviet president Mikhail Gorbachev came to understand, that bureaucratic monopolies don't work and that reform won't fix them. We have run our schools the way the Soviet Union and its client states ran their entire economies, and the results have been just as disillusioning."[45]

Rather than trying to reform the system, future efforts should be directed at ending the monopoly that public schools currently have over education by giving parents the freedom to choose between private and public schools. A program of tax credits or vouchers of a sufficient amount to allow parents to choose a private school if they so desire would transform parents from hostages into customers. Placing parents on an equal par with customers of other services would deprive DCPS of its monopoly position and would allow existing and new private schools to help students whose present options are limited to poorly performing schools.

Choice that is common in most sectors of the economy is slowly becoming more prevalent in education. For more than five decades, the courts have permitted school districts to reimburse parents of children in religious schools for public transportation costs.[46] Since 1955, K–12 schools in Minnesota have allowed low-income parents to have a small tax credit for private education.[47] Milwaukee became the first district in the country with a publicly funded K–12 school choice option. Private donors have also come forward to finance scholarships for low-income children in New York City, Dayton, San Antonio, Indianapolis, and Washington, D.C. Cleveland's school choice program, which passed the scrutiny of the U.S. Supreme Court, now provides vouchers to more than 3,700 schoolchildren.[48] If the public schools were educating every child, it might make less sense to challenge the government's monopoly on educating students whose parents can't afford to pay for private schooling. But in a system in which a large percentage of students are achieving at low levels, it is more difficult to accept limiting educational choices to public schools.

Researchers have generally found positive gains for students in school-choice programs that include both public and private schools. For example, Caroline Hoxby of Harvard University observed, "Overall, an evaluation of Milwaukee suggests that public schools made a strong push to improve achievement in the face of competition from vouchers. The schools that faced the most potential competition from vouchers raised achievement dramatically."[49]

Paul Peterson and his colleagues at Harvard University have shown that choice programs benefit black students in particular. Their findings revealed that black students who attended private schools after winning vouchers through lotteries had higher test scores than comparable students who had entered the same lotteries but remained in public schools.[50] Cecilia Rouse, a Princeton University economist and a former staff member of the Clinton administration's Council of Economic Advisers, analyzed data from Milwaukee and found that "students selected for the Milwaukee Parental Choice Program . . . likely scored 1.5 to 2.3 percentile points per year in math more than students in the comparison groups."[51]

The District of Columbia must find a way to create competition within the system, thereby giving parents power over the education of their children, fostering an environment that will create a climate for education entrepreneurs to flourish, and taking education out of the hands of feuding politicians. Instead of worrying about "saving" the public schools by limiting choices to just a handful of schools, the emphasis must be on setting up a system whereby schools are competing for each child.

Blocking the Exits

Local officials have resisted past efforts to allow children to escape failing public schools. In 1981, an initiative placed on the ballot by the D.C. Committee for Improved Education would have allowed families earning less than $20,000 a year to receive a $1,200 local income tax credit to be used for private school fees or to pay for supplemental programs at government schools. At the time, the average per-pupil cost at private schools was $2,857. D.C. residents voted 9 to 1 against the measure.[52] Bill Keyes, then chairman of the local affiliate of the National Taxpayers Union, which mounted the tax credit drive, claimed the measure was defeated by a "vigorous smear campaign."

According to the *Washington Post*, "A group of labor unions, spearheaded by the American Federation of Teachers, said they would spend up to $200,000 in fighting the measure."[53] Up to that point, supporters had raised about $114,000. Opponents denounced the initiative as "racist."[54] Floretta D. McKenzie, superintendent of DCPS, urged defeat of the educational tax credit, saying it would "hurt young people and our struggling District government."[55] The League of Women Voters, the American Federation of Teachers, the D.C. Federation of Civic Associations, the American Civil Liberties Union, the D.C. Congress of Parents and Teachers, the entire city council, the school board, the Washington Teachers Union, Parents United for Full Funding, the American Federation of Government Employees Council 211, D.C. delegate Walter Fauntroy, the local chapter of the NAACP, and every candidate for mayor opposed the initiative.[56] D.C. Mayor Marion Barry, who said the city would have to increase property taxes 20 to 40 percent if the initiative passed, joined city officials and residents in filing challenges to the education tax credit initiative.[57] The D.C. Board of Elections eliminated the initiative from the ballot, although the D.C. Court of Appeals later reversed the decision.[58]

The District is not the only urban school system struggling with educating its residents, but it is the only one for which Congress has clear constitutional authority to "exercise exclusive legislation in all cases whatsoever."[59] In 1998, Congress passed a voucher plan for the District. The District of Columbia Student Opportunity Scholarship Act (H.R. 1797), cosponsored by House Majority Leader Dick Armey (R-Tex.) and Rep. William Lipinski (D-Ill.), was vetoed by President Clinton.[60] That $7 million plan would have offered up to $3,200 in tuition subsidies to 2,000 low-income students for use at the public, private, or parochial school of their choice.

In April 2001, Sen. John McCain (R-Ariz.) announced that he would offer a voucher proposal on the Senate floor as an amendment to an education bill.[61] Called "Educational Choices for Disadvantaged Children," the proposal would have created a $25 million fund for vouchers. The D.C. Board of Education would have been empowered to select low-performing schools and make scholarships worth $2,000 a year for four years available through a lottery for students to use at public or private schools.[62] After a storm of criticism from D.C. officials and activist groups, McCain withdrew the bill. In a letter to McCain, D.C. Del. Eleanor Holmes Norton, the district's nonvoting representative, denounced the bill as "a disservice to the high standards of education accountability for every child the District of Columbia has set for itself."[63]

Has the District been able to establish "high standards of education accountability for every child"? That may be the goal, but it is not the reality. The problems in D.C. schools are so entrenched that we should allow children to seek education outside of the government-run education system. Unfortunately, city leaders and voters continue to resist efforts to provide educational choice for students and families dissatisfied with the system, although the system clearly is failing.

Statehood: A Barrier or an Excuse?

District officials have repeatedly waved the red flag of statehood to oppose congressional reform of D.C. public education, arguing that Congress attempts to "impose" policies on defenseless citizens who lack representation in Congress and thus can't fight back. In response to Armey's bill, the D.C. Board of Education approved a resolution entitled "Opposing the Congressional Imposition of Vouchers on the District of Columbia." Council member Kevin Chavous stated, "Congress, which does not understand the culture or climate of our city, should not impose a decision on our residents—even if it is proposing funding it."[64] Eleanor Holmes Norton has been quoted at various times denouncing Congress for intervening into District issues, especially education.[65] Norton, however, has championed choice for college students in the District. Norton worked with Congress to pass and later expand the District of Columbia College Access Act of 1999, which provided $17 million in federal funding to create the D.C. Tuition Assistance Grant Program.[66] The bill allows D.C. residents to attend any public college or university anywhere in the United States at in-state tuition rates or to receive $2,500 to attend any private college or historically black college or university in the country.[67] In a May 24, 1999, press release, she praised the bill, saying it addressed "a critical educational deficit that not only affects students and other residents, but the revitalization of the city itself."[68] In the first year of the program's existence, more than 3,200 D.C. high school graduates attending schools in 37 states received grants averaging $5,270.[69] If choice is effective in higher education, then why not in K–12?

Whatever the merits of the cause, the issue of statehood should not be a reason to avoid giving students more choice. Offering students more choices won't "impose" anything on students who would benefit from a more competitive education sector.

Public School Choice Options within the District

The number of choices within the District has been cited as a reason that vouchers or tuition tax credits are not needed. "With its 42 charter schools, 15 transformation schools, and out-of-neighborhood attendance, the city already has proven alternatives to the public-school system," says D.C. Del. Eleanor Holmes Norton.[70] How much choice do those programs offer to parents now looking for choices? A review of the out-of-boundary, transformation schools, and charter schools, reveals that the options are limited.

The public school system in March 2003 reported receiving more than 6,000 applications for 5,254 out-of-boundary placements. Virginia Walden-Ford, executive director of D.C. Parents for School Choice, says, "The out-of-boundary placement program is a joke. Parents who have been waiting for out-of-boundary placements for years never get in."[71]

In congressional testimony, Jefferson Junior High School PTA President Jackie Pinckney-Hackett also questioned the number of choices offered by the out-of-boundary program.[72]

Out-of-boundary enrollment applicants are considered only if a school has space after accepting all of its in-boundary students. Parents are not allowed to apply to more than three out of 146 schools in D.C. for each child.[73] Ms. Pinckney-Hackett testified that Woodrow Wilson Senior High School, considered one of the top schools in the District, received 520 applications. It had zero spaces available. Deal Junior High, a feeder school for Wilson, had 532 applications, but only 10 openings.

In contrast, Anacostia Senior High School had 80 spaces available, but only 7 applicants. Ballou SHS had 220 available spaces, but only 3 applicants. In 2002, fewer than 800 of the 7,000 children who applied for out-of-boundary spots were granted permission, mainly because many of the available slots are in low-performing schools.

What about spaces available in transformation schools, the low-performing schools that have been targeted with extra resources? According to the D.C. public-schools Web site, 12 of the 15 transformation schools listed on the site have 453 seats available for out-of-boundary transfers.[74] Of those 12 schools targeted for improvement, 5 (Stanton, Turner, Walker-Jones, and Wilkinson elementary schools and Evans Middle School) had no out-of-boundary spaces available. More than 25 percent of the available transformation school spaces are at Kramer Middle School, which had 120 available spaces, but only 4 applicants.

The District of Columbia Public School system has identified 15 schools as being "In Need of Improvement" under the Bush administration's No Child Left Behind Act. Students at those schools are eligible for supplemental services. However, there are still many troubled public schools in the District that have not been identified as being in need of improvement (see Table 5-9).

The city's charter schools have increased the amount of choice offered within the city. But an estimated 14,000 children are now enrolled in those institutions, and parents often complain about long waiting lines. "Despite often inadequate or crowded facilities," Delegate Norton has said, "these schools have long waiting lists because of their small class sizes and tight curriculums."[75] So, instead of seeing the long waiting list as a reason to expand choice, opponents of the voucher program say the waiting list is a reason to limit choice.

It is ironic that charter schools, now cited as an adequate option, just a few years ago were attacked with language similar to that used against vouchers today. "They are taking away from the basic premise of education to allow public funds to go to private schools," Board of Education President Wilma R. Harvey (Ward 1) said in 1995 as she lobbied against the charter-school proposal.[76] Former school-board member Jay Silberman (At Large) said the committee's decision to endorse charter schools was a "cut and run" approach. Former D.C. council member Harry Thomas (D-Ward 5) said, "We don't need nobody to come in and run our schools." Mr. Thomas also said, "I don't think this is the way to go. My position is very loud and clear. I'm against privatization, I'm against charter schools in the city."[77] Barbara Bullock, the former president of the Washington Teachers Union who was accused by the FBI earlier this year of

Table 5-9
DISTRICT OF COLUMBIA PUBLIC SCHOOLS NOT
"IN NEED OF IMPROVEMENT"

			Reading			
School	Ward	SAT	Below Basic	Basic	Proficient	Advanced
Bell	1	724	44	49	6	1
Cardozo	1	662	51	46	3	0
Dunbar	5	736	50	46	4	0
Phelps	5	627	68	31	1	0
Spingarn	5	704	51	43	6	0

			Math			
School	Ward	SAT	Below Basic	Basic	Proficient	Advanced
Bell	1	724	53	34	11	2
Cardozo	1	662	70	27	3	0
Dunbar	5	736	77	21	2	0
Phelps	5	627	94	6	0	0
Spingarn	5	704	70	22	7	0

SOURCE: Paul L. Vance, *A Five-Year Statistical Glance at D.C. Public Schools: School Years 1997–98 through 2001–02* (Washington: Division of Educational Accountability, Student Accounting Branch, November 2002).

embezzling millions from the union, said, "They are basically giving public money to create private schools. If you have extra money, put it in for security, textbooks, teacher training."[78]

Private School Options in the District

The percentage of students in private schools in the District has increased over the last four decades. During the same time, the number of children in D.C. public schools has decreased markedly, from a high of 149,000 in 1969 to 68,000 in 2001, its lowest number in seven decades.[79] This is partially due to a drop in the number of school-age children in the District. However, even given that drop, the number of students in private schools has remained relatively stable. In 1960, 20,466 children attended private and parochial schools in the District.[80] According to the D.C. Board of Education, today there are more than 18,000 students attending private schools in the District of Columbia.[81] Thousands of D.C. parents have made it clear that they want school choice. One indication of this desire is the Washington Scholarship Fund, a private fund set up to distribute partial scholarships to low-income students. Every year thousands of low-income students apply for approximately 100 scholarships given out each year. Eligible families must reside in the District, qualify for the federal school lunch program, and have a child entering kindergarten through eighth grade.

Students are chosen from a randomly-based lottery drawing in February. The maximum amount of the scholarship ranges from $2,000 for K–8 to $3,000 for high school.[82] The D.C. public school system is spending more than $10,000 per student yet yielding disastrous educational results. Although spending on education has grown 39 percent since Mayor Williams took office in 1998, there are still demands to further increase spending.[83] In March 2001, in response to complaints that education spending had not increased fast enough, Mayor Williams asked, "But really, how can you justify increasing funds for a school system that is losing students?"[84]

He was right. But a more important question is, How much longer can the District justify forcing children to attend schools that most people acknowledge are troubled? The failure of the D.C. public schools didn't happen overnight and there is little reason to believe that administrators have the ability to overcome several decades of failure. Spending more money, changing administrators, and even giving the mayor more power over the schools have not improved the system.[85]

Reversals

In response to the public schools' troubles, some city leaders finally decided in 2003 to introduce a school-choice program within the District. The mayor and the president of the D.C. Board of Education cited the failure of the D.C. public school system as a reason for ending their opposition to vouchers. The president and members of Congress have proposed school-choice plans that would allow families to use federal education dollars to buy education services from private providers, further increasing educational options. Because private schools charge less on average than public schools spend and often subsidize tuition for low-income students, taxpayers in the District would realize savings, and students would have more educational opportunities.[86] What is the capacity of private schools in the Washington metropolitan area to absorb more students?

Private School Capacity

Private schools in Washington could immediately accommodate about 2,925 students now attending public or charter schools. Allowing all independent and parochial schools in the Washington metropolitan area to participate in a school-choice program could add almost 3,500 more spaces because there are more than 6,000 seats available in local, nonpublic schools.

There are more than 80 private elementary and secondary schools in Washington, D.C., according to the U.S. Department of Education and a Cato Institute survey.[87] Surveys conducted in recent years suggest that private and parochial schools could play a significant role in offering more choices for children in the nation's capital. In 1997 a Washington Scholarship Fund survey found 4,000 available seats in the Washington metropolitan area, half of which were in the District.[88] The superintendent of Washington Archdiocese schools in 1998 testified that Catholic schools "are eager to serve more of the District's children." He estimated that up to 2,000 additional students could be accommodated in area Catholic schools.[89] Surveys conducted during the last year indicate that local private schools could accommodate about 2,000 children. Archdiocese officials estimated that 1,200 children could be accommodated immediately.[90] A survey of private schools in the Washington metropolitan area by the Washington Scholarship Fund found at least 4,000 available spaces, with almost 1,800 in the District. The Washington Scholarship Fund asked schools about their class sizes and current enrollment to calculate the number of available seats.[91]

A Cato Institute survey conducted in June of this year asked private schools how many more students they believed they could accept. Seventy private schools in the District reported that they could make space for another 2,500 students, an average of 35 available seats per school. Extrapolating that average to the remaining 15 schools, there could be 2,925 seats available in D.C. private schools.[92] The same Cato Institute survey found that about 75 private schools in Virginia (703 area code) and Maryland (301 area code)

Table 5-10
NUMBER OF STUDENTS THAT COULD BE ACCOMMODATED IN
PRIVATE SCHOOLS IN THE D.C.-METROPOLITAN AREA

Private school spaces currently available in D.C.	2,925
Private schools spaces currently available in Md. and Va.	3,407
Total available spaces in the D.C.-metropolitan area	6,332

SOURCE: Cato Institute survey.

could accommodate an additional 3,407 students (see Table 5-10). There are at least 25 private schools within a 10-mile radius of Washington. Filling those seats could reduce D.C.'s public school enrollment by almost 10 percent.[93]

And of course, the introduction of vouchers to the District could stimulate an expansion of private school capacity that would rival the growth in the number of charter schools within the city. In 1995 charter schools were virtually nonexistent in the nation's capital. Today the District has about 40 charter schools serving more than 11,000 students. A voucher program may start small, but within a decade it could serve as many students as charter schools now do. It could also change the makeup of private schools. Parochial schools currently dominate because subsidies from religious institutions keep their costs low. The number of nonparochial schools may increase with vouchers making more schools affordable for families.

Cost of Schools in the Nation's Capital

There is little agreement about the cost of public education in the nation's capital (see Table 5-11). Estimates range from $8,536 per student to $15,122, depending on who does the counting and what is counted.

In comparison, the Cato Institute's analyses reveal that private schools in the nation's capital cost much less than public schools in the area.[101] The average cost of private elementary schools in the District is $4,500, the average cost of secondary schools is $16,075 (see Table 5-12). More than half of private elementary and secondary schools in the District cost less than $7,500 per year. Almost 70 percent (69.4 percent) of private elementary schools and 18.2 percent of private high schools in the District cost less than $7,500 per year. Private schools in northern Virginia and southern Maryland are

Table 5-11

THE COST OF PUBLIC EDUCATION IN THE NATION'S CAPITAL
DEPENDS ON WHO DOES THE COUNTING

Source	Per-Pupil Funding
U.S. Census Bureau	$15,122 (all costs included)[94]
National Education Association	$13,525[95]
U.S. Census Bureau	$10,852 (operating fund)[96]
U.S. Department of Education	$11,009[97]
DCPS Superintendent's Office	$10,477[98]
Parents United for the D.C. Public Schools	$10,031 (including federal grants)[99]
Parents United for the D.C. Public Schools	$8,536 (local funds only)[100]

SOURCES: U.S. Census Bureau, National Education Association, U.S. Department of Education, DCPS Superintendent's Office, Parents United for the D.C. Public Schools.

Table 5-12
COST OF PRIVATE SCHOOLS IN THE D.C.-METROPOLITAN AREA

Area	Type of School	Per-Pupil Cost
District of Columbia	Private Elementary	$4,500
District of Columbia	Private Secondary	$16,075
Maryland and Virginia	Private Elementary	$4,288
Maryland and Virginia	Private Secondary	$6,920

SOURCE: Cato Institute survey.

somewhat more affordable than those within the borders of the District of Columbia. Eighty-eight percent of private elementary schools and 60 percent of private secondary schools in the area charge less than $7,500 annually. The median private elementary school tuition in those areas is $4,288 annually, and for private secondary schools the cost is $6,920, almost $10,000 less than private high schools in D.C. Allowing D.C. residents to use vouchers to transfer to cheaper schools in northern Virginia and southern Maryland would result in increased choices for D.C. schoolchildren and greater savings for D.C. taxpayers. Private schools already heavily subsidize the tuition of low-income students. About 25 percent of Washington Archdiocese schools have tuition rates that cover only 50 to 70 percent of the real cost of educating a child.[102] According to a 1998 study by the U.S. Department of Education, tuition revenues provide 82 percent of total operating funds at most U.S. parochial schools.[103]

If vouchers paid the full cost for students to attend parochial schools, such schools would be able to expand their facilities and even build new schools.

D.C. Public Schools Under Capacity

According to C. Vanessa Spinner, acting director of the D.C. State Education Agency, the District's public school system is barely operating at half capacity. The system can accommodate 120,000 students. There are about 66,000 students currently in the system.[104]

Numerous underused facilities are being kept open, even when they are not economically feasible. Superintendent Paul L. Vance said at a December 2002 news conference that the public school system had 14,000 open work orders and needed money to pay for repairs.[105] The D.C. public school system needs to consider closing its most decrepit schools rather than continuing to spend money on repairs to schools operating under capacity.

With almost 150 public schools in a system that has been losing students, the D.C. public school system could merge several schools to save taxpayer money. In October 2002 Mayor Anthony A. Williams suggested establishing a commission to determine whether some schools and other city buildings should be closed because of underuse.[106] Sixty school buildings have been declared surplus within the last few years, yet the District is building more schools.[107]

Instead of closing or merging schools operating at half capacity and cutting back on operating costs, city leaders have sought to renovate every school, at a total cost of $2 billion over the next 10 to 15 years.[108] The city and the school system should close schools with the fewest students and most in need of renovation.

Charter schools in the District, which must currently acquire their own facilities, could use buildings currently underused by the public school system. Other facilities could be given to or auctioned off to private entrepreneurs who agreed to operate them as schools. Because of the political sensitivities that come with closing schools, army bases, or fire stations, an independent group should determine which schools should be closed.

Instead of spending billions of taxpayer dollars to renovate underused schools, the District could stimulate the expansion of a private school market with vouchers. Maine and Vermont have financed education for students attending private schools for decades. About 35 percent of all students enrolled in Maine's private schools are publicly funded. Towns receive full or partial reimbursement from the state of Maine for the part of the tuition they pay for each child.[109] Since 1869 Vermont has operated a voucher program, which pays tuition for students to attend public and private schools.[110] With political and educational leaders in the District of Columbia reversing their opposition to vouchers, residents of the city will finally have the opportunity to increase the number of educational choices available to children. In testimony before Congress in late June, Mayor Williams did not rule out the possibility that the voucher program could eventually be expanded to include Virginia and Maryland.[111]

Conclusion

The problems with public schools in the District of Columbia have been documented in numerous studies. The city government, taxpayers, and families in the D.C. area would benefit if D.C. children were allowed to spend the education dollars allocated for them on private schools. The city would benefit from resources now wasted by schools operating at half capacity. Taxpayers would benefit because children would be educated at lower-cost private schools in the area. Low-income families would benefit from being able to choose among a range of public, private, and charter schools to serve their needs. Most of all, children in the District would benefit from competition created by public, private, and charter schools vying for their tuition dollars.

The problems plaguing DCPS are not with particular administrators, as critics often charge, or with congressional interference, as defenders of the status quo allege. Instead, the problems are with a system that tolerates incompetent people, passes along students even when they are not academically prepared, and restricts the choices of parents to public schools and charter schools. A review of standardized test scores since 1978 reveals that D.C. children show up for school achieving at the national average, but that they get farther behind the longer they remain in DCPS. The D.C. system spends more than $10,000 per student yet yields disastrous educational results. The failure of the D.C. public schools didn't happen overnight, and there is little reason to believe that current administrators have the ability to overcome several decades of ingrained failure.

The Control Board identified many of the system's problems in 1996, but it failed to do one key thing: Suggest a way to allow children to opt out of D.C.'s historically dysfunctional education system. In addition to the empirical case, there is also a basic moral case for school choice. Parents are the ones best equipped to decide what is in the best interests of their children. School choice would introduce an element of competition desperately needed in the system. The District of Columbia has not established "high standards of education accountability for every child." Instead, the record shows that the District has failed miserably in its mission to educate children. The best way to hold schools accountable is to give parents an opportunity to withdraw their children from schools that are failing them.

The reversal by local officials has helped pave the way for a rational discussion of how to increase school choice options for District children, resulting in the modest D.C. voucher plan created by Congress and President Bush in early 2004.

"When Dunbar Was Dunbar"

The case of Paul Laurence Dunbar High School is particularly poignant.[112] As noted earlier, Dunbar High School is one of the District's high schools that is struggling academically. The students are divided into two parts: The regular high school and the SWSC (School Within a School) that focuses on pre-engineering. Today 99 percent of Dunbar's regular students score below the proficient level in math and 96 percent do so in reading.[113] The pre-engineering students, who must do well on a proficiency test to get into the program, score slightly above district averages on the Stanford-9 and well above the averages of grades 9–12.[114]

The school has seen brighter days. A 1956 newspaper series on DCPS schools notes that despite the inferior performance of predominately black schools, there was one clear exception: "Dunbar High School, virtually all-Negro, had the city's best college-entrance record both last year and the year before, and a big quota of its graduates got scholarships."[115]

Historically, performing at a high level wasn't anything out of the ordinary for Dunbar High School. The first high school for blacks in the United States, Dunbar was also the first high school for children of any race in Washington.[116] Founded in 1870 by a group of freed slaves, it produced an honor roll of firsts, including the first black Cabinet officer, the first black Army general, the first black federal district judge, the first black U.S. senator since Reconstruction, as well as Charles Drew, the discoverer of a superior way to store blood plasma.[117] As of the 1950s, when the school was still segregated, Dunbar was sending 80 percent of its graduates to college, the highest percentage of any school in the District, regardless of race.[118] Dunbar students performed at or above the national average

(continued next page)

(continued)

on standardized tests. As early as 1892, Dunbar outperformed students at both white and black schools.[119] A study of the backgrounds of African-Americans with doctorates found that more had graduated from Dunbar than any other school in the country.[120] Until the mid-1960s, Dunbar graduates dominated the city's black institutions. In 1964, a Dunbar alumnus led almost every black public school in the District. Influential graduates within the District now include former D.C. Delegate Walter Fauntroy, current D.C. Delegate Norton and scores of black professionals, educators, and scholars around the country.[121]

Dunbar achieved these impressive results despite lacking many amenities, such as small student-teacher ratios and new facilities, now considered necessary to student achievement. The class size was above 40, with some classes having as many as 90 students, compared with today where class size at Dunbar is less than 20 students per class.[122] During most of its history, the school operated in inferior facilities.[123] The school required two years of foreign language, along with biology, chemistry, physics, American history, and algebra.[124] More than one-third of Dunbar's students studied Latin.[125] Its extracurricular organizations were academically oriented—student-run banking, biology, chemistry, contemporary literature, and library clubs.[126]

Several reasons are cited for Dunbar's success in the face of segregation and unequal allocation of funds during the Jim Crow era, but three stand out:

1. Dunbar was able to draw the best and brightest black students from the region, educating them with a rigorous curriculum. Ironically, the *Brown v. Board of Education* decision is credited with undermining Dunbar by forcing it to become a neighborhood school. By 1960, a newspaper story on the school was titled "Black Elite Institution Now Typical Slum Facility."[127]

(continued next page)

(continued)

2. Dunbar's teaching force included educated blacks who had limited employment options in a segregated society. Although it appears that many of the teachers in Dunbar pre-1960 were not certified, they were highly educated people handpicked by principals with the discretion to hire them.[128]

3. White school officials in D.C.'s segregated system basically left Dunbar alone, allowing local administrators to determine what was best for students.[129]

Notes

1. Hobart M. Corning, then superintendent of District of Columbia Public Schools, issued to the D.C. Board of Education a report titled "Your Child and the Schools" on May 16, 1951. Corning advised the Board of Education, school personnel, and the community to scrutinize the system, as Jefferson had advised Virginians to do about Virginia's education system. See "The Letters of Thomas Jefferson: 1743–1826, The University and the Schools." See www.odur.let.rug.nl/~usa/P/tj3/writings/brf/jefl266.htm.

2. DCPS, "Brief History of the Public Schools of the District of Columbia," Office of the Statistician, August 28, 1946. Copies can be obtained from the Charles Sumner School Museum and Archives in Washington, D.C.

3. The text continues, "and they shall receive such other instruction as is given to pay pupils, as the board may from time to time direct; and pay pupils shall, besides, be instructed in geography and in the Latin language." Ormond J. Wilson, "Eighty Years of the Public Schools of Washington—1805 to 1885," Washington, Columbia Historical Society, October 30, 1895, vol. I, p. 5. Copies can be obtained from the Charles Sumner School Museum and Archives in Washington, D.C.

4. Sixty-Seventh Congress, "Hearings before a Subcommittee of the Committee on the District of Columbia, United States Senate," Washington, Government Printing Office, May 5, 6, and 13, 1921.

5. District of Columbia Financial Responsibility and Management Assistance Authority, "Children in Crisis: Foundation for the Future," November 12, 1996. See www.washingtonpost.com/wp-srv/local/longterm/library/dc/control/part1.htm.

6. Michael Powell, "Red Flags Lined Road to City's Education Crisis," *Washington Post*, September 5, 1996, p. 1.

7. Frank Ballou, then superintendent of schools, delivered this report to the Board of Education of the District of Columbia on January 18, 1939; to civic organizations, home and school associations, and the parent-teacher associations on February 7, 1939; and to all school officers on February 10, 1939. Copies of the full report can be obtained from the Charles Sumner School Museum and Archives in Washington, D.C.

8. "Sorry System," *Washington Post* editorial, March 19, 1947, p. 14.

9. George F. Strayer, *The Report of a Survey of the Public Schools of the District of Columbia* (Washington: Government Printing Office, 1949), p. III.

10. Erwin Knoll, "D.C. Pupils Top Last Year's Marks in Standard Tests of 15 Subjects," *Washington Post and Times Herald*, June 26, 1959, p. A17.

11. A. Harry Passow, "Toward Creating a Model Urban School System: A Study of the Washington D.C. Public Schools," Teachers College, Columbia University, 1967, p. 2. The summary and findings of the report are available at www.lweb.tc.columbia.edu/exhibits/passow/summary.html.

12. "The Silent Disaster," *Washington Post*, April 18, 1967, p. A12.

13. Valerie Strauss and Sari Horwitz, "Students Caught in a Cycle of Classroom Failures," *Washington Post*, February 20, 1997, p. A1.

14. Ibid., p. A1.

15. The District of Columbia uses the U.S. Department of Education's definition of a dropout when reporting student dropouts for the National Center for Education Statistics on the Common Core of Data survey. The CCD dropout definition is based on a snapshot count of students at the beginning of the school year. A dropout (1) was enrolled in school time during the previous school year and did not enroll on October 1 of the current school year, (2) was not enrolled on October 1 of the previous school year but expected to be in membership (i.e., was not reported as a dropout the year before), (3) has not graduated from high school or completed a state- or district-approved educational program, and (4) does not meet any of the following exclusionary conditions: (i) transfer to another public school district, private school, or state- or district-approved education program; (ii) temporary school-recognized absence due to suspension or illness; or (iii) death. See U.S. Department of Education, National Center for Education Statistics, "Common Core of Data Dropout Statistic: Reporting Instructions for the 1999–2000 School Year," Government Printing Office, January 2001, Appendix G. DCPS has a graduation rate of 59 percent. The national average is 71 percent. Jay P. Greene, "High School Graduation Rates in the United States," New York, Manhattan Institute, November 2001, Table 2. See www.manhattan-institute.org/html/cr_baeo.htm.

16. Ben W. Gilbert, "The People of the District of Columbia: A Demographic, Social, Economic and Physical Profile of the District of Columbia by Service Areas," District of Columbia Office of Planning and Management, January 19, 1976, p. 40. Copies of this report can be obtained from the Martin Luther King Jr. Library in Washington, D.C.

17. This analysis is based on information from a series of five-year statistical reports prepared by the superintendent of schools. Most recently, see Paul L. Vance, *A Five-Year Statistical Glance at D.C. Public Schools: School Years 1996–97 through 2000–01* (Washington: Division of Educational Accountability, Student Accounting Branch, February 2002). Copies of these reports can be obtained from the D.C. Board of Education.

18. The District proudly announced this fact in a 1983 news release, "Elementary Student Test Scores Surpass National Norms," District of Columbia Public Schools, June 22, 1983. Copies can be obtained from the Charles Sumner School Museum and Archives in Washington, D.C.

19. College Board, "2001 Profile of College-Bound Seniors, High School Information, the District of Columbia," New York, College Board, 2001, p. 19. Fifty-six percent

of test-takers in the District are from public schools, 44 percent are from private schools.

20. Vance, p. 42.

21. Ibid., pp. 43–44.

22. The D.C. State Education Agency was established under the federal Adult Education and Family Literacy Act to help fund programs for adults over the age of 16 who don't have a high school diploma. Housed at the University of the District of Columbia, SEA funds 23 local programs to help men and women improve their reading, math, or computer skills or learn to speak English. See www.easternlincs.org/DCsite/factsstats.htm for more information.

23. Corning.

24. Justin Blum, "Half of District Teachers Weak, Board Chief Says," *Washington Post*, February 22, 2001.

25. Sari Horwitz and Valerie Strauss, "A Well-Financed Failure: System Protects Jobs While Shortchanging Classrooms," *Washington Post*, February 16, 1997, p. A1.

26. Ibid.

27. Sari Horwitz, "D.C. Study Challenges School Enrollment Data; Census Figures Show 13,000 Fewer Students," *Washington Post*, April 28, 1995, p. A1.

28. Ibid.

29. Ibid.

30. David E. Cooper, "D.C. Public Schools' Modernization Program Faces Major Challenges," Washington, General Accounting Office, April 25, 2002.

31. In FY 2001, there were 10,967 full-time employees. "Government of the District of Columbia, FY 2003 Proposed Budget and Financial Plan," Office of the Chief Financial Officer and Office of Budget and Planning, 2002, p. D-5.

32. This information is according to Harcourt, designer of the Stanford-9 test. An official from the Division of Educational Accountability of the Public Schools of the District of Columbia faxed the definitions to the author.

33. "I am no apologist for D.C. public schools or for any of the rest of these public schools that are not educating our children." Eleanor Holmes Norton; *NewsHour with Jim Lehrer*, April 29, 1998.

34. College Board, "2002 Profile of College-Bound Seniors, High School Information, the District of Columbia," New York, College Board, 2002, p. 19. Slightly less than half of the test-takers in the District were from D.C. Public Schools. DCPS: 1740; Religiously affiliated schools: 912; Independent schools: 459; Unknown (typically charter, correspondence, home, and nonaccredited schools): 374.

35. Paul L. Vance, *A Five-Year Statistical Glance at D.C. Public Schools: School Years 1996–97 through 2000–01* (Washington: Division of Educational Accountability, Student Accounting Branch, February 2002). Copies of these reports can be obtained from the D.C. Board of Education.

36. The D.C. State Education Agency was established under the federal Adult Education and Family Literacy Act to help fund programs for adults over the age of 16 who don't have a high school diploma. Housed at the University of the District of Columbia, SEA funds 23 local programs to help men and women improve their reading, math, or computer skills or learn to speak English. See www.easternlincs.org/DCsite/factsstats.htm for more information.

37. National Center for Education Statistics, "The Nation's Report Card Trial Urban District Assessment, Reading 2002 and Writing 2002," July 22, 2003. See http://nces.ed.gov/commissioner/remarks2003/7_22_2003.asp.

38. District of Columbia Public Schools News Release, District of Columbia Public Schools is one of six large urban districts to participate in first Trial Urban National Assessment Education Progress (NAEP), July 22, 2003. See http://www.k12.dc.us/dcps/dcpsnews/newsrelease/NAEP%20Release%20-%20July%2021%202003.pdf.

39. Vaishali Honawar, "D.C. Parents Lack School Choice Notice; Officials Scramble to Help Students Transfer under New Law," *Washington Times*, July 31, 2002, p. A1.

40. Adam Smith, *An Inquiry into the Nature and Causes of the Wealth of Nations* (New York: The Modern Library, 1937), p. 721. "Those parts of education, it is to be observed, for the teaching of which there are no public institutions, are generally the best taught. When a young man goes to a fencing or a dancing school, he does not indeed always learn to fence or to dance very well; but he seldom fails of learning to fence or to dance."

41. John Stuart Mill, *On Liberty* (Indianapolis: Bobbs-Merrill, 1975), pp. 129–30. "The objections which are urged with reason against State education, do not apply to the enforcement of education by the State, but to the State's taking upon itself to direct that education: which is a totally different thing. That the whole or any large part of the education of the people should be in State hands, I go as far as any one in deprecating. All that has been said of the importance of individuality of character, and diversity in opinions and modes of conduct, involves, as of the same unspeakable importance, diversity of education. A general State education is a mere contrivance for moulding people to be exactly like one another: and as the mould in which it casts them is that which pleases the predominant power in the government, whether this be a monarch, a priesthood, an aristocracy, or the majority of the existing generation, in proportion as it is efficient and successful, it establishes a despotism over the mind, leading by natural tendency to one over the body. An education established and controlled by the State, should only exist, if it exist at all, as one among many competing experiments, carried on for the purpose of example and stimulus, to keep the others up to a certain standard of excellence."

42. "Governments could require a minimum level of education which they could finance by giving parents vouchers redeemable for a specified maximum sum per child per year if spent on 'approved' educational services. Parents would then be free to spend this sum and any additional sum on purchasing educational services from an 'approved' institution of their own choice. The educational services could be rendered by private enterprises operated for profit, or by non-profit institutions of various kinds. The role of the government would be limited to assuring that the schools met certain minimum standards such as the inclusion of a minimum common content in Milton Friedman, *Capitalism and Freedom* (Chicago: University of Chicago Press, 1962), p. 89.

43. Caroline M. Hoxby, "How School Choice Affects the Achievement of Public School Students," in *Choice with Equity*, ed. Paul T. Hill (Stanford, Calif.: Hoover Institution Press, 2002). Also see, Linda Gorman, "School Choice Improves Student Achievement," National Bureau of Economic Research, August 2002, pp. 1–2.

44. John E. Chubb and Terry M. Moe, *Politics, Markets, and America's Schools* (Washington: Brookings Institution, 1990), p. 3. "Until the first few decades of the 1900s, there was really nothing that could meaningfully be called a public 'system' of education in the United States. Schooling was a local affair."

45. David Boaz, "The Public School Monopoly: America's Berlin Wall," in *Liberating Schools: Education in the Inner City*, ed. David Boaz (Washington: Cato Institute, 1991), pp. 11–12.

46. *Everson v. Board. of Education,* 330 U.S. 1, 16 (1947).

47. Minnesota House of Representatives Research Department, "Minnesota's Public School Fee Law and Education Tax Credit and Deduction," December 1998. "The deduction has been in effect since 1955 and allows parents to subtract from their taxable income up to $2,500 for qualifying expenses on behalf of each child in grades 7–12, and up to $1,625 for each child in grades K–6." See www.house.leg.state.mn.us/hrd/pubs/feelaw.pdf.

48. "[The Cleveland Scholarship program] provides a maximum of $2,250 each to the families of about 3,700 mostly low-income students, enabling them to attend religious or secular private schools." Charles Lane, "Court Upholds Ohio School Vouchers; Ruling Says Program Offers Poor Families Freedom of Choice," *Washington Post,* June 28, 2002, p. A1.

49. Hoxby, p. 150.

50. William G. Howell and Paul E. Peterson, *The Education Gap: Vouchers and Urban Schools* (Washington: Brookings Institution, 2002), pp. 145–7.

51. Cecilia Rouse, "Private School Vouchers and Student Achievement: An Evaluation of the Milwaukee Parental Choice Program," *Quarterly Journal of Economics* 113, no. 2 (May 1998): 593.

52. Eric Pianin and Lawrence Feinberg, "D.C. Voters Reject Tax Credit; District Voters Soundly Reject Tax Credit Initiative," *Washington Post,* November 4, 1981. For a full analysis of the 1981 education tax credit initiative, see E. G. West, "An Analysis of The District of Columbia Education Tax Credit Initiative," Cato Policy Analysis D, October 27, 1981. See www.cato.org/pubs/pas/pa00d.html.

53. Lawrence Feinberg, "National Unit Backs Tax Credit; $114,000 Contributed to D.C. Campaign; National Group Finds Education Tax Credit Drive," *Washington Post,* October 16, 1981. Judith Valente, "2 Challenges to D.C. Education Tax Credit Initiative Are Filed," *Washington Post,* July 19, 1981, p. B9.

54. "It's a racist initiative [and] this is a predominantly black city," said council member John A. Wilson (D-Ward 2), one of the coalition members. "If it passes here, it will let them say that there is nothing racist about it." Keith B. Richburg, "Coalition Fights Educational Tax Credit Initiative: Educational Tax Credits Opposed by City Coalition," *Washington Post,* July 8, 1981, p. B1.

55. Lawrence Feinberg, "McKenzie Blasts Tax Credit; Pledges School System Fight; Superintendent Pledges Fight on Tax Credits," *Washington Post,* September 22, 1981.

56. The League of Women Voters joined five other civic groups in forming the D.C. Coalition for Public Education, a new organization to fight the education tax credit. The Save Our City Coalition, headed by City Council Chairman Arrington Dixon, tried to derail the initiative "by raising a long series of challenges about how the tax credit petition was conducted." The D.C. Elections Board ruled in early August that most of the signatures had been collected by out-of-towners who were not properly registered D.C. voters. Lawrence Feinberg, "McKenzie Blasts Tax Credit"; Judith Valente, "Candidates Criticize Tax Credit Proposal," *Washington Post,* October 8, 1981, p. C1; and Lawrence Feinberg, "Barry Says Vote for Initiative Means Tax Hike; Barry Says Vote for Referendum Means Tax Increase," *Washington Post,* October 17, 1981, p. A1.

57. Barry said at a press conference, "We make no bones about it. We will mobilize the D.C. government and do all we can to defeat this ill-conceived proposal." Lawrence Feinberg, "Barry Says Vote for Initiative Means Tax Hike."

58. Judith Valente, "2 Challenges to D.C. Education Tax Credit Initiative Are Filed," *Washington Post*, July 19, 1981, p. B9. Lawrence Feinberg and Benjamin Weiser, "Tax Credit Initiative Ordered on Nov. 3 Ballot by Appeals Court," *Washington Post*, October 14, 1981.

59. "To exercise exclusive legislation in all cases whatsoever, over such District (not exceeding ten miles square) as may, by cession of particular states, and the acceptance of Congress, become the seat of the government of the United States, and to exercise like authority over all places purchased by the consent of the legislature of the state in which the same shall be, for the erection of forts, magazines, arsenals, dockyards, and other needful buildings." U.S. Constitution, Article I, Section VIII.

60. "Message to the Senate Returning Without Approval the 'District of Columbia Student Opportunity Scholarship Act of 1998,' " *Weekly Compilation of Presidential Documents* 34, (May 20, 1998); 935.

61. Supporters asked him to withdraw the bill once it became evident there were not enough votes to pass it. See Perry Bacon Jr., and Yolanda Woodlee, "McCain Backs Away from D.C. School Vouchers," *Washington Post*, June 21, 2001, p. T2.

62. Ibid, p. T2.

63. Marlene L. Johnson, "Catania in Running for Housing Award," *Washington Times*, June 13, 2001, p. C2.

64. Kevin P. Chavous, "Let the District Choose for Itself," *Washington Post*, July 7, 2002, p. B3.

65. According to the *Washington Informer*, D.C. Del. Eleanor Holmes Norton (D) "fumed" about the bill saying, "In short, the voucher bill uses District's children gratuitously for political purposes. Congress seems to want either to continue to abuse or use the District." "Congressional Intrusion," *Washington Informer*, May 13, 1998, p. 12. According to the *Washington Times* in 2002, Norton said, "This is the same old anti-democracy story at a new low—and we are going to fight it every step of the way." Honawar Vaishali, "D.C. Leaders Oppose Voucher Bill; GOP's Armey Proposes $45 Million for Disadvantaged," *Washington Times*, July 11, 2002, p. B3.

66. Amy Argetsinger, "D.C. Youths Branch Out with U.S. College Aid," *Washington Post*, July 24, 2000, p. A1.

67. The District of Columbia College Access Act of 1999, sec. 38-2704 (c)(1)(B), D.C. Official Code. See www.house.gov/norton/20020315.htm.

68. C. Boyden Gray, "Choice in Education; Vouchers for D.C.'s K–12 Students Make Sense," *Washington Times*, July 18, 2002, p. A21.

69. Spencer S. Hsu, "Senate Votes to Expand Tuition Plan; D.C. Students to Get Aid For All Black Colleges," *Washington Post*, March 16, 2002, p. B1.

70. Eleanor Holmes Norton, "D.C. Wants Accountable Schools—Not Vouchers," *Washington Post*, May 11, 2003, p. B8.

71. As quoted in Casey Lartigue, "Real Choices: Giving D.C. Kids the Best Education Available," *National Review Online*, October 7, 2003.

72. Jackie Pinckney-Hackett, Testimony before the Committee on Government Reform, May 9, 2003. See http://reform.house.gov/UploadedFiles/Parent%20-%20Pinckney-Hackett%20Testimony.pdf.

73. District of Columbia Public Schools, DCPS Out-of-Boundary Policy and Information, Selection Criteria. See http://www.k12.dc.us/dcps/outofbounds/oobcriteria.html.

74. The District of Columbia Public Schools Web site includes a list of schools. See http://www.k12.dc.us/dcps/T9/main/schools.asp.The author counted the number of seats available according to the DCPS out-of-boundary information. See http://www.k12.dc.us/dcps/outofbounds/pdfs/seatsavailable.pdf.

75. Norton, May 11, 2003.

76. Hamil R. Harris, "D.C. Council Committee Endorses Congress's Charter School Plan," *Washington Post*, October 24, 1995, p. C3.

77. Maria Koklanaris, "Critics Say No to Council School Plan," *Washington Times*, June 1, 1995, p. C6.

78. Valerie Strauss, "House Moves To Reshape D.C. Schools; Proposal for Vouchers Draws Loud Criticism," *Washington Post*, November 3, 1995, p. B1.

79. Bart Barnes, "Enrollment Drop Causes Problems for Local Schools; Schools Face Pupil Drop; Too Many Teachers," *Washington Post*, July 30, 1977, p. A1; Vance, p. 7.

80. "Metropolitan Washington Council of Governments, Statistics: Washington Metropolitan Area," Metropolitan Washington Council of Governments, January 1968, Table 17.

81. The numbers were given to the author by Sharon Dunmore, coordinator of NonPublic Schools for the District of Columbia Public Schools.

82. See the Washington Scholarship Fund at www.wsf-dc.org.

83. The Board of Education denounced Williams's budget for fiscal 2002 as being inadequate although it increased spending by 4.5 percent. Robert E. Pierre, "Williams Reaching Out to Poor in Budget Plan," *Washington Post*, March 12, 2001, P. A1.

84. Jabeen Bhatti, "Williams Says Schools Should Get Private Aid; Suggests Edison as Viable Option," *Washington Times*, March 15, 2001, p. A1.

85. The District recently announced the t9 Initiative in which schools that have scored in the lowest 10 percent of all schools in the last five years and showed no hint of progress were scheduled for "transformation." DCPS employees in nine schools have had to reapply for their jobs. Although highly touted by District administrators, this initiative amounts to little more than reshuffling employees. One principal estimated that 35 to 40 percent of employees had been rehired. Arlo Wagner, "Vance Puts His Faith in Transformations," *Washington Times*, August 29, 2002, p. B1. Rep. William Lockridge (District 4) said he wished there was more new blood, especially for the transformation schools, for which Vance had promised new leadership but hired only one principal from outside of the District. Lockridge said, "In my opinion , all we're doing is shuffing principals from one school to another. So we're still suffering." Debbi Wilgoren, "Many Schools Reopen under New Leadership," *Washington Post*, August 30, 2001, p. T9.

86. The Archdiocese of Washington estimates that it saves taxpayers approximately $200 million in annual educational expenditures. See Archdiocese of Washington, "National Research on Catholic Schools." See www.adw.org/education/edu_research.html.

87. According to the search engine of the National Center for Education Statistics, Office of Non-Public Education, there are 83 private schools in the District of Columbia. See http://nces.ed.gov/suveys/pss/privateschoolsearch. The Cato Institute identified 85 private schools in the District.

88. Samuel Casey Carter, "A Question of Capacity," *Policy Review*, January–February 1999.

89. Quoted in Coalition for American Private Education Outlook Newletter, "Congress Approves Historic School Choice Legislation," May 1998. See www.capenet.org/Out5-98.html.

90. Marc Fisher, "Cafritz Rolls with the Polls," *Washington Post*, April 17, 2003, p. B1.

91. These data were obtained directly from the Washington Scholarship Fund. It conducted a survey over several months in mid-2003. WSF received answers in writing to a host of questions about enrollment, tuition, admission fees, and class size.

92. The Cato Institute attempted to contact all 85 D.C. private schools by telephone. Fifteen schools either did not provide information or could not be reached after several attempts.

93. The D.C. public school system currently has about 66,000 students. The exodus of 6,300 students to private schools in the D.C. metro area would reduce the public school system's enrollment by almost 10 percent.

94. U.S. Census Bureau, *Public Education Finances 2001*, March 2003, Table 11.

95. National Education Association, *Rankings & Estimates: Rankings of the States 2002 and Estimates of School Statistics 2003*, May 2003, Table H-11.

96. U.S. Census Bureau, Table 11.

97. Lena M. McDowell and Frank Johnson, National Center for Education Statistics, *Early Estimates of Public Elementary and Secondary Education Statistics: School Year 2001–02*, April 2002, Table 7. See http://nces.ed.gov/pubs2002/2002311.pdf.

98. Paul L. Vance, *A Five-Year Statistical Glance at D.C. Public Schools: School Years 1996–97 through 2000–01* (Washington: Division of Educational Accountability, Student Accounting Branch, February 2002).

99. Parents United for the D.C. Public Schools, "D.C. Public School Funding: Myth & Reality," Washington D.C., February 2003, p. 11.

100. Ibid.

101. Cato Institute survey; and David Salisbury, "What Does a Voucher Buy? A Closer Look at the Cost of Private Schools," Cato Institute Policy Analysis no. 486, August 28, 2003. Private school costs in Maryland and Virginia were obtained from the Children's Scholarship Fund and by telephone contact with the private schools.

102. Valerie Strauss, "Tuition, Pay to Jump at Catholic Schools; Shortage of Teachers Forces Changes," *Washington Post*, January 27, 2000, p. B1.

103. Lana Muraskin and Stephanie Stullich, "Barriers, Benefits and Costs of Using Private Schools to Alleviate Overcrowding in Public Schools," U.S. Department of Education, Office of the Undersecretary, November 1998, p. 13.

104. Connie Spinner appeared as a guest on WOL 1450-AM, discussing the impact of vouchers in the District of Columbia, June 11, 2003.

105. Yolanda Woodlee and Justin Blum, "NE School's Woes Leave Staff, Pupils Cold; Balky Boiler, Broken Windows Make for Chilly Conditions at Taft Junior High," *Washington Post*, December 3, 2002, p. B3.

106. "D.C. Schools Get a Lesson in Economics; Cost of Renovations Is Far Above Projections," *Washington Post*, October 2, 2002, B1.

107. "Mayor Illegally Blocks Schoolhouse Door," *Washington Times*, September 18, 2002, p. A16.

108. Justin Blum, "Despite Sinking Enrollment, Proposal Calls for Rebuilding," *Washington Post*, December 7, 2000, p. B2.

109. Frank Heller, "Lessons from Maine: Education Vouchers for Students since 1873," Cato Institute Briefing Paper no. 66, September 10, 2001. See www.cato.org/pubs/briefs/bp-066es.html.

110. Libby Sternberg, "Lessons from Vermont: 132-Year-Old Voucher Program Rebuts Critics," Cato Institute Briefing Paper no. 67, September 10, 2001. See www.cato.org/pubs/briefs/bp-067es.html.

111. Anthony Williams, Testimony before the House Committee on Government Reform, May 9, 2003.

112. Colbert I. King, "The Dunbar Determination; Excellence was the Expectation at D.C.'s Premier Black School," *Washington Post*, June 14, 1992, p. C8. The title of this section is derived from King's article.

113. Vance, p. 70.

114. Ibid, p. 71.

115. James G. Deane, "Crisis in the Schools 3: Merging Two Levels Discloses Problems," *Washington Star*, March 6, 1956, p. 5.

116. For a more extensive analysis of the rise and fall of Dunbar High School, see Thomas Sowell, "Patterns of Black Excellence," in *Education: Assumptions Versus History, Collected Papers* (Stanford, Calif.: Hoover Institution Press, 1986), p. 29.

117. William Raspberry, "Good Students, Good Schools," *Washington Post*, February 21, 1994, p. A29.

118. King, 1992, p. C8.

119. Thomas Sowell, "Black Excellence: The Case of Dunbar High School," *The Public Interest*, Spring 1974, pp. 1–21.

120. Hewitt, Colby, "A Ray of Hope in Urban Education," *Boston Herald*, April 5, 1999, p. A27.

121. King, 1992.

122. Tucker Carlson, "From Ivy League to NBA; A Great Urban High School Falls through the Hoop," *Policy Review*, Spring 1993, p. 36.

123. Sowell, 1986, p. 31. According to Sowell: "The school was in operation more than 40 years before it had a lunchroom, which then was so small that many children had to eat lunch out on the street. Blackboards were 'cracked with confusing lines resembling a map.' It was 1950 before the school had a public address system."

124. Carlson, 1993, p. 36.

125. Ibid.

126. Ibid.

127. Thomas Sowell, 1986, p. 32.

128. Andrew J. Coulson, *Market Education: The Unknown History* (New Brunswick, N.J.: Transactions Publishers, 1999), pp. 133–135.

129. David L. Lewis, *District of Columbia: A Bicentennial History* (New York and Nashville: W. W. Norton & Company and American Association for State and Local History, 1976), p. 110.

6. Undermining Teacher Quality: The Perverse Consequences of Certification

Chaim Karczag

In the fractious realm of education policy analysis—in which premises, methods, and conclusions are hotly disputed—it is now widely agreed that the improvement of teacher quality is the single policy outcome most likely to elevate the achievement levels of public school students.[1] So-called value-added research that seeks to isolate the consequences of effective or ineffective instruction has reinforced this claim by finding a surprisingly large effect attributable to teacher quality.[2] Today, enhancing the effectiveness of teachers to improve student outcomes is a common priority among education reformers who agree about little else.

The new consensus only accentuates the difficult question of "Who may teach?" Because the politics of teacher certification are of most interest to teachers, they and their self-appointed representatives tend to dominate the political process of setting requirements for entry into the classroom; the general public has little input. The dramatic conclusions of value-added research and the new emphasis on teacher quality—which coincide with a renewed focus on achievement, standards, and accountability—demand a reexamination of questions about teacher supply. As if the results of research and the dictates of common sense are not enough, two other factors command that we focus our attention on teacher supply issues. The first is the demographic squeeze imposed by an aging teacher force and a swelling school-age population, which will require that we put well over two million teachers into the classroom over the next decade.[3] The second pressure originates in a provision in Title II of the No Child Left Behind Act that mandates a "highly qualified teacher" in every classroom.[4]

Given these various pressures, now is the time to think about the future of the teacher supply. Although the labor market for teachers is affected by many things (e.g., relative performance of the outside

109

economy, methods of teacher recruitment, preparation, and compensation), we can learn a great deal about who enters the classroom by understanding a single step in the production of new teachers: teacher certification. Even without other much-needed education reforms, successful reform of the current system of teacher certification would go a long way to improving lagging student achievement in the United States.

Teacher Certification: A Short History

A brief foray into the history of teacher certification laws will help us understand the present system and the motivations and assumptions of those who created it. As will become evident, the political context that gave rise to our current system was very different from the ideas and values of the present day.

For the past century, certification laws have been under state jurisdiction. This largely remains the case today, although as part of the No Child Left Behind Act, the federal government requires states to set their certification laws within certain parameters. In fact, this is just the latest step in a process of centralization stretching back to the 19th century.

In early America, the job of ensuring that teachers were of good moral character and qualified for their tasks was the work of local church authorities. As the 19th century progressed, the job increasingly became the work of local and county governments and became more centralized.

The history of teacher certification laws is marked by the ceaseless and often successful efforts of the teaching profession to gain more control over the process of teacher certification. The case of New York state—the first state to have a uniform system consolidated under state control—is instructive. In 1834, a state law was passed that provided for the specialized education of teachers in separate departments in private academies that were nevertheless subsidized by the state. In 1856, the state superintendent was empowered to create rules for certification exams administered at the county level. By 1894, the state superintendent was allowed to set questions for the certification exams, score the exams, and establish the cut-off score for admission to the teaching profession. In a final consolidation of power in 1899, the teacher institutes themselves were placed under the state superintendent's office. Thus New York had established the first uniform, state-controlled system of teacher certification.

By and large, teacher certification laws did not take root until the early 20th century. At the turn of the century, 28 states certified teachers solely on the basis of graduation from a "normal school" (teachers college) while only three states—New York, Rhode Island, and the then-territory of Arizona—had requirements that all teachers be certified by the state. By 1937, 41 states required state certification.

This trend was driven by the intellectual elites of the first third of the 20th century who, concerned with rapid urbanization and the destabilization of American life brought on by industrialization, had a clear model of reform for all levels of American society. Specifically, the opinion leaders of the Progressive Era placed a high degree of faith in science, hierarchic organization, the reliability of expertise over political solutions, and centralized rather than localized governance. Although the Progressive movement of that era is extinct, the teacher certification system they created lives on. The educational philosophy of the Progressives is nicely summarized by education historian David Angus:

> Administrative progressives never wavered from the view that a higher quality, more professional teaching corps could only be produced by requiring more and more training in colleges of education . . . that their claim to scientific arcane knowledge should be legitimated by issuing increasingly specialized certificates based on longer and longer periods of formal training; that control of entry should rest with the profession itself; that eliminating the local certificate (and the examination on which it was based) was key; that state certification laws should be written only in broad strokes, leaving the details to a state bureaucracy controlled by their members; and finally that neither legislatures nor state education departments should exercise close supervisory authority over the curriculum and organization of teacher education programs and that institutional autonomy should be the watchword.[4]

Urbanization and the industrial revolution had taken hold, giving rise to a larger school system serving more students. Because of high levels of immigration, population growth, and the fact that Americans were staying in school longer, high school enrollment swelled from 630,000 in 1900 to 4.7 million in 1938. From 1900 to 1930 the number of colleges of teacher education jumped from 4 to 150.

The Progressive reaction to the growth in the size and complexity of the American education system was to concentrate power in the hands of the experts, eliminating the provincialism and variation in quality inherent in localism. During this era, Progressives invented and implemented new forms of professional training. The old requirement of basic examination of subject-matter knowledge was jettisoned in favor of a lengthier process of specialized education through certification programs with required coursework. (Progressives hated exams because they were seen as a "backdoor" through which infiltrators could enter the teaching profession.) In 1919, Vermont became the first state to replace exams with a training program requirement for certification; by 1937, 28 states required professional training for certification rather than exams. Exams did not disappear; instead states began using training as a prerequisite for taking the exams. Over time, the number and type of certificates grew (e.g., kindergarten, junior high school, junior college) as did the specializations offered in schools of education (school administration, educational psychology, guidance counseling, etc).[5]

After a brief respite stemming from teacher shortages during World War II, the ratcheting up of restrictions for entry into the profession resumed in midcentury. In 1946, the National Education Association (then still a professional association rather than a union) created its Commission on Teacher Education and Professional Standards (TEPS), which undertook to combat "low standards of preparation and of admission to teaching" by creating yet another bureaucracy.[6] The National Council for the Accreditation of Teacher Education sought to raise the standards of teacher preparation programs by accrediting those schools that it deemed worthy and eventually taking direct control of all "approved programs." By the 1950s, it became clear to outside observers such as James Koerner, Mortimer Smith, and, most notably, Harvard president James Conant that an alliance of interests had coalesced into an "interlocking directorate" or "educational establishment" forming around what Smith called "a cohesive body of believers with a clearly formulated set of dogmas and doctrines."[7]

After the 1950s, the professional model for teachers began to suffer setbacks. One such setback was the rise of a new, more militant form of teacher unionism that was more interested in traditional union concerns of pay, benefits, and job protection than with the progressive goal of establishment and enforcement of high professional standards and professional autonomy. Criticism of the so-called education trust also came both from academics in the liberal arts (who derided its model teacher preparation as academically insufficient in the face of *Sputnik* and the Soviet threat) and from rank-and-file teachers themselves who sought the devolution of power on issues related to professionalism and preparation.

Despite the waning of the Progressive ethos in politics, the system of teacher certification that they created has endured. Today, all 50 states require a bachelor's degree from an accredited college as well as pedagogical coursework. The vast majority also require some student teaching. Beyond these commonalties, prerequisites for classroom entry vary. Some states require a bachelor's degree in education, while others require a degree in an academic subject. Many require coursework in special education. More than a dozen require prospective teachers to study issues related to health, drugs, and alcohol. A few require them to study nutrition.[8]

Rather than replacing Progressive institutions, subsequent reforms have layered new approaches over old ones, often in an attempt to address the defects of the existing system. For instance, in 1984, New Jersey became the first state in the nation to adopt an "alternate route" to certification, allowing teachers into the classroom who had not first attained a degree in education. Today, 46 states have such an alternative certification program.[9]

In response to concerns over the academic qualifications of teachers, there has been a sharp rise in the number of states requiring teachers to take tests. Some form of testing is now required for certification in 44 states. Tests of basic skills in the form of the Educational Testing Service's Praxis I and of subject-matter knowledge in the form of the Praxis II are the most prevalent, although many states have their own versions. Although proponents argue that teacher licensure testing does more than simple "college credit counting" to ensure quality, these requirements generally add to approved program requirements rather than replace them.[10]

Are Children Learning?

Given the expensive, elaborate certification system that has evolved, we might expect that the result would be a high-quality education for every child. Sadly, this has not proved to be the case. By any reasonable measure, American students are achieving too little in school. In general terms, there are two ways to assess our national standing in regards to student achievement. We can compare our student achievement levels against those of students from other countries, or we can examine student achievement against an independent standard such as scores on a given test over time. Analysis by either method yields gloomy evidence about American achievement.

In the 1999 Third International Math and Science Study, American 8th-graders came in 17 out of 38 countries in math, trailing such proud world powers as Slovakia, Slovenia, Bulgaria, and Canada. They evinced a similar mediocrity in science, and were trounced by Australia, Belgium's Flemish half, and Hungary. Their scores in both subjects were statistically closest to those of Bulgaria. (Ironically, American 8th-graders did much better in self-esteem: almost 60 percent said math was one of their strengths, placing us at 4th in the world.) American 12th-graders did even worse. They finished 16th out of 22 nations in science and 20th out of 22 nations in math. The only nations that performed worse in science were Cyprus and South Africa, while Lithuania, Iceland, and the Czech Republic had better math scores. This trend is particularly alarming given that American 4th-graders do relatively well on the same tests. It seems that the longer students are in American schools, the worse they perform on international comparisons.[11]

To use data that are more familiar to Americans, we might look at SAT data over time. Between 1966 and 1967 and 2001 and 2002, SAT scores fell 40 points even though real per-pupil expenditures more than doubled. Because of this decline, the SATs were "re-centered" to reflect a lower average in 1996.[12]

Losing Ground

For all its flaws, perhaps the most damning is that the American public school system has failed to educate students equally, regardless of race or socioeconomic background. Despite the abolition of Jim Crow laws and the integration of public schools since the 1950s, it is clear that the United States is failing to educate white and minority students equally.

114

The facts on this matter are both clear and frightening. According to test scores on the SAT and the National Assessment of Educational Progress, black 17-year-olds score at the same level on math and reading as white 13-year-olds.[13] Even worse, white 13-year-olds score marginally *better* than black 17-year-olds at science.[14] Coupled with data that indicate a strong positive correlation between educational achievement and lifetime earnings, this is a recipe for social disaster.

It is clear that many public schools have failed to provide all children with the education that is necessary for future economic success. The statistics are grim.[15] According to the National Center for Education Statistics, African-American 17-year-olds read at the same level as white 13-year-olds in 1990, and there has been no progress since then. Among college-bound high school seniors, according to the Educational Testing Service, white students had an average of 527 on verbal section of the SAT and 533 on the math, while African Americans scored 430 and 427, respectively.[16] The black-white test gap is equivalent to one standard deviation, the difference between reading at a 4th-grade level and an 8th-grade level or, similarly, doing math at an 8th-grade or 12th-grade level.[17]

As grim as the situation is when looking at the SATs, we must remember that the SATs are taken by only about 46 percent of high school seniors. Many minority students never become college-bound high school seniors. In 2001, black students were about 50 percent more likely to drop out than whites, while Hispanics were nearly four times as likely to quit school.[18]

There can be little doubt of a racial achievement gap when the National Assessment of Education Progress data show that in five out of seven categories—math, science, history, civics, and geography—most blacks are performing at "Below Basic," the lowest level. In reading, the average score of a black 12th-grader is at the 23 percentile for whites (or below 77 percent white students). In math, it's below 86 percent for whites and in science, 90 percent.[19]

Another way to approach the achievement gap is to look at the top score. Less than 5 percent of blacks are scoring at or above "Proficient" in math, science, or geography, and scores are not much better in writing, civics, and history. By contrast, whites are five to seven times as likely to attain such scores. Twenty-nine percent of whites scored as well as the top 5 percent of blacks in math; 36 percent of whites attained scores that are as high as the top 5 percent of blacks in science. Only .1 percent of black students achieve "advanced" proficiency in science. The number for white students is 34 times as high; for Asians, it is 37 times as high.[20]

Unsurprisingly, such stark contrasts in test scores have troubling consequences downstream. According to the National Educational Longitudinal Study, black students are more than twice as likely as whites to drop out of college. Also, as is commonly acknowledged, greater levels of educational achievement are closely tied to higher earnings. This "return on education" is substantial. According to census data, the median annual income for whites with a two-year degree is $30,000, while those with a four-year degree get $40,000.[21] (Statistics for blacks and hispanics are similar.) Researcher Christopher Jencks has shown that a large proportion of the black-white earnings gap can be attributed to the racial achievement gap.[22] In the absence of educational equality, can anyone seriously argue that racial equality is more than a dream?

Achievement and Teacher Quality

While most observers can agree on the importance of teacher quality in adding to student achievement, there is less agreement about what attributes contribute to it. Are master's degrees a good indicator of teacher quality? Does certification matter? How much of what makes a good teacher can be attributed to native intelligence? How much to experience in the classroom? Despite a current dearth of reliable data, sophisticated assessments are beginning to quantify the evidence, reinforcing the urgency of rationalizing our teacher supply and helping us to consider which teacher attributes are correlated with student achievement.

Economist Eric Hanushek found that a difference of one full year of learning is attributable to effective and ineffective teachers and this effect is persistent over time.[23] Well-designed studies in Dallas and Tennessee have produced similar results—students with math teachers whose effectiveness is in the top quintile for three straight years were *50 percentile points* ahead of peers who had had three straight years of bottom quintile teachers. The effect for reading was similar, if less dramatic in scale.[24] Clearly, an ample supply and equitable distribution of high-quality teachers is a requirement for a fair and effective education system.

There is ample evidence that the overall quality of American teachers is lower than it ought to be. Although 99 percent of teachers have a bachelor's degree, only 38 percent have a degree in an academic field rather than in education. Although such a specialized academic degree may not be necessary for those who seek to teach elementary education, among middle and high school teachers the rates are still only 44 percent and 66 percent, respectively.[25] Research indicates that teachers who have a greater knowledge of their subject matter are more effective at improving student achievement—it stands to reason that you can't teach what you don't know—making these relatively low rates worrisome. Furthermore, as noted by education policy analysts Dan Goldhaber and Dominic Brewer, "most college students selecting education majors tend to be drawn from the lower part of the ability distribution."[26] On the one hand, only 14 percent of education majors have SAT or ACT scores in the top quartile, while twice as many score in the bottom quartile. On the other hand, those who do *not* major in education are relatively overrepresented in the top quartile of SAT/ACT scores: social sciences majors at 26 percent; humanities majors at 31 percent; math/computer/natural science majors at 37 percent.[27] The recitation of these statistics is not an exercise in snobbery; teacher quality is strongly linked to cognitive (particularly verbal) ability.[28] Clearly, the system of teacher recruitment is broken insofar as it deters too many talented students from becoming teachers.

Although teacher quality in general is low, the situation in high-minority urban areas is positively dire. It is widely agreed that such schools have the worst staffing problems.[29] Urban school systems rely heavily on inexperienced teachers and "late fill" staffing, and are often characterized by high levels of teacher turnover and out-of-field teaching.[30] Given the importance of teacher quality, policies that systematically reinforce the urban disadvantage would have a disparate impact on minorities.

The Problem of Out-of-Field Teaching

One of the simplest yet most telling measures of the teacher supply problem is the extent of out-of-field teaching, which occurs when teachers are assigned to teach subjects for which they do not have a major, minor, or equivalent demonstrated competence. Sociologist Richard Ingersoll has studied out-of-field teaching in the United

States and found it to be alarmingly common. Analyzing public secondary schools (grades 7–12), Ingersoll finds that 24 percent of students learn English from a teacher without an English background. Likewise, 31 percent of math teachers, 20 percent of science teachers (including 57 percent in the physical sciences), and 53 percent of history teachers teach out-of-field. The numbers are somewhat better if grades seven and eight are excluded. But even by the end of 12th grade, 24 percent of students in math, 14 percent of students in English, and 62 percent of students in history are learning from out-of-field teachers.[31]

These numbers are even worse if one considers that only 37 percent of math teachers have a major or minor in mathematics (or physics or engineering). By way of comparison, 30 percent have a degree in "math education," a major that is widely considered to be less rigorous. Indeed, according to the Schools and Staffing Survey (from which Ingersoll gathered his data) only 38 percent of teachers have any sort of academic major as opposed to a less-rigorous education-specific major.[32]

Perhaps worst of all are the statistics from high-poverty schools, in which one quarter of English teachers, 43 percent of math teachers, 28 percent of science teachers (fully 65 percent in physical sciences), and 60 percent of history teachers are out-of-field. Since ample data show that teachers with a background in subject matter are better than those that are out-of-field, the skewed distribution of out-of-field teaching is one indicator of inequity in our current system.[33]

The Paradox of Certification

It is intuitively difficult to understand how a system that seeks to ensure the quality of teachers through high professional standards can ultimately reduce competence and hurt student achievement. Similarly, it can be difficult to see how a system that takes no account of race or class can nevertheless have a disproportionately harmful effect on minorities and the poor.

But consequences are not identical with intentions. Any law setting minimum requirements to enter a profession will have an effect on both the size and the composition of the labor pool in that profession, since even the most lax regulation will diminish the number of entrants into a field. Proponents of a given barrier to entry almost always contend that such a diminution is necessary to ensure the welfare of the consumer. They argue that the regulation that they favor is a "quality screen," while critics of restrictive licensure question whether the regulation does, in fact, serve to protect the public. Some even note that it is in the self-interest of members of a profession to limit the number of new entrants because these entrants are their competition. Unless the entry criteria are carefully tailored to measure the skills needed for occupational competence, critics contend, the effect of such "barriers to entry" is merely to exclude qualified potential entrants. Along these lines, there is a large body of economic literature arguing that occupational licensure leads to artificial shortages, higher prices, and little net benefit to the consumer.[34]

It's not surprising, then, that there is little evidence linking teacher certification to student achievement. An exhaustive meta-analysis by Kate Walsh at the Abell Foundation catalogs more than 200 studies between 1950 and the present day on the relationship between certification and improved student achievement. Although Walsh's survey points to several teacher characteristics that *are* linked to student achievement—including subject-matter mastery, selectivity of college, experience, and (interestingly) verbal ability— she fails to find a correlation between certification and student achievement.[35]

Even worse, there is reason to believe that certification actually lowers the quality of the applicant pool. The tedious certification process imposes a large opportunity cost on potential teachers and thereby dissuades some of the best candidates. Typically, potential teachers must familiarize themselves with the bureaucracy, pay tuition for a teacher education program, engage in uncompensated student teaching for 8 or 12 weeks, and be ready to endure the process again should they wish to teach in another state. There is also a widespread perception that education classes are a waste of time, amounting to nothing more than another hoop to jump through to gain entry to the classroom. In the words of Frederick Hess, schools of education generally are "not selective, fail out few if any students for inadequate performance, and see that more than 95 percent of their graduates receive teacher licenses."[36] Although some bright and talented students with a strong desire to teach will undoubtedly persevere, it is reasonable to expect that this perception will disproportionately deter high achievers who have other oppor- tunities. In other words, those who are deterred by the certification requirements will be precisely the types of teachers our schools desperately need. As Richard Riley, Secretary of Education under President Clinton, put it, "too many potential teachers are turned away because of the cumbersome process that requires them to jump through hoops and lots of them."[37]

A System by the Bureaucracy, for the Bureaucracy

Given the pernicious effects of certification requirements, what accounts for their growth? In large part, this process has been driven by powerful establishment groups who have portrayed themselves as custodians of the public interest but are also directly affected by the legislation and regulatory structures that they have helped to enact. The tight hold of the regulatory model on today's policies is better understood if one is familiar with these vocal and powerful advocates.

The National Council for Accreditation of Teacher Education was founded by TEPS and the American Association of Colleges for Teacher Education (AACTE) in 1950 and today controls 540 of the 1,300 teacher training programs that produce 70 percent of new teachers each year. NCATE accreditation is only quasi-voluntary. NCATE has partnerships with 46 states to conduct joint reviews of schools of education, while eight states explicitly require that their schools of education become NCATE accredited. Critics contend that NCATE accreditation is expensive, burdensome, and overly reliant on peer- and self-assessment rather than measurement of its graduates' classroom results. NCATE program standards largely ignore the candidates' demonstrated skills and knowledge, focusing instead on required inputs and processes. Critics also question whether there is a single best approach to teacher preparation given the absence of evidence linking particular types of preparation to student achievement.

Like NCATE, the National Board for Professional Teaching Standards (NBPTS) is a quasi-voluntary organization that has integrated itself into the teacher certification process. Formed in 1987 in response to the 1983 *A Nation at Risk* report, NBPTS set out to meet the challenge of underperforming teachers by establishing a voluntary national certification of "master" teachers. Today, the NBPTS is only somewhat voluntary. In 29 states taxpayers foot the bill for NBPTS, with states usually paying the $2,300 application fee for applicants in addition to a bonus to NBPTS-certified teachers. These bonuses can be quite substantial: In Georgia, they amount to a 10 percent salary increase for the life of the 10-year certificate; in North Carolina, it's 12 percent. Thus far, there is little evidence that Georgia, North Carolina, and other states that pay for NBPTS are getting their money's worth. In addition, studies have found that NBPTS-certified teachers are far more likely to be in affluent districts. NBPTS subsidies are therefore a transfer of wealth from state coffers to rich districts. Finally, critics wonder about the value of a subjectively graded test that looks only at teacher behavior rather than a teacher's impact on student achievement.

The Interstate New Teacher Assessment and Support Consortium (INTASC) was created in 1987 as an alliance between state education agencies and private education groups, including the NEA and AFT. Today, 34 states participate in INTASC's efforts to establish uniform quality standards and assessments for both teacher preparation programs and prospective teachers and to align licensure policies across states.

As the growing influence and success of INTASC, NBPTS, and NCATE make clear, teacher certification is becoming increasingly homogenous and restrictive. These three organizations are but a fraction of the teacher professionalism movement. These and other organizations, including the American Association of Colleges for Teacher Education, the National Commission on Teaching and America's Future, the National Education Association, the American Federation of Teachers, and the American Association of School Administrators, have combined into an "interlocking directorate" that is not only powerful but vast.

Mired in the frustration of seemingly permanent defeat, would-be reformers have dubbed this coalition "the blob." Many contend that American education has become producer-dominated, serving the interests of its members rather than those of students or the general public. Its steady growth should therefore be a cause for concern.

This growth would not be possible if interest group-dominated bureaucracy did not exercise almost complete control over entry into the teaching profession through state licensure laws. The structure of teacher certification is the result of regulatory capture, a term used by economists to describe cases in which a regulating organization is "captured" by those it is charged with regulating. Economists have found that captured regulatory bodies tend to serve the narrow economic interests of those doing the capturing ("the blob") over those of the wider public (students and their parents). The process of certification was not created by teachers and precedes their unionization. But, given the existence of the process today, unions are loath to see any relaxation of the levels of control of entry into the profession. Today, ingrained habits of thought and bureaucratic inertia are all that sustain the status quo, a system that does more to undermine the quality of teachers in the classroom than to ensure it.

Despite the danger of regulatory capture, there may be good reasons for licensure laws in some industries. In particular, when there exists a widely shared cannon of professional knowledge and there are information asymmetries between the practitioner and consumer's knowledge, it can be beneficial to consumers to restrict entry into a profession. In the case of neurosurgery, for example, the complexity of neurosurgical operations and the high cost of mistakes might justify government licensing to screen out the incompetent practitioners.

However, education is very different from medicine—which is, not coincidentally, the model most often cited by advocates of certification—in that there is no widely accepted knowledge base for pedagogy. Although there is a deep literature in medicine based on the scientific method and a commitment to quantitative research, the instruction in pedagogy is marked by fads, conflicts, and a dearth of scientific research. Controlled experiments, randomized trials, and use of large-scale longitudinal data are all rare. In their place is a large body of jargon-laden theory, pseudopsychology, and radical social criticism.

Genuine professional standards are all but nonexistent. The National Board for Professional Teaching Standards—a voluntary certification organization that certifies classroom instructors as "master" teachers who are awarded bonuses from the school districts in participating states—has standards that are laughably fuzzy. Among them: "Teachers are committed to students and their learning." "Teachers are responsible for managing and monitoring student learning." "Teachers think systematically about their practice and learn from experience." "Teachers are members of learning communities." It is no wonder, then, that certification has little relation to student achievement.

122

Even in the absence of professional standards based on scientific knowledge, *something* must be taught. Schools of education have become incubators of a radical worldview. Besides being wedded to a "constructivist" or "student-centered" philosophy of learning— that is, one that denies that the world is knowable or that teachers should instruct students on it—professors of education tend to teach as received wisdom that the larger society is fundamentally racist, that sexism is pervasive and must be fought, and that inequality of wealth is a problem to be eradicated. Such political propaganda is a poor placeholder for pedagogy. In its semiofficial interpretation of the National Council for Accreditation of Teacher Education, the American Association of Colleges for Teacher Education (an NCATE member organization) insists that teacher training programs must "first and foremost [be] dedicated" to "equity," "diversity," and "social justice," further opining that "we are convinced that [programs] living the three themes will not have difficulty in meeting NCATE's standards."[38]

Stumbling toward Solutions: Increase Certification Requirements or Deregulate?

Due to the persistence of American underperformance and the achievement gap, all observers agree on the need for education achievement to improve and equalize. In the area of teacher certification, education policy analysts are divided into two camps on the basis of a single question: Should teacher preparation be more regulated or should it be largely deregulated? Advocates of these two positions can be grouped neatly into two camps called "teacher professionalism" and "competitive certification," respectively.

Teacher professionalism is a descendent of the Progressive-inspired approach that dominated the profession until the 1950s when the field became unionized. The professionalism movement seeks to raise the prestige and performance of teaching by raising the formal education requirements for teaching (such proposals as requiring that all teachers receive a graduate degree), granting full control over teacher certification policy to professional standards boards made up of teachers, requiring more student teaching, increasing professional development, and raising pay both across the board and as "extra credit" for National Board certification. Plainly put, the animating idea is that teachers need *more*: more

123

classes in education school, more graduate degrees, more pre- and in-service training, and higher pay.[39]

Competitive certification advocates support a more flexible approach. They seek to reduce requirements for education coursework, lower barriers to entry, and expand alternative routes to the teaching profession.[40] By and large, they only wish to simplify and minimize the restrictions, not to abolish the state role in certification. A typical proposal would require students to have a bachelor's degree, pass a criminal background check, and pass a test of basic skills and content knowledge. To make the market for teachers more flexible, responsive, and outcome-oriented, advocates of competitive certification seek greater flexibility for local administrators and schools in teacher hiring, firing, and compensation. As part of the broader "standards and accountability" movement, boosters of competitive certification believe that regulation and accountability are substitutes rather than complements. Therefore, they argue that schools, administrators, and teachers ought to be held accountable for measurable student achievement (through incentives and sanctions) while inputs and process decisions should be decentralized.

It is barely an oversimplification to say that the teacher professionalism and competitive certification models are diametric opposites. Nevertheless, the teacher quality provisions of the No Child Left Behind Act were informed by both of them.

No Child Left Behind?

Since its passage in 2001, discussions of primary and secondary education in the United States are overwhelmingly informed by a single piece of federal legislation: the No Child Left Behind Act (NCLB). It is a sweeping law, widely considered to be the most radical overhaul of education since the first Elementary and Secondary Education Act (of which NCLB is only the latest reauthorization) was passed in 1967. The important change with respect to certification is a new requirement that all classroom teachers be "highly qualified" by the 2005–2006 school year. The states retain flexibility in implementing this requirement, but NCLB requires that "highly qualified" teachers have a bachelor's degree, demonstrated subject-matter knowledge, and full certification (alternative certification is acceptable). It bans uncertified teaching or teaching with an emergency, provisional, or temporary certificate or by someone who is "on waivers." The architects of NCLB want to end the practices of out-of-field teaching and "any warm body will do" inattention to teacher qualifications.

The statements of the Department of Education in its Non-Regulatory Draft Guidance and the law itself emphasize that NCLB is *not* meant to outlaw alternative certification. Indeed, the Secretary of Education has explicitly signaled in the Department's annual report on teacher quality that states should reexamine their certification regimes, removing unnecessary hoops and lowering barriers to entry that do not ensure improved student achievement to both enlarge and raise the quality of the teacher supply.[41]

In the grand tradition of American lawmaking, NCLB is a huge compromise. With regard to teacher certification, it is a compromise between those who believe in teacher professionalism and those who believe in competitive certification. For teacher professionalism, it mandates certification and outlaws out-of-field teaching. Partisans of competitive certification note that while it mandates content knowledge for teachers, it has no mandate for pedagogy requirements, allowing states to streamline or eliminate them. It also gives a specific endorsement to alternate routes to the classroom, even highlighting programs that it believes are less burdensome on candidates while ensuring strong subject-matter knowledge.[42]

NCLB presents us with a paradigmatic example of the opportunities and risks of trying to impose reform through regulation from above. The authors of NCLB hope that increased federal involvement and funding can be leveraged to raise educational standards and, in turn, raise student achievement. States are encouraged to reexamine licensure and streamline the certification process to broaden the candidate pool. A new federal approach seeks to shake up moribund educational bureaucracies at the state level and give new ideas an opportunity to be implemented.

The question, then, boils down to state compliance with federal mandates. Will state agencies responsible for teacher certification comply with the federal government? Or will they resist? Will they seek to undermine the spirit of the law by obstinate misinterpretation of the law or perhaps by special pleading—claiming that the law's mandates cannot possibly be met in their jurisdiction?

Thus far there is little evidence regarding the level of compliance among the states. No state has dramatically streamlined its teacher certification process by trading meaningless coursework and credit counting for tests of competency, nor has any state dramatically expanded alternative routes to the classroom. This does not prove that the highly qualified teacher provision of NCLB is a failure, only that it has yet to succeed. States may be biding their time, waiting to see if the next presidential election will yield a different administration with a different outlook on regulatory enforcement in this area. Of course, to the extent that NCLB seeks to end the harmful practice of out-of-field teaching and improve the competence of classroom teachers, this sort of regulatory gamesmanship on the part of the states ultimately only causes students to suffer.

School Choice and Competitive Certification

In the coming years the American education system is likely to include increasing levels of school choice. In recent years, the number of public charter schools and magnet schools has exploded. The Supreme Court's *Zelman vs. Simmons-Harris* decision upholding the constitutionality of vouchers opens the door to experiments in choice at the district or state level. Milwaukee, Cleveland, and Florida already have voucher programs. Colorado recently enacted a voucher program, and Congress is set to introduce a voucher program for the District of Columbia. Although public opinion on vouchers varies from year to year and especially depending on the wording of the question, vouchers are supported by more than 40 percent of the population and possibly by a majority.[43] Among African-Americans and urban residents, the proportion is higher.[44] It is difficult to avoid the conclusion that with constitutional issues resolved, choice will be expanded, even though it may never become universal.

If school choice grows by even a fraction as much as some expect, it is bound to have far-reaching effects on every aspect of American education, including the recruitment, preparation, certification, and distribution of teachers. It is reasonable to expect that the process of teacher production will be radically transformed as education begins to be affected by the introduction of market forces. Specifically, we can expect prospective teachers to have many more possible routes into the profession as private schools experiment with different methods for selecting teachers. The near monopoly granted to schools of education is unsustainable in a market environment.

Although it is clear that true school choice would require a functioning market for teachers, deregulation of teacher preparation may come first. Interpolating from the example of New Jersey—where 23 percent of teachers enter via the alternative route—it may be accurate to say that the liberalization of labor market for teachers will precede any significantly sized program of school choice and that the lessons of alternative certification in the current public school system will inform the shaping of the teachers' market for private schools.

Forty-six states have some form of alternative certification, with Rhode Island the last to join the fold in 2003. Since the size and scope of alternative certification programs vary widely, it is difficult to make blanket generalizations about them. In many states, alternative certification remains tightly regulated, statutorily limited in size, and requires candidates to complete the same education coursework requirements as traditional program graduates.[45]

Since it is difficult to characterize "alternative certification" because of the diversity of programs falling under that label, it is similarly difficult to predict whether the future will see such programs flourish in response to increasing demand for highly qualified teachers or perish under the weight of new regulations. On the one hand, the federal government has sought to encourage alternative certification programs, going so far as to create and/or fund several alternative routes to the classroom. These include Troops-To-Teachers, the American Board for Certification of Teacher Excellence (a standardized test of content knowledge and pedagogy that states can adopt to certify teachers), and, most famously, the Teach for America program. These three federally supported programs indicate our current administration's support for expanding the number of routes into the classroom.

On the other hand, NCLB's enacting regulations also contain language that might choke off alternative certification. By legislatively defining the characteristics required of an alternative certification program—including teacher mentorship and professional development—the administration may have unwittingly taken a large step toward unnecessary, detrimental standardization and away from a diverse system of alternative certification.

If the future of teacher preparation and certification will be shaped by a broad program of liberalization that will make America's currently sclerotic education sector more closely resemble its dynamic business sector, we can expect more emphasis on the bottom line ("student achievement") and less on the processes employed to get there. Put another way, "best practices" will not be imposed from above by panels of experts; they will *emerge* from a competitive process.

Just as they do today, experts in a system of school choice will often disagree about the best methods of teacher preparation. For instance, some advocate that teachers use direct instruction to impart knowledge to students. Others argue that the teacher's role is to act as a facilitator of a child's own discoveries, where learning is student-centered and constructed by the learner. Should a teacher be a "sage on a stage" or a "guide by the side"? This is the essence of the long-running debate between traditionalist and progressive educators. In the current context of a dominant, near-monopolistic "traditional" route to the classroom, this debate has led to an intense struggle for control of the schools of education: the winner would control the pedagogical philosophy imparted to the vast majority of the cohort that would teach America's children.

Strong disagreements will undoubtedly persist under a system of voluntary, competitive certification. Part of this is due to a genuine diversity of preferences in the realm of teacher attributes, while part is owed to ambiguity of the data on student achievement (which will presumably diminish over time).

Some choice opponents contend that in the absence of state-mandated educational standards, educational quality will suffer. Yet the opposite result is more likely. Schools will be free to experiment with new and innovative educational approaches, and the need to attract students will drive them to monitor new developments in the educational field and adopt those approaches that prove to be most effective. Successful approaches will thrive; failing approaches will wither. It might be helpful to think more specifically about exactly how this will happen.

Over the first decade or so of a regime of competitive certification, teachers will enter the classroom from different sorts of preparation programs. As new graduates replace retiring teachers and those leaving the profession, the number of teachers from different types of schools of education will steadily increase. Longitudinal data on the outcomes of students taught by different sorts of teachers will accumulate.

We might imagine any number of extrinsically valid tests that would be useful as a basis of comparison—standards that might vary from proportion of admission to selective colleges to standardized test data such as SAT, NAEP, or state achievement test scores. Over time, these data will accumulate and patterns will emerge. Schools with high achievement will trumpet their scores while lower-achieving schools may seek to explain them away. Nevertheless, we can expect that all schools will feel pressure to improve student achievement and will seek teachers that can provide it.

Imagine two schools. School A is a private school that accepts vouchers and is run by a traditionalist principal who believes that there is a certain body of content knowledge that students must learn to be educated adults. The philosophy of the school emphasizes order, discipline, study, repetition and memorization of facts, and places less emphasis on creativity, exploration, and self-discovery. School B is a charter school that prides itself on innovative learning techniques. Its operational outlook emphasizes individualized styles of learning, self-paced study, and nonhierarchical classrooms. Students rarely encounter tasks that require memorization, or even graded assignments.

These schools have very little in common with regard to curriculum or how they treat their students. It would be difficult to imagine that they might choose to evaluate their employees in exactly the same way.

Over time, teachers with certain types of training—those proven to correlate with increased student achievement—will likely be more attractive to employers. Schools will bid up the price of teachers with these types of training. To ensure that teachers have this type of proficiency, one can easily imagine a burgeoning industry of teacher certification. Diverse forms of certification will complement the various goals of schools and parents. Some schools and parents are extremely focused on academic achievement while others are devoted to the creation of a well-rounded child. Some parents and schools may seek to emphasize certain content areas such as the arts or sciences while others want the broadest liberal education possible.

One distinct possibility is the elimination of certification altogether. Around 10 percent of American students currently attend private schools. By and large, such schools are free to hire whom they please; they can dispense with the entire certification process if they so desire, and many do just that. These schools—with a relatively wealthy clientele and high outcomes—generally hire teachers who lack certification. Given the existence of specialized programs for teacher training, why would they do this? These schools believe that it is possible and prudent for them to perform the screening process themselves. Perhaps they devote their time, energy, and better judgment to the process because they believe that staffing decisions are too subtle, time-consuming, and important to be reduced to—or even benefit from—a credentialing process. Just as management firms and newspapers can recruit consultants and journalists from the pool of general liberal arts graduates—selecting for hard-to-measure characteristics such as tenacity, patience, and intellectual curiosity—schools may decide that no mechanism of certification can convey the information necessary to make highly individualized staffing decisions.

Perhaps the most likely outcome is something in between. A "thin" form of voluntary or competitive certification might help schools narrow their candidates. Teacher preparation programs might be directly linked to a certain type of certification agency (say, one with a "direct instruction" philosophy or another with a "critical pedagogy" approach). Or the certification agencies might offer free-standing tests that can be taken by anyone. The pressure to make these tests rigorous and meaningful would come from the market; flimsy, easy-to-pass tests would confer little value on the test-taker.

How will the market for standards of certification play itself out? Will there be different agencies for certification of different subject areas? Will the certification agencies tightly control the curriculum required for their types of certification or instead ask only for broad outlines?

The answer is that we cannot be sure. The process of competition is a discovery process in which solutions that meet the demands of the marketplace evolve. Over the course of time, we can expect knowledge to increase. What type of teacher education produces teachers who are best at improving achievement? What principles must be required by such a program and which are optional? Does such a broadly applicable program of teacher education exist?

These are questions of the utmost importance, but we cannot know the answers in our current one-size-fits-all system. It will take patience, time, hard work, and experimentation to learn these answers. But the promise of American education—of social equity through universal opportunity—cannot be fulfilled without this sort of reform. In the interest of American children, schools, and our society at large, we must immediately reform our teacher certification system.

Conclusions

The ideal of teacher professionalism has largely succeeded in transforming the rhetoric of regulation to the reality of restriction. America's labyrinthine licensure laws are a paradigmatic example of good intentions gone awry. Rather than simply ensuring the qualifications of all educators, U.S. teacher certification laws have the unintended consequence of depressing teacher quality. Originally envisioned as a prudent gatekeeper that would ensure the qualifications of teachers entering the profession, teacher certification instead serves as the worst sort of barrier to entry. It drains the pool of qualified candidates, perversely selects for prospective teachers who are willing to overcome senseless bureaucratic hurdles, imposes extra costs on future teachers, and ultimately diminishes the competition for teacher positions. What is often overlooked is the fact that school districts on the margin—those in which teaching vacancies are plentiful, classrooms are bulging, and salary money is scarce—are the ones that are most often left in the lurch by the artificially limited supply of excellent teachers. Fundamental reform of the system of teacher certification is a prerequisite for providing adequate education to students in urban districts.

Notes

1. As an example of the wide range of consensus on priorities, see the following reports by the generally conservative Thomas B. Fordham Foundation, *The Teachers We Need and How to Get More of Them: A Manifesto* (Washington: 1999), and the generally liberal National Commission on Teaching and America's Future, *What Matters Most: Teaching for America's Future* (New York: 1996).

2. William L. Sanders and June C. Rivers, "Cumulative and Residual Effects of Teachers on Future Student Achievement" (Knoxville, Tenn.: University of Tennessee Value-Added Research and Assessment Center, 1996). See also Heather Jordan, Robert Mendro, and Dash Weerasinghe, "Teacher Effects on Longitudinal Student Achievement" (Indianapolis: National Evaluation Institute, 1997), and Boston Public Schools, "High School Restructuring," (Boston: March 9, 1998).

3. W. Hussar, *Predicting the Need for Newly Hired Teachers in the United States to 2008–09* (Washington: National Center for Education Statistics, 1999). See also Cheryl

C. Sullivan, *Into the Classroom: Teacher Preparation, Licensure and Recruitment* (Alexandria, Va.: National School Board Association, 2001).

4. David L. Angus, *Professionalism and the Public Good: A Brief History of Teacher Certification* (Washington, D.C.: The Thomas B. Fordham Foundation, 2001), p. 15.

5. On mulitiplication of certificates: Ibid., 19. On multiplication of educational specialties, see Diane Ravitch, "A Brief History of Teacher Professionalism." Paper presented at White House Conference on Preparing Tomorrow's Teachers, March 5, 2002, available at http://www.ed.gov/admins/tchrqual/learn/preparingteachers-conference/ravitch.html.

6. Ibid., p. 23.

7. Ibid., p. 25.

8. Dale Ballou and Michael Podgursky, "Teacher Training and Licensure: A Layman's Guide" in *Better Teachers, Better Schools*, ed. Marci Kanstoroom and Chester E. Finn Jr. (Washington: The Thomas B. Fordham Foundation, 2001). See also Frederick Hess, *Tear Down This Wall: The Case for a Radical Overhaul of Teacher Certification* (Washington: The Progressive Policy Institute, 2001). For a complete, if opaque, listing of teacher licensure requirements by state see the National Association of State Directors of Teacher Education and Certification manual, available at http://www.nasdtec.org.

9. The quality and scope of these programs vary widely. New Jersey's remains one of the best; the Garden State gets about a quarter of its public school teachers through this route. For New Jersey, see Leo Klagholz, *Growing Better Teachers in the Garden State* (Washington, D.C.: The Thomas B. Fordham Foundation, 2000). Other states, crippled by powerful interest groups that oppose the existence of alternative routes to the classroom, have systems that barely function. By contrast, Ohio's woefully dysfunctional alternative certification system graduated only 31 teachers in its first 11 years of existence. See C. Emily Feistritzer and David T. Chester, *Alternative Teacher Certification: A State-by-State Analysis, 2003* (Washington: National Center for Educational Information, 2003).

10. See Education Commission of the States, available at http://www.ecs.org.

11. Math scores are from the International Association for the Evaluation of Educational Achievement, Third International Mathematics and Science Study, 1999. Ina V.S. Mullis et al., *TIMSS 1999 International Mathematics Report* (Boston: International Association for the Evaluation of Educational Achievement, 2000). Science Scores are from the International Association for the Evaluation of Educational Achievement, *Mathematics and Science Achievement in the Final Year of Secondary School: IEA's Third International Mathematics and Science Study, 1998*. Ina V.S. Mullis et al. (Boston: International Association for the Evaluation of Educational Achievement, 1998). Information also available in National Commission on Education Statistics, *Digest of Education Statistics 2002* (Washington: NCES, 2003), Tables 398 and 407, respectively.

12. National Commission on Education Statistics, *Digest of Education Statistics 2002* (Washington: NCES, 2003), Table 134.

13. Ibid., Table 123 and Table 114.

14. Ibid., Table 129.

15. Cf. Christopher Jencks and Meredith Phillips, "The Black-White Test Score Gap: An Introduction" in *The Black-White Test Score Gap*, ed. Christopher Jencks and Meredith Phillips (Washington: Brookings Institution, 1998).

16. *Digest of Education Statistics 2002*, Table 133.

17. For an overview of the extent of the achievement gap, see Abigail Thernstrom and Stephen Thernstrom, *No Excuses: Closing the Racial Gap in Learning* (New York: Simon and Schuster, 2003), Chapters 1–2. For a useful and accessible explanation applying the statistical concept of standard deviation to measures of educational achievement, see Paul Peterson, "Ticket to Nowhere" *Education Next* 3, no. 2 (Spring 2003): 39–46, available online at http://www.educationnext.org/20032/39.html.

18. U.S. Department of Education, *The Condition of Education* (Washington: National Center for Education Statistics, 2003), Table 17-1.

19. Abigail Thernstrom and Stephen Thernstrom, *No Excuses*, Chapter 1.

20. Ibid.

21. Ibid., Figure 2-4, p. 38.

22. Jencks and Phillips, *The Black-White Test Score Gap*, p. 6.

23. Eric A. Hanushek, "The Trade-off between Child Quantity and Quality," *The Journal of Political Economy* 100, no. 1 (February 1992): 84–117.

24. William L. Sanders and June C. Rivers, *Cumulative and Residual Effects of Teachers on Future Student Achievement* (Knoxville, Tenn.: University of Tennessee Value-Added Research and Assessment Center, 1996). See also Heather Jordan, Robert Mendro, and Dash Weerasinghe, *Teacher Effects on Longitudinal Student Achievement* (Indianapolis: National Evaluation Institute, 1997), and Boston Public Schools, *High School Restructuring* (Boston: Boston Public Schools, 1998).

25. U.S. Department of Education, *Meeting the Highly Qualified Teachers Challenge: The Secretary's Annual Report on Teacher Quality* (Washington: Office of Post Secondary Education, 2002), p. 12.

26. Dan D. Goldhaber and Dominic J. Brewer, "Does Teacher Certification Matter? High School Teacher Certification Status and Student Achievement," *Educational Evaluation and Policy Analysis* 22, no. 2 (Summer 2000): 139.

27. U.S. Department of Education, *Meeting the Highly Qualified Teachers Challenge: The Secretary's Annual Report on Teacher Quality* (Washington: Office of Post Secondary Education, 2002), p 14.

28. Kate Walsh, *Teacher Certification Reconsidered: Stumbling for Quality* (Baltimore: The Abell Foundation, 2001).

29. Jessica Levin and Meredith Quinn, *Missed Opportunities: How We Keep High Quality Teachers Out of Urban Classrooms* (Washington: The New Teacher Project, 2003).

30. Patrick J. Murphy and Michael M. DeArmond, *From the Headlines to the Frontlines: The Teacher Shortage and Its Implications for Recruitment Policy* (Seattle: University of Washington, Center on Reinventing Public Education, 2003). See also Richard M. Ingersoll, *Out-of-Field Teaching, Educational Inequality, and the Organization of Schools: An Exploratory Analysis* (Seattle: University of Washington, Center for the Study of Teaching and Policy, 2003).

31. For the purposes of meeting the "Highly Qualified Teacher" provision of the No Child Left Behind Act, teachers of the 7th and 8th grades will have to be certified in their subject rather than receiving an elementary or general education degree.

32. Richard M. Ingersoll, "The Problem of Underqualified Teachers in American Secondary Schools," *Educational Researcher* 28, no. 2 (1999): Table 1, p. 28.

33. A perfectly equitable system might suffer from some out-of-field teaching, but one would not expect it to be concentrated in, say, schools with one type of minority or students of a certain income level.

34. See, for example, Morris M. Kleiner, "Occupational Licensing," *Journal of Economic Perspectives* 14, no. 4 (Fall 2000): 189–202.

35. Walsh.

36. Frederick Hess, *Tear Down This Wall: The Case for a Radical Overhaul of Teacher Certification* (Washington: The Progressive Policy Institute, 2001), p. 13.

37. Richard W. Riley, "New Challenges, A New Resolve: Moving American Education into the 21st Century," Sixth Annual State of American Education Speech, Long Beach, Calif., February 16, 1999.

38. Quoted in J. E. Stone, "NCATE: Whose Standards?" in *Better Teachers, Better Schools*, ed. Marci Kanstoroom and Chester E. Finn Jr. (Washington: The Thomas B. Fordham Foundation, 2001), p. 204.

39. For a de facto teacher professionalism manifesto, see National Commission on Teaching and America's Future, *What Matters Most: Teaching for America's Future* (New York: NCTAF, 1996).

40. For paradigmatic models of competitive certification, see Hess, *Tear Down This Wall: The Case for a Radical Overhaul of Teacher Certification*. See also, Michael Podgursky, *Improving Academic Performance in U.S. Public Schools: Why Teacher Licensing is (Almost) Irrelevant* (Washington: American Enterprise Institute, forthcoming).

41. U.S. Department of Education, *Meeting the Highly Qualified Teachers Challenge: The Secretary's Annual Report on Teacher Quality* (Washington: Office of Post Secondary Education, 2002).

42. U.S. Department of Education, *Meeting the Highly Qualified Teachers Challenge: The Secretary's Second Annual Report on Teacher Quality* (Washington: Office of Post Secondary Education, 2003).

43. Compare, for instance, the results of a Washington Post/Kaiser/Harvard poll of April 2001 with American Viewpoint of October 1997. Both are available at http://www.publicagenda.org/issues/major_proposals_detail.cfm?issue_type = education&list = 13.

44. Public Agenda survey of 800 African-American and 800 white parents, March 26–April 17, 1998. Available at http://www.publicagenda.org/issues/nation_divided_detail2.cfm?issue_type = education&nation_graphic = nd4.gif.

45. For the full range of alternative certification programs, see C. Emily Feistritzer and David T. Chester, *Alternative Teacher Certification: A State-by-State Analysis, 2003* (Washington: National Center for Educational Information, 2003).

7. Private and Public School Desegregation in Atlanta 50 Years after *Brown v. Board of Education*

Eric Wearne

Introduction

With the 50th anniversary of the lauded decision to desegregate America's public schools in *Brown v. Board of Education*[1] coming in May 2004, it is an appropriate time to take stock of what that decision has accomplished in the lives of the students it affects today. How were students' experiences in the fall of 2003 different than they were in the fall of 1953? This decision was an important victory for individual freedom, as state governments were no longer legally able to force significant portions of their populations into substandard schools. The South saw the most dramatic changes in education policy because of *Brown*, although the case actually involved a few separate decisions concerning segregated schools in Kansas, Delaware, and Washington, D.C., as well as northern Virginia and South Carolina. Because of the demographics of the city and its history of resistance to desegregation, as well as its current prominence in the South, the city of Atlanta is an especially appropriate place to examine the effects of public school desegregation half a century after *Brown*. This chapter will show that, while some integration has occurred in Atlanta's public schools since *Brown*, public schools are still much more segregated than are private schools in the city.

History of Atlanta Public Schools

In 1950, a complaint was brought against Atlanta Public Schools (APS) in *Aaron v. Cook*, charging that the school system was providing separate and unequal schools for the city's black and white students.[2] After the complaint was filed, several editorials in the *Atlanta Journal* and the *Atlanta Constitution* spoke out against the

135

plaintiffs. Citing improvements in black schools between 1944 and 1950, one editorial said: "The School Board repeatedly has said its ultimate aim is full equalization of funding for white and Negro pupils. The record shows this is not an idle announcement or one voiced to placate the Negroes. It is being carried out as fast as financial conditions will permit. There can be no question of the Atlanta School Board's good faith."[3] While the segregated schools did improve between 1944 and 1950, the board's "good faith" still resulted in vastly unequal school experiences for black and white children. In 1954, *Brown v. Board of Education* was decided, rendering segregation in all of America's public schools unconstitutional and illegal. *Aaron v. Cook* was dismissed in 1956.

Eugene Cook, the Georgia state attorney general at the time, declared that the decision did not affect the state of Georgia, and joined other southern officials in declaring "massive resistance" to the ruling.[4] Many white parents in 1954 and the years following either moved or withdrew their children from public schools across the South, including Atlanta Public Schools, and placed them in private (and still segregated) schools. In some places public schools had to close down completely because of huge drops in enrollment. Some states, community groups, and labor unions aided white parents in the creation of these "segregation academies" by providing funding for white children to leave the newly desegregated public schools.

In the 1960s, Atlanta took very small steps to desegregate. After the second *Brown* decision, which came a year after the first one, school districts were required to desegregate with "all deliberate speed."[5] In 1961—seven years after *Brown*—just nine black high school seniors were enrolled in four different Atlanta high schools. Under the Freedom of Choice plan, black students were allowed to transfer into white schools, but in 1970 the U.S. Supreme Court held that such plans were not adequate desegregation plans.[6]

In 1970, the Freedom of Choice plan was replaced by a "majority to minority" transfer plan, in which students could transfer from a school in which they were in the majority into one in which they would be in the minority. This plan also included a transfer of teachers intended to "achieve a racial ratio in each school close to the citywide ratio which at the time was 60 percent black in the elementary schools and 52 percent in the high schools."[7] A biracial committee was also set up to advise the school board on desegregation.

During the 1970s, as Fulton County (which encompasses Atlanta) was under its own desegregation orders and students were being bused through the city, Atlanta underwent a power shift in which the black business and political communities gained more and more control over APS. In 1974, Judge Albert J. Henderson Jr., in a case that had been in the courts since 1958, lifted Atlanta's desegregation order by holding that "the administrative staff of the system is over two-thirds black and is under the able supervision of Superintendent Alonzo A. Crim, a black educator and an administrator with an impressive list of credentials and accomplishments. In short, it would be difficult to attribute to those presently charged with the operation of the Atlanta Public Schools any intention to discriminate against black students enrolled in that system or to continue the effect of past discrimination."[8]

The Settlement Plan approved by Judge Henderson included four main provisions:

1. A student assignment plan, in which all schools were required to have at least a 30 percent black enrollment. In practice, because of the changing demographics of the city, many schools became or remained all black and were considered desegregated;
2. A plan for staff desegregation;
3. An expanded majority to minority transfer program; and
4. A plan for administrative desegregation, which included the creation of several new positions.[9]

Before *Brown*, APS consisted of 600 schools serving 18,664 black students separately from the city's white students.[10] Each school was 100 percent de jure segregated. At the turn of the 21st century, APS consists of 96 schools serving 55,812 students of all races.[11] And more than three quarters of them are still de facto segregated.

Atlanta's private schools now, however, are very different from the segregation academies of the 1950s and 1960s. Though they draw students from the same general geographic area as APS, they are significantly less segregated than are the public schools.

Private and Public Schools in Atlanta

The schools examined in this report include all schools in the Atlanta Public Schools system listed in the Common Core of Data and all private schools with enrollments above 50 students in K–12 classes in Atlanta listed in the Private School Universe Survey, both produced by the National Center for Education Statistics.[12]

Racial enrollment data were also taken from the Common Core of Data and the Private School Universe Survey. The latest data available for private and public schools were used. In the case of private schools, the latest results were for the 1999–2000 school year; for public schools, the latest results were for the 2001–2002 school year.

The percentage of the majority race in each school (whatever race that might be) was used to determine how segregated a school was. Schools in which the majority race constituted 90 percent or more of the total school population are considered to be "highly segregated."

Integration Rates 50 Years after *Brown*

Using a 90 percent majority as a benchmark, the National Center for Education Statistics data show that there is a lower percentage of "highly segregated" private schools than of "highly segregated" public schools in Atlanta. About 60 percent of Atlanta's 53 private schools are "highly segregated," while nearly four fifths of Atlanta's 96 public schools (79 percent) are so segregated (see Appendix).

Despite the fears of many opponents of school choice, it appears that in Atlanta the government is more likely to segregate students by race than are individual parents making their own private choices.

Because students are assigned to schools on the basis of where they live, segregated housing patterns are reproduced in the public schools. One way to overcome this obstacle would be to implement a strong system of school choice in Atlanta Public Schools. Parents in poor, segregated sections of Atlanta deserve the right to send their children to higher achieving, more integrated schools if they think those schools will better serve their children's needs. They should not be forced to send their children to unsafe, low performing schools simply because of their socioeconomic status or their address.

Besides the fact that private schools seem to do a better job of creating diversity in their populations, it is hard to imagine a system better able to keep public schools segregated than the one we have now. Wealthier parents, if dissatisfied with their children's neighborhood schools, can choose to either send their children to private schools or buy a house in a district with a better public school system. These families are already able to choose their children's schools based on location, safety, academic reputation, and special programs. The only options for dissatisfied poorer families, who may not be able to move, are to either hope they live near a charter school or to take advantage of a private scholarship program.

Spending more money on public school does not appear to be a solution. While Atlanta Public Schools spent almost $10,000 per student in 2002, two neighboring districts—Gwinnett and Cobb counties—achieve better results while spending less (Gwinnett spent $7,107 and Cobb spent $7,074).[13] More spending does not equal better schools, but higher home prices and a lack of school choice do keep poor students from leaving the failing public schools to which they have been forcibly assigned.

Meanwhile, the National Center for Education Statistics reports that across the country, the average tuition among all private schools was just $4,689 in 1999–2000[14]—much less than what the Gwinnett and Cobb school districts spend, and less than half what APS spends on its students.

A system of choice within the city of Atlanta, therefore, makes sense for several reasons. A small voucher worth $5,000, for example, could be a way to both foster desegregation and allow the city to save money, which it could then, if it chose, reinvest in APS. If a really bold system were enacted and the full amount of money the government already spends followed children, it would nearly cover tuition at some of the most prestigious schools in the city.

Resegregation in the Classroom

While these data do show that private schools in Atlanta are less segregated than public schools, over half of them still clear the 90 percent benchmark. Private schools overall averaged an 87 percent single-race majority, which is slightly less than the public school average of 92 percent (see Appendix). Also, though looking at school-level data presents a more accurate picture than does looking at district-level data, schools often resegregate within themselves through tracking in individual classrooms and programs. These problems are noteworthy, but if integration is still a valued goal for our schools, then, in Atlanta at least, the private school sector seems to be doing a better job of reaching it than are our public schools.

Conclusion

The demographics of the city of Atlanta overall include a majority of black citizens (61 percent)[15] and students in the public school system (89 percent),[16] but Atlanta's public schools are significantly more segregated than are the private schools. In this sense, the promise of *Brown v. Board of Education* has not been fulfilled. The government still forces students into segregated schools through attendance zone assignments, rather than strictly by race, and the results are nearly the same. But, if given a choice, the citizens of Atlanta have shown that they want to send their children to more integrated schools. This is not to say that school choice would instantly equalize every school and eliminate segregation and racism, but it would be a more effective way to address the problem of highly segregated schools than is our current reliance on legislation and court-ordered remedies. *Brown* itself was an important court order, but the situation in Atlanta today is evidence that educational quality now takes precedence over race when parents choose their children's schools. In a unanimous decision, Chief Justice Warren wrote that segregated schools were unconstitutional and could not be made equal.[17] In effect, we acknowledged that all students deserved to receive a good education and promised that they would not be excluded from high-achieving, academically rigorous schools because of their race. Fifty years on, it's about time we lived up to that promise.

Notes

1. *Brown v. Board of Education*, 347 U.S. 483 (1954).

2. *Aaron v. Cook*, (Atlanta) 522.Ga.a (1950).

3. "The School Board Has Clean Hands," *Atlanta Journal*, editorial, September 21, 1950.

4. "Attorney General Cook's Response to *Brown v. Board of Education*," *Atlanta Constitution*, May 18, 1954.

5. *Brown v. Board of Education*, 349 U.S. 294 (1955).

6. *Green v. School Board of New Kent County, Va.*, 391 U.S. 430 (1968).

7. In Barbara L. Jackson, "Desegregation: Atlanta Style," *Theory into Practice 17*, no. 1, Ohio State University, Columbus, Ohio (1978).

8. *Calhoun v. Cook*, 487 F2d 680 (1974).

9. Jackson.

10. "The School Board Has Clean Hands."

11. Georgia Department of Education, "2001–2002 Georgia Public Education Report Card, Atlanta City System Report," http://accountability.doe.k12.ga.us/Report02/.

12. U.S. Department of Education, National Center for Education Statistics, Private School Universe Survey, http://nces.ed.gov/surveys/pss/privateschoolsearch/ and Common Core of Data, http://nces.ed.gov/ccd/schoolsearch/.

13. Paul Donsky, "Spendthrift Schools?" *Atlanta Journal-Constitution,* June 25, 2003.

14. NCES, *Digest of Education Statistics 2002,* Table 61. Private elementary and secondary enrollment and schools, by amount of tuition level, http://nces.ed.gov/programs/digest/d02/tables/dt061.asp.

15. U.S. Census Bureau, Public Information Office, "U.S. Census 2000 Population by Race and Hispanic or Latino Origin: Places in Georgia."

16. Georgia Department of Education, "2001–2002 Georgia Public Education Report Card."

17. *Brown,* 1954.

Appendix ATLANTA PUBLIC SCHOOLS	
School	Percent Majority Race
Adamsville Elementary	99
Anderson Park Elementary	99
Arkwright Elementary	99
Beecher Hills Elementary	100
Benteen Elementary	67
Bethune Elementary	99
Blalock Elementary	100
Boyd Elementary	99
Brandon Elementary	89
Brown Middle	99
Bunche Middle	99
Burgess Elementary	99
C.W. Hill Elementary	99
Capitol View Elementary	93
Carver High	98
Cascade Elementary	99
Centennial Place Elementary	91
Charles R. Drew Charter School	99
Cleveland Elementary	97
Coan Middle	99
Collier Heights Elementary	99
Connally Elementary	99
Continental Colony Elementary	99
Cook Elementary	100
Crim Evening Classes	98
Crim High	99
D.H. Stanton Elementary	99
Dobbs Elementary	99
Douglass High	99
Dunbar Elementary	98
East Lake Elementary	99
F.L. Stanton Elementary	99
Fain Elementary	95
Fickett Elementary	99
Garden Hills Elementary	55

Atlanta Public Schools (cont.)

Gideons Elementary	94
Grady High	63
Grove Park Elementary	100
Harper/Archer High	98
Herndon Elementary	99
Hope Elementary	83
Howell Elementary	98
Hubert Elementary	84
Humphries Elementary	99
Hutchinson Elementary	73
Inman Middle	58
Jackson Elementary	77
Kennedy Middle	99
Kimberly Elementary	99
King Middle	88
Lakewood Elementary	92
Lin Elementary	55
Long Middle	93
M.A. Jones Elementary	99
Mays High	99
McGill Elementary	83
Miles Elementary	98
Mitchell Elementary	77
Morningside Elementary	70
North Atlanta High	70
Oglethorpe Elementary	98
Parks Middle	96
Parkside Elementary	74
Perkerson Elementary	96
Peterson Elementary	99
Peyton Forest Elementary	96
Pitts Elementary	88
Price Middle	95
Ragsdale Elementary	100
Rivers Elementary	40
Rusk Elementary	98
Scott Elementary	97
Slater Elementary	95
Smith Elementary	85

Atlanta Public Schools (cont.)

South Atlanta High	94
Southside High	92
Sutton Middle	44
Sylvan Hills Middle	95
Therrell High	99
Thomasville Heights Elementary	99
Toomer Elementary	97
Towns Elementary	95
Turner Middle	99
Usher Middle	98
Venetian Hills Elementary	99
Walden Middle	98
Washington Evening High	100
Washington High	99
Waters Elementary	92
West Fulton Middle	99
West Manor Elementary	99
White Elementary	99
Whitefoord Elementary	99
Williams Elementary	99
Woodson Elementary	99
Young Middle	99
Average Majority %	92
% of "highly segregated" schools	79

SOURCE: U.S. Department of Education, National Center for Education Statistics, Private School Universe Survey, http://nces.ed.gov/surveys/pss/privateschoolsearch/.

ATLANTA PRIVATE SCHOOLS

School	Percent Majority Race
Archbishop T. Donnellan School	88
Atlanta Adventist Academy	48
Atlanta Country Day School	93
Atlanta International School	80
Atlanta New Century Schools	63
Atlanta North School of SDA	49
Atlanta School	70
Atlanta Speech School Inc.	97
Believers Bible Christian Academy	100
Ben Franklin Academy	89
Brandon Hall School	84
Cascade Adventist Elementary	59
Children's School	64
Christ the King Elementary	92
Clara Mohammed Elementary	99
Dar Un-Noor School	72
Davis Academy	97
Epstein School	100
First Montessori School of Atlanta	85
First Steps School Inc.	100
Galloway School	92
Heiskell School	75
Holy Innocents Episcopal School	95
Horizons School	51
Howard School Central	95
Imhotep	99
Immaculate Heart of Mary School	74
International Preparatory Institute	100
Intown Community School	97
Johnson's Learning Center	100
Greenfield Hebrew School	99
Laurel Heights Academy	58
Light of the World Atlanta	100
Lovett School	90
Marist School	90
Masters Christian Academy	44

Altanta Private Schools (cont.)

Mt. Vernon Baptist Church Academy	100
Mt. Vernon Presbyterian School	88
New Generation Christian Academy	100
Northwoods Montessori School	55
Our Lady of Lourdes School	97
Our Lady of the Assumption School	96
Pace Academy	95
Paideia School	82
Renaissance Montessori Inc.	100
St. Anthony's Catholic School	94
St. Jude the Apostle School	94
St. Martin's Episcopal School	97
St. Pius X Catholic High	83
Schenck School Inc.	99
SW Atlanta Christian Academy	98
Trinity School Inc.	94
Whitefield Academy	81
Average Majority %	87
% of "highly segregated" schools	60

Source: U.S. Department of Education, National Center for Education Statistics, Common Core of Data, http://nces.ed.gov/ccd/schoolsearch/.

8. Building Futures with Private Scholarships: The Washington Scholarship Fund

Tracey Johnson

> *What future can children have if they have not been properly educated? How can our kids function in mainstream America if they attend poor or mediocre schools? If you look around you'll see they are passed from grade to grade and graduate unable to read or use measuring cups to measure ingredients. It's time for a change.*
> — Barbara Mickens, a Washington Scholarship Fund parent

These are the words of a parent coming to grips with a public education system she believes has failed to provide the best for her children. The public education system was supposed to assist parents like her in the intellectual nourishment of their children—and provide equal access to education for all citizens, regardless of economic standing. A subtle intent behind the creation of this public education system was to prevent the development of an elitist society in which the wealthy would have exclusive rights to quality learning. The public education system was to be an equalizer, propelling America ahead of other countries by providing all of our young with superior intellectual training.

Unfortunately, today equality in education is more the exception than the rule. The best public schools are often found attached to wealthy neighborhoods where high student expectations, pristine school facilities, and engaged students entice the best and brightest teachers to teach. Meanwhile, low-income neighborhood schools are beset with a lack of expectations, resources, and enthusiastic personnel, resulting in a continual educational dichotomy between the haves and have-nots.

The reality is that the parents who need the greatest level of assistance in preparing their children for the future receive the least

147

help. Low-income parents grapple with what may be the greatest civil rights issue of our time. It's a civil rights issue based on economic standing rather than race. As poor children are forced to remain in schools deemed unsafe and low performing, their wealthier counterparts avail themselves of the benefits of financial choice by either moving to better public school districts or attending private school.

As we became further distanced by time from the foundation of our public school system, it became clearer and clearer that a great disparity was arising and that low-income families were being left behind. Recognizing this, 15 years ago, an individual acutely aware of the plight of low-income parents undertook a novel approach to help these children. J. Patrick Rooney, an Indianapolis businessman and owner of Golden Rule Insurance Company, created and launched the first private scholarship program in the United States. What made this program so revolutionary was that it focused exclusively on pre-collegiate students from low-income families. The program's aim was to provide these parents with assistance in sending their children to private school.

On a small scale, the program helped address the underlying equality issue facing education. Wealthy parents (by moving to an area with a preferred public school or sending their children to private school) had the ability to choose the way in which their children were educated. The Golden Rule program sought to allow low-income parents the same options. Though it was not feasible to move families from one neighborhood to another, this program was able to offer the financial boost parents needed to send their children to private school. In its first year in 1991, the Golden Rule program served almost 750 students in the company's hometown of Indianapolis.

The program was remarkably successful—and word quickly spread about its effectiveness. Nationwide efforts began to create similar programs in other neighborhoods and communities. In 1992, four additional programs began in Atlanta, Battle Creek, Milwaukee, and San Antonio. Each of these programs was successful and created a culture of optimism in the areas they served.

By the following year, seven additional scholarship programs cropped up nationwide, including the program in Washington, D.C.—the Washington Scholarship Fund. The end of the 1993 school year found more than 5,000 low-income students nationwide engaged in private scholarship programs.

Scholarship programs continued to emerge over the next few years. As programs began they revised their operational plans and, although based on the initial Golden Rule model, programs modified their approach to respond to each individual community's needs.

Remarkable developments were taking place. The D.C. program, for instance, noted that parents who were well below the poverty line when they entered the program were taking on additional jobs to help pay their portion of tuition—and some even returned to school themselves to qualify for better job opportunities. One key element of the new scholarship programs was that parents pay a portion of the tuition and so scholarship programs provided partial tuition assistance to ensure a level of parental involvement and commitment. The parents demonstrated incredible ownership for their children's education, with schools reporting a high degree of parental school participation among scholarship recipients. What began as an endeavor to focus on low-income student education started to have far-reaching benefits throughout low-income communities.

By 1997, the private elementary scholarship movement had gained a great deal of attention. Public policy analysts were interested in the implications of the effectiveness of the programs for public education, while parents were simply interested in having their children gain access to better schools. Families both in and out of scholarship programs were beginning to believe that participation in a private scholarship program was their only means of providing their children with the education they needed. The story of Shawna is typical of other Washington Scholarship Fund parents:

> After doing a few "shadow visits" at the local public school that her daughter Leslie would have attended, Shawna realized that she could not send Leslie to that school. "The school was bad. In terms of safety and education, it was just a bad school." Shawna applied to the Washington, D.C., out-of-boundary public school program multiple times, which would enable her to send Leslie to a school outside of her neighborhood, but she never once received a response to her applications. Thousands of parents apply each year to gain access to a few spaces in those quality public schools that exist in Washington, D.C. Shawna became exasperated with the fact that the D.C. public school system did not give her a choice. After trying to work with the school system, and

149

having failed, she looked into sending her daughter to private school.

The cost of private school was almost prohibitive. Shawna explored every option she could before locating the Washington Scholarship Fund. Once she was accepted she immediately enrolled her daughter in a private school. Shawna says that there have been many struggles and a lot of sacrifices to keep both of her children in private school. She has at times had to work two or three jobs to keep up with tuition payments, but it has been well worth it. "Who knows what could have happened to Leslie?"

— Shawna, a Washington Scholarship Fund parent

These scholarship organizations sparked a great deal of interest as well as a number of questions in educational circles. Educators, public policy analysts, and researchers began wondering aloud what impact these scholarship programs would have on public education, about the true advantage of the access to private education that these programs allowed, and whether this scholarship system was ultimately benefiting the students in the programs.

Tied to these queries was the question about the role the government should play, if any, in the alternative education of students.

The dawn of 1997 brought with it an important turning point in the debate about educational choice. Two philanthropists, John Walton and Theodore Forstmann, came into the forefront by making a multiyear financial commitment to one of the first scholarship programs, the Washington Scholarship Fund. This private contribution enabled 1,000 student scholarships to be awarded via random lottery in Washington, D.C., a school district noted for consistently having the poorest performing public school system in the United States.

Because these new scholarships were to be awarded randomly, researchers took interest in the possibility they could study the effect of private school education on low-income students. Although anecdotal information and the observation of individual student performance held that students who left low-income neighborhood public schools to attend private schools met with greater academic achievement, researchers were excited by the prospect of providing empirical evidence attesting to the benefit of these programs, or lack thereof.

Private scholarship program administrators and parents attested to the scholastic success of students in these programs. And although there was no single component of private schooling cited as being "the" key ingredient for this success, parents and teachers alike saw the increased performance:

> My son was labeled "learning disabled" by the D.C. public school system and was to be placed in special education classes. I didn't believe it. I knew my son was not learning disabled, so before they transferred him to the special education classes, I registered him at [a private school], and had him tested on his grade level, and he did fine on the test. I did not know where the extra funds would be coming from to keep him in that school, but found out later through the school about WSF. Thanks, words can't express how grateful I am. My son is now at [a private high school] and making the second honor roll. . . . Thank you, thank you, thank you.
>
> — Kendra, a Washington Scholarship Fund parent

Parents in scholarship programs across the nation were expressing their gratitude for the assistance the programs provided. These parents, though low-income, knew better than anyone that education enables Americans to flourish in society. Because America is a monetary society that places great importance on material items, socioeconomic stature is a key determinant of "success" in the United States. Education is what enables citizens to transcend economic barriers and excel because they can use what they have learned to enhance their opportunities for social growth and enrichment.

Parents and teachers of individual students were grateful that doors were being opened, allowing at-risk students to access quality educational opportunities because they believed that these schools were preparing children for the future. Still, skeptics asserted that the success of students in scholarship programs was not a result of quality private schools but rather an indication of the quality of students being tested. They believed the self-selection of high-performing students unfairly skewed the anecdotal results the scholarship programs boasted.

Those who promoted this idea (sometimes referred to as "creaming") also maintained that the average low-income student would not benefit from a private education and, further, that typical parents from impoverished areas lacked both the education themselves and the inclination to properly determine the best educational environment for their children.

In fact, in an outspoken criticism of publicly funded vouchers, opponents of private schooling asserted that parents, especially the most disadvantaged, lacked the information and the ability to make wise choices and were likely to be overly influenced by factors as school convenience and the degree to which the school was supportive of their own religion or ideology. Critics contend that vouchers require parents to be informed consumers of education, even though most parents have neither the time, the ability, nor the information that would enable them to make good assessments of their alternatives.[1]

Despite these assertions, private scholarship programs around the country knew that the thousands of parents who applied to the programs each year had an unquenchable desire for something better for their children. They longed to have their children receive the type of educational nourishment they knew was essential to future success, nourishment that oftentimes, these parents had not received themselves:

> I am writing to say thank you for helping my family to send Carl to school of my choice. Thank you. At one time I was a little girl with no mother, father, or teacher to whisper in my ear, "Sharon do good in school, do your homework, study for spelling tests" or tell me that I could be anything in the world: a teacher or a nurse. Later I did know. I was so dirty with no clothes. All I could think of was being clean when I grew up. I went to the Detroit public schools. Teachers did not help, they looked down on me and just passed me on until the ninth grade. I quit. I gave up. No one cared. But with Carl, I care. I'll pay and pay and pay until Carl gets his education and knows he is somebody.

> — Sharon, a Washington Scholarship Fund parent

These opposing sides, and the implementation of a randomized environment within which student performance could be assessed, interested researchers at Harvard University who ultimately undertook a study to determine the benefit of providing private school scholarships to students in inner-city environments.

Harvard researchers coordinated the awarding of the 1,000 scholarships in Washington, D.C., which were given out through random lottery. The researchers administered a grade-appropriate standard-ized test to each of the students who applied for the scholarships. Students who were offered a scholarship were designated as "test" subjects while those who were not were designated as "control" subjects for the purposes of further testing. This set up the program so that the effects could be studied in a scientific manner. More than 7,500 students applied for these 1,000 scholarships, an incredible testament to the parental demand for the opportunity these scholar-ships provided.

After seeing the incredible demand for scholarships in Washing-ton, D.C., Forstmann and Walton organized a national scholarship effort based on the Washington Scholarship Fund's model.

In 1999, the Children's Scholarship Fund was created to provide the same type of hope, opportunity, and access to quality educational options on a national level that the Washington Scholarship Fund and other scholarship organizations provided locally. Within the first 100 days, 38 cities arranged to create scholarship programs for their communities.

Meanwhile, researchers were continuing their task of assessing the progress of the original 1,000 students awarded scholarships through the Washington Scholarship Fund program. The initial test-ing results showed that before receiving the scholarship award, both sets of students were equal when it came to academic performance. There were no inherent educational or achievement differences between the students who received the scholarship offer and those who did not. This finding had powerful implications because it would serve to dispel the myth that only the "best and brightest" received the scholarship.

As the testing progressed, differences between the two groups began to emerge. The students who had been a part of the scholarship program excelled. They scored the equivalent of a full grade level above those students who remained in public schools. Advocates of scholarship programs and critics alike were astounded with these results. In addition, the research showed that the parents of students in private schools were far more satisfied with the environment their children were in; the schools were safer, more disciplined, and interestingly enough, promoted the appreciation of cultural diversity better than public schools.[2]

These results were no surprise to the parents in the program.

[R]eceiving a scholarship for my daughters was one of the best things that ever happened to me. At a downtime in my life, your scholarship was the beginning of my fortunes changing for the better. When I divorced my wife in 1998, my children started to go down the wrong path. They started fighting, using profanity, and talked about joining gangs. They also were left home alone at night with their brother (10 years old at the time). So their mom sent them to me in D.C. D.C. public schools are not what they were when I attended, so I did not want to send them there. Working two part-time jobs, I could not afford to send them to private school.

That's when I applied for the WSF and was pleasantly surprised that we were selected. It's been a blessing. My children have done a complete turnaround. They both received honors throughout the school year. They perform in all the school plays and dance recitals. My oldest daughter is an outstanding basketball player. My youngest just completed K–5 and she can cursive write, do multiplication tables to 15, and read every word in this letter. They have memorized scriptures and songs from the Bible. Now they sing in the youth choir at my church.

— Duane, a Washington Scholarship Fund parent

The most recent development in private scholarship programs has been the progress of scholarship students through high school. Because many of these programs placed an age-based entrance requirement that limited applicants to kindergarten through 8th grades, the original students are just beginning to complete their high school education.

The initial objective of these programs was to see that low-income students received a quality elementary and high school education. There were no stated objectives pertaining to college. However, at least in the Washington, D.C., program, an interesting phenomenon has occurred. More than 90 percent of the program's graduating high school seniors go on to enter college. The students graduating from the 2002–2003 school year may boast as high as 100 percent college acceptance, once the final figures are tallied.[3]

Recent research into the progress of the Washington Scholarship Fund's high school students shows that these students are going on to some of the finest learning institutions in the nation. One of the individuals working on this project spoke about her experience interacting with the high school students in the program:[4]

> The last two summers I worked at the Washington Scholarship Fund, a private organization in Washington, D.C., which raises money to send children to private and parochial schools. From the research, we knew that the schools these children attended improved their testing results, but we were interested in the long-term results. I contacted the recent graduates to learn about their lives after high school and found out that 19 out of 20 were going to college. One student was at art school, another at school in New York City to become a sports broadcaster, another at Stanford, and another at U Penn. Three students were majoring in education, one in dance, and two were studying abroad in Europe and Africa. Each one said their mother was their most important role model.
>
> After talking to these students, I forgot the stereotypes about black inner-city families. The media often portrays inner-city parents as dysfunctional and drug addicted and has made claims that these families are incapable of understanding how to best educate their children. When I spoke to these families I saw dedication, love, intelligence, hard work, and respect. The parents had worked hard for their children's futures and they had achieved their dreams.
>
> I only spoke with 20 graduates, but the same is true for the thousands of other students helped by these programs. I always believed that the only way to achieve equality in this country is for every person to have the right to a good education. This summer I learned that, when given the opportunity, people can surpass your expectations, and I met people who didn't take life for granted but were working to make theirs better.
>
> — Eliza Gray, program researcher

The common theme throughout the history of the scholarship movement has been the ongoing struggles of families to provide for all of their children's needs. Scholarship parents and parents still looking for scholarships have always recognized that they needed to do more to nourish their children than simply feed and house them. They needed to nourish their minds and give them the tools to succeed in American society, a society focused on critical thinking and education.

Parents have always known. We are the ones who did not see. It took the first scholarships and the overwhelming response of parents who understood and to make clear how important education was to their children. Low-income parents desire scholarships because they understand it is their best hope. Their children are sinking into the worst school systems in America while the children of wealthier families are educated by some of the best. When given the opportunity to succeed through a scholarship, these children flourish. Scholarships enable these children to compete equally with their wealthier counterparts which, once again, enable education to equalize the playing field and to remove a barrier that separates those born into economic good fortune from those who are not.

As we move forward into the 21st century, the scholarship movement continues to spread, demand continues to grow, and children continue to receive the best education possible to provide them with the options many of their parents have lacked and the future they always dreamed of. Today, there are more than a hundred private scholarship programs across the nation, serving countless thousands of children. These programs are serving as an oasis of hope in deserts of lost opportunity and broken dreams. But these programs do not simply provide hope to our low-income populations. By properly educating our youth, we are investing in our own future and the future of this nation. The success of these programs is success for each of us ... because these children are our hope ... they are our future.

Notes

1. These criticisms are described by Isabel V. Sawhill and Shannon L. Smith, "Vouchers for Elementary and Secondary Education." Paper prepared for the Urban Institute, Brookings Institution, and Committee for Economic Development conference held October 2–3, 1998. Available at http://www.macalester.edu/courses/econ50-01/vouchers.pdf.

2. William G. Howell, Patrick J. Wolf, Paul E. Peterson, and David E. Campbell, "Test-Score Effects of School Vouchers in Dayton, Ohio; New York City; and Washington, D.C.: Evidence from Randomized Field Trials." Paper prepared for the annual meetings of the American Political Science Association, Washington, D.C., September 2000.

3. Eliza Gray, "Washington Scholarship Fund Senior Survey 2003." Available from Washington Scholarship Fund, 1133 15th Street NW, Suite 550, Washington, D.C. 20005.

4. Eliza Gray, Personal Interview, November 18, 2001.

9. Success as a Charter School: The Cesar Chavez Experience

Irasema Salcido

Introduction

The Cesar Chavez Public Charter High School for Public Policy (Chavez) was born out of the desire of a small group of individuals to improve the way urban high schools educate low-income, minority students. Founded in 1998 in Washington, D.C., Chavez has already developed a reputation as a model high school, providing at-risk students with a high-quality education that prepares them for college and future civic engagement. In the short span of five years, we are proud to have achieved such success and recognition. But this success certainly did not come easily, and we have learned many valuable lessons along the way.

The Chavez story is not unlike the stories of many other charter schools throughout the country. It is a story filled with big ideas, passionate leaders, students struggling to meet high academic standards—often for the first time in their lives—and everyday triumphs and disappointments. I believe the Chavez story reveals a great deal about urban education in America. In particular, it exposes the limitations of the traditional public school structure, which is ill-suited to respond thoughtfully and flexibly to specific student needs.

I am neither a policymaker nor an expert in education reform. I believe in charter schools and, indeed, in any reform that truly addresses the needs of children. My area of expertise is my own institution—its history, struggles, and successes, the latter of which I never take for granted. The story of Chavez is, of course, still unfolding, but I hope that in sharing its experience so far, I can inspire others to seek their own way to help ensure that every child—whatever the race, whatever the family income level—has the opportunity to attend an excellent school, gain entry to college, and become an engaged citizen.

Overview: Responding to the Needs of the District of Columbia Students

The Cesar Chavez Public Charter High School for Public Policy is very much a home-grown institution: it was created in response to the terrible lack of quality educational opportunities available for low-income students in the District of Columbia, but it was designed to leverage the best resources this city has to offer.

Despite its status as the capital city of the world's wealthiest nation, Washington, D.C., seems to be one of the most unfortunate places to live in America if you're a child. Approximately 32.1 percent of District children under the age of 18 are now living below the poverty level. This ranks the District of Columbia first in this category compared with the 50 states (the national average is 16.4 percent).[1]

And while the District of Columbia Public Schools serve some students well, far too many students—predominantly low-income and minority students—are not attaining the education they will need to be competitive in the 21st century. Approximately half of D.C. students (50.5 percent in 1999) are dropping out, and half of those students who drop out are leaving by the 8th grade.[2] Those who remain in school and graduate are not necessarily prepared for college or competitive careers: Stanford-9 Achievement Tests show that D.C. students' performance declines as they proceed through the grades.

This begins to explain why the District of Columbia has the lowest levels of adult literacy proficiency in the nation when compared with the 50 states, according to the National Adult Literacy Survey of 1993.

The founders of Chavez—who included a former DCPS assistant principal, three teachers, and an active board—agreed that the key to breaking these cycles of low literacy and poverty was twofold: first, every child must have the opportunity to attend an excellent school, and second, all students must acquire the knowledge and skills needed to engage in their community's development and to have an impact on public policy. Given our location in the District of Columbia, we knew that the resources for teaching children about civic engagement, government affairs, and public policy were easily within reach, if yet untapped by the traditional public schools.

There was another concern among the Chavez founders that helped determine the focus and specific character of the school. The

158

District's public schools are often criticized for their inadequacy in serving the city's majority African-American student population, but frequently overlooked are the many new challenges that have arisen in terms of the educational needs of its rapidly growing Hispanic population.

Currently, more than 1,000 language minority students are dropping out annually in D.C., reflecting national statistics that show Hispanics dropping out at a rate of 21 percent, nearly three times that of whites, and nearly two times that of African-Americans.[3] Many of these students are recent arrivals who lack the language skills to succeed in school. Providing these students with an English-as-a-Second Language (ESL) class is not enough: immigrant students need to be gradually moved into mainstream English-only classes after first being provided with transitional classes that also provide content like, for example, bilingual history and bilingual biology.

Those who helped found Chavez had grown increasingly frustrated by the inability of the traditional public school system to meet these and other needs of our city's children. Thus we left our respective positions in local traditional schools and created a charter school that would—

- Provide District students with a top-notch academic program
- Give District students the tools and skills they could use for a lifetime of successful civic engagement
- Ensure that the specific needs of *all* students were addressed

The Chavez mission states:

> Drawing on the vast policy resources in the nation's capital, the Chavez School will challenge students with a rigorous curriculum that fosters citizenship and prepares them to excel in college and in life. The school will use public policy themes to guide instruction and will provide students direct experience with organizations working in the public interest.

As the founding group worked through the design and development of the school, several questions arose again and again: Would local students be able to reach high academic standards despite damage already done by underperforming schools? Could a public policy focus really make a difference in the way that students considered themselves and the future of their city? How would we fund the educational atmosphere we were hoping to create—would the city's contribution plus fund-raising cover all of the personnel, programming, and facility needs we predicted? Even more basic, would students sign up for such a challenging program? What would these students look like in terms of their academic histories and personal histories? And just what sort of teachers would be most effective in teaching them?

Like many charter school founders, we had to take the plunge without all the answers to these questions or any guarantees that we would receive the adequate support and funding we would ultimately need to succeed. We opened our doors to our first set of 60 ninth-graders on September 2, 1998, with the plan to add a grade level each year for the next three years. We knew we were facing incredible challenges and entering largely unexplored territory. At the time—and this is still very true—the practices and procedures of successful charter schools had not been documented and disseminated widely by either chartering authorities or support services. And, of course, by their nature charter schools are highly individualized, so it is difficult to make generalizations about what specific practices work. Although we had some guidance from the board of trustees that we assembled and from the D.C. Public Charter School Board—which authorized our charter—we primarily had to learn by doing.

Our primary focus in the early stages was the design and fine-tuning of our school program. We created standards for each grade level in terms of curriculum, standardized test scores, the public policy program, attendance, and diverse assessment tools. We decided that Chavez students would be required to pass all classes with a C or better, compared with DCPS schools that pass students with a D or better. Chavez students would also be required to complete yearly portfolios to collect their work and demonstrate progress. In addition, we set a number of targets for Stanford-9 achievement, both in terms of the absolute score and "normal curve equivalent" gains. Many of our original ideas are still a major part of the school program, but others, like aspects of the Public Policy Program, were revised several times as we learned from doing.

Essentially, Chavez's unique Public Policy Program evolved and expanded as we learned how to navigate and use the vast resources available in the District. During the first year, the ninth-graders' program was largely characterized by in-house weekly seminars

and "Capstone Units," which had small groups of students participating in interdisciplinary studies of public policy issues (e.g., one
group of students studied immigration trends in the District, focusing on Vietnamese, Ethiopians, and Salvadorans). However, the
founders noted in the 1999 Annual Report that "it has become clear
to the staff that the public policy program is in a nascent stage. . . .
While the general public policy goal has not changed (that is, teaching Chavez students skills and knowledge in the field of public
policy), the school has developed new strategies for meeting that
goal."

Starting in the second year, tenth-graders were divided into
groups of five to seven students and placed with local nonprofit
organizations to complete what has now become the focal point of
the tenth-grade public policy curriculum: the "Community Action
Project." The goal of the project is to turn a traditional community
service requirement into a more robust project that teaches students
tools and skills to influence policies that affect their communities.
Groups meet weekly with local organizations like the Alliance for
Justice, Campaign for Tobacco-Free Kids, Amnesty International,
and the National Campaign to Prevent Teen Pregnancy to research
an issue and design a strategic campaign focused on policy solutions.

In year three, the "Junior Fellowship" was put into place. In this
program, eleventh-grade students are placed individually with local
public policy organizations to gain further understanding of specific
policy issues and practice applying their public policy and research
skills. The Fellowship is intensive: fulltime for three weeks. In addition to gaining further knowledge of the public policy field, students
also work on acquiring important professional skills, including
resume writing, interviewing, computer-based presentations, time
management, and office and phone etiquette. Chavez students have
fulfilled their fellowships at such diverse places as the Office of the
U.S. Vice President, the Urban Institute, the Heritage Foundation,
the Sierra Club, and D.C. Action for Children.

Finally, the Chavez senior year is dedicated to writing a public
policy research paper and further developing important public policy leadership skills. Seniors are enrolled in a year-long thesis writing
class, working with two advisers—a Chavez faculty member and
an outside expert—on their thesis topics from the public policy community. Chavez students have prepared papers on topics like racial

profiling, genetic engineering, missile defense systems, homelessness, Latin American immigration, child abuse, and the foster care system. At the conclusion of the school year, seniors must present their research to a panel of public policy professionals.

In Chavez's fifth year of operations, we also added a mandatory ninth-grade class called "Foundations in Public Policy" when we determined that Chavez students needed more preparation before venturing into the community for their following years' assignments. There are additional aspects to the Chavez Public Policy Program— and we continue to improve it—but these essential programs reflect the greater part of its curriculum.

Today, Chavez serves 250 students in grades 9 through 12. Our students come from all four quadrants of the District and reflect its diversity: the population is currently 51 percent Hispanic, 45 percent African-American, 1 percent Asian, 1 percent White, and 2 percent identified as "other." Seventy-six percent of Chavez students qualify for free or reduced-price lunch through the federal program.

Chavez has developed a solid reputation as a school that does not cut corners or ever lower its high expectations for students. The *Washington Post* has published several favorable articles on Chavez, most notably two that followed our first graduation, largely inspired by the fact that all Chavez graduates had been accepted to college. *Post* columnist Marc Fisher wrote, "Chavez has emerged as one of the most exciting in the city's charter school movement. There is something different about the students. In every case, somewhere along the line, someone reached for something different, something better."[4]

In February 2001, Founder and Principal Irasema Salcido was awarded Oprah Winfrey's "Use Your Life Award," which provided $100,000 for the Chavez School. Along with the Oprah show, the success of Chavez has been featured in several National Public Radio stories, the *Washingtonian*, *The Economist*, *El Tiempo Latino*, *El Pregonero*, the *Christian Science Monitor*, and on several local news stations.

Ms. Nathea Lee, the mother of a Chavez student, characterized the school well in a June 2002 Letter to the Editor of the *Washington Post*: "Chavez is a success story born of vision, dedication, flexibility, and attention to the needs of all students, regardless of the advantages or disadvantages they bring to the school."[5]

Challenges of the First Five Years

Like any start-up enterprise, a charter school's development brings many, often unexpected challenges. The 10 greatest challenges we faced during the first 5 years of operating Chavez were—

1. Overestimation of Student Skill Level
2. Establishing a Strong School Culture
3. Managing Business Operations
4. Maintaining High Standards
5. Facility and Location
6. Yearly Expansion
7. Curriculum Development
8. Staffing
9. Testing the Vision
10. Accountability

The nature of each of these challenges and how we have dealt with them are briefly described below.

1. Overestimation of Student Skill Level

We had anticipated that our students would be behind academically, but we were not prepared for the degree to which they would need remedial attention. Most of our ninth-grade students have arrived at Chavez far below grade level, with many functioning at a fourth- and fifth-grade level. Many of these students have never written an essay, and many have difficulties with even basic addition and subtraction. Of our first class of 60 students, 81 percent scored below basic on the math portion of the Stanford-9 Achievement Test in their first year at Chavez, and 52 percent scored below basic on the reading portion. We were astonished that these students had been so underserved by their elementary and middle schools. With each passing year, we have become better equipped to evaluate our incoming students and to provide them with individualized attention to address their deficiencies. We have also learned to deal creatively with those fortunate few who arrive ready for accelerated coursework (through AP courses, etc.) in addition to the many students arriving below grade level.

2. Establishing a Strong School Culture

Many of our students deal with difficult emotional, family, and social problems (teen pregnancy, abusive or unstable homes, violence in their communities, low academic skills, etc.). Because of these issues, our students have difficulty keeping their focus on learning and often react negatively to structure and academic pressure to perform. Again, we had anticipated strong reactions to our strict discipline plan and high academic standards, but we did not realize how much of our time would need to be devoted to enforcing them. In the early years, so much energy was invested in surmounting the problems our students had with structure and discipline that it often became impossible to teach. We asked ourselves: How do we build from nothing a culture of high academic and high moral expectations in which students know right from wrong, a culture in which students understand and care that their behavior affects the learning environment for everyone?

We knew that we had to model the behavior we expected of our students. Patience, consistency, and example were critical components of demonstrating how we would hold our students and parents accountable. Over time, we began to establish a culture in which students saw a direct connection between actions and consequences. Often we had to make difficult decisions that affected the lives of these students—suspending, expelling, and retaining many of them. By handling these challenging situations with courage, setting important precedents, and enforcing consequences, we began to shape the life of the school.

3. Managing Business Operations

Charter schools function like independent businesses in many ways. Our challenges with running the business operations of the school were heightened by our—the founders'—lack of business experience (we were all lifelong educators). In the beginning, our Board took responsibility for nearly every aspect of the operations of the school: contracts, checking, setting up the phone system, and pricing equipment and services. However, this arrangement was only temporary, and we eventually transitioned to handling most operations in-house. With each passing year, we had to manage more staff, a bigger budget, and more personnel positions. We grew from one principal and three teachers (for 60 students) to 10 administrative and support staff and 25 teachers (for 250 students) in 5 years: a growth of 400 percent!

As we grew, we had to create and fill new positions: Dean of Students, Chief of Operations and Finance, Technology Resource

Coordinator, Director of Development, and so on. Fund-raising for the school became a much greater concern, and managing the budget and making decisions about which programs to fund (summer school, after-school programs, technology and college prep programs, etc.) posed ever greater challenges.

4. Maintaining High Standards

Fulfilling our commitment to high academic standards often requires us to make very difficult and unpopular, decisions. We retained three-quarters of our first class to repeat the ninth grade—which some considered drastic. But one year was simply not enough to make up for our students' academic deficiencies and to teach our students that there are consequences for not completing all of the required work. We refused to perpetuate what many other schools do—that is, simply pass students along regardless of performance and growth. We wanted something better for our students and knew that this was their last chance to prepare for their adult lives. We invested significant time talking to parents and students about the importance of being prepared for college, and convincing them that a high school education is not just about getting a diploma and graduating with your friends. It was the right thing to do and that tough decisions following year one made similar decisions in the following years easier. We set a precedent and kept our standards high—and our students have been stronger for it.

5. Facility and Location

Along with business operations, we also must find, finance, and manage our own facility. For the first five months, we were located in a basement with 300 students from another school, where we had to use dividers as walls. Then we moved into a somewhat larger space with another school and paid rent to an outside organization that helped manage security and maintenance for both schools. At the end of that first year—in August 1999—we moved again because the arrangement with the management organization was no longer viable, and because we needed to accommodate 60 incoming students. Our new site was located (and still is) in Columbia Heights, a neighborhood that unfortunately has many unsafe areas and gang-infested parks, street corners, and schools. When we first moved in, we shared space with another school whose culture was drastically

165

different than ours. During that time, our students were often the victims of bullying by those in the less academically focused school. We managed to officially separate our space by the third year of our existence, but the location remains less than optimal. We are currently evaluating the feasibility of raising funds to acquire a better and larger facility for the 2004–2005 school year.

6. Yearly Expansion

Because our student numbers increase each year, our individual student problems increase as well. Dealing with larger numbers of students with emotional and social problems—on top of a lack of basic skills—is a challenge that we soon realized would required additional personnel and resources but, as a small school, this put a strain on finances. We had to find extra resources to serve a growing Hispanic population, a growing special education population, and teen mothers. As a rule, we want to place all of our money in the classrooms—to compensate effective teachers, reduce class size, and give students more academic attention. Nevertheless, we know that learning does not occur unless we address specific student needs as well, which requires hiring counselors and other student support staff. With more people came more personalities, more ideologies, and a need to set up institutional structures to formalize procedures. Unlike many other schools, we are committed to keeping most of our resources in-house and, in so doing, to retaining control over nearly every aspect of our students' school lives. Although this method is more challenging, we find it to be more effective for educating the whole student.

7. Curriculum Development

It became obvious early on that our college prep standards would require coursework far above the skills of our students. We struggled a great deal with this issue and, as a staff, often disagreed on the best approach and curriculum. In the beginning, we adhered rather strictly to the Modern Red Schoolhouse curriculum model, a well-respected national model of schoolwide reform. Over time, though, we began to tweak many aspects of the curriculum to deal with our student population and to include more national standards, while still remaining true to many of the original MRSh standards. For example, we adjusted our math curriculum to reflect the National

Council of Teachers in Mathematics standards and an integrated, spiraling approach (versus traditional sequencing).

Because we added a grade level each year for four years, we were, in a sense, unable to plan backward. In theory, this is possible, but for us, given the needs of our population and the standards we were intent on maintaining, vertical and horizontal planning was challenging and somewhat chaotic until we institutionalized departments (English, history and politics, science, foreign language, math, ESL/bilingual, and public policy) and grade-level teams.

8. Staffing

As in probably every start-up organization, some hiring mistakes were made—in our case, with regard to teachers. Teaching our diverse student population requires a certain balance of experience, expertise, and courage to try new and creative measures in the classroom. We are demanding of our teachers, and our curriculum requires certain skills and certainly a level of subject expertise. In addition, because we are a small school, getting along with others is critical to maintaining our nurturing, family-like environment. One benefit to charter school staffing is our one-year contract policy, which enables us to quickly repair poor hiring decisions. Of course, like most organizations with an independent-minded and intelligent staff, Chavez does experience its share of staff conflicts. Charter schools attract independent thinkers, which is refreshing and truly beneficial to students, and yet also the cause for internal strife.

9. Testing the Vision

During the early years, given our population, we questioned our vision: Can we really prepare all of our students to attend college? Should we instead be focusing as much on vocational opportunities for students? The Chavez board of directors, teaching staff, and administration had several discussions to evaluate whether changing the vision to reflect the reality of our students' academic levels was necessary. We ultimately agreed, though, that the vision would necessarily become a component of academic success and achievement. Students would succeed, not in spite of the vision, but because of it. In fact, the proof is very much in our second graduating class; many of whom were forced to repeat the ninth grade after our first year. Their courage, both academically and socially, has contributed to the Chavez culture. At Chavez, there is not a stigma attached to repeating grades. To fulfill the mission, we (Chavez students and staff) do what we must.

10. Accountability

As a public charter school, we welcome the opportunity to set forth goals, implement measures to meet them, and then report publicly our successes and also where we have fallen short. Four student achievement goals are stated in our accountability plan. The D.C. Public Charter School Board monitors our progress with each of these goals, all of which have annual targets: (1) Chavez graduates will demonstrate high school competency, (2) Chavez students will improve their Stanford-9 reading and math scores, (3) Chavez graduates will enroll in two- or four-year colleges, (4) Chavez students will graduate with skills in and knowledge about the discipline of public policy. At the beginning of the 2001 school year, we had the opportunity to revise some of our targets, which we adjusted to reflect our baseline data. Also, our original goals were created in a vacuum, without having had a student set foot in the school. After a few years with our students, we were able to adjust our targets to make them attainable, while keeping our standards high. In addition, we've had to deal with the challenge of being publicly judged on only one of our four academic goals: standardized tests. Although we have made great gains on our Stanford-9 scores and will likely meet the five-year target at our Charter Board Review, as an academic institution striving to create strong thinkers, we generally believe that our other assessment tools are better indicators of the progress (or, in some cases, lack thereof) of our students.

Successes of the First Five Years

Not surprisingly, the challenges we faced during Chavez's start-up and early operating years resulted in some of our greatest successes. We are proud to note this because we believe it indicates the strength of our organization and our ability to tackle challenges head-on with perseverance and flexibility. Some of our greatest successes during the first five years had to do with—

1. Student Retention, Satisfaction, and Progress
2. Building a Dynamic Staff and Staff Confidence
3. Institutionalizing Meaningful and Effective Structures

4. Public Policy Program
5. Quantitative Results
6. Role of a Supportive Board of Trustees
7. Creation of Programs in Response to Assessed Needs
8. Support of Charter Board, Funders, Policy Community, and Volunteers
9. Parent Satisfaction and Involvement
10. Student Satisfaction

Some observations about each of these successes follow.

1. Student Retention, Satisfaction, and Progress

After our first year, 40 of our 60 students decided to return for their second year, even though 29 of the 40 would be repeating the 9th grade. These 40 students gave us hope. Their belief in Chavez empowered us to continue on our journey of providing students the quality education they deserve. Their return was a testament to the theory that when you hold young people to high expectations, they rise to the occasion. The students that were repeating 9th grade came back convinced that they made the right decision, and prepared to honor their mistakes with hard work and persistence. Over the next four years, our retention rates improved, with each class passing more and more classes, and more students earning promotion.

2. Building a Dynamic Staff and Staff Confidence

Those of us running the school became even more committed to our work as time went on. We saw the injustice done to the young people we served, and began to see our role more clearly, that is, as a legitimate choice local parents could make to ensure that their child would find a better education and a better life. Coming to this realization was energizing and motivating. It pushed us to be creative and to be open-minded about the ways we achieve our goals. Although year two presented some problems in terms of staffing, by year three we had put together a strong staff that worked well together; this same group is nearly unchanged three years later. We were helped by the fact that, by the time we were recruiting teachers and staff for our third year, our reputation was beginning to develop positively.

In that year, many of our teacher applicants came from private schools, bringing along enormous talent. We had to convince them that Chavez offered a setting conducive to student success. Many of these teachers were concerned with the lack of structure and precedent that often characterizes charter schools, but we explained that with such newness came opportunity. Ultimately, teachers and administrators alike became excited to meet the challenge of not only making a difference for students but also contributing to the development of the organization's policies and procedures. In years three and four we worked hard to preserve the family-like, tight-knit fabric that we had created, and to continue to ensure that the school was a great place to work. By hiring intelligent, progressive teachers and staff, we have created an intellectually stimulating environment for educators, one that challenges them to creatively serve students and engage each other on issues ranging from curriculum and standards to politics.

3. Institutionalizing Meaningful and Effective Structures

The Chavez School has been and continues to be a work in progress. There are, however, certain structural and procedural components of the school program that we believe are particularly important to our effectiveness as an organization. The grade-level teams and departments that we institutionalized in years three and four ensure that teachers and staff are meeting regularly and planning curriculum horizontally and vertically. This effort also greatly helps the administration hold staff accountable through shared goals and deliverables. In addition, our programs and services—from after school to college prep to mental health—are better integrated and managed, largely due to our efforts to define staff roles clearly.

4. Public Policy Program

As mentioned before, fine-tuning the Public Policy Program and, indeed, institutionalizing it has taken a full five years. We can say now, though, that the program is one of our most successful and distinguishing characteristics. Our public policy curriculum prepares our students to become effective citizens dedicated to improving their communities. To achieve this goal, we collaborate with a vast network of Washington public policy experts and organizations to establish one of the most innovative public policy programs in the country. To date, we have collaborated with more than one hundred organizations to provide our students with a truly unique and meaningful high school education. In addition, students take courses that expose them to social issues and solutions; they complete community action projects and fellowships with local nonprofit organizations and nationally (and internationally) renowned public policy institutions; and they research and write a public policy thesis that analyzes and proposes solutions to a compelling social issue. This curriculum provides students with skills and knowledge to participate—actively and successfully—in civic life. In June 2002, Chavez became just one of 11 schools nationally to become a First Amendment School, a joint project of the Freedom Forum and the Association for Supervision and Curriculum Development. In February 2003, Chavez Principal Irasema Salcido was selected to contribute a paper to "The Civic Mission of Schools," sponsored by the Carnegie Corporation of New York and the Center for Information and Research on Civic Learning and Engagement.

5. Quantitative Results

As the years passed, we began to see great academic results from our students that had been with us for more than two years. For example, in year three, our 11th-grade students (i.e., our first class of 9th-graders) outscored D.C. public school students in all 16 content clusters of the Stanford-9 Achievement Tests; and all of our graduates of the class of 2002 were admitted to college, perhaps our most significant achievement to date. Students have been accepted to some of the world's best schools, including Brown, Columbia, and Georgetown as well as strong local schools like the University of Maryland—College Park, Howard, and American University.

6. Role of a Supportive Board of Trustees

Following the advice of the Public Charter School Board and other charter school founders, we assembled a board with a wide range of areas of expertise, including finance, education policy, facility and real estate, governance, and business management. The Board was critical on a *daily* basis in the first year, cutting checks, working with the budget, and helping with decisions about curriculum. As the years passed, the board empowered staff members to take over these tasks and assisted with a successful transition. Today, our board is primarily involved with fund-raising, facility search, balancing the budget, and evaluating school leadership.

7. Creation of Programs in Response to Assessed Needs

One of our most critical successes has been in effectively analyzing our student population and then responding with innovative programs to serve their needs. In the first few years, this was challenging because we didn't have the capacity to staff extra programs. By year three, however (and more firmly in years four and five), we began to dedicate more funding and personnel to programs that we created, such as the Bilingual/ESL Program, the Reading Program, Summer School, and the School-Wide Literacy Initiative, among others. These programs were created by Chavez staff members to serve the diverse needs of our students and to individualize the attention provided to all Chavez students. Because of the freedom offered to educators through the charter law, we were able to take the initiative and individualize our programs, which has been critical to the success of our students with the college prep curriculum.

8. Support of Charter Board, Funders, Policy Community, and Volunteers

The Chavez founders firmly believed that schools cannot and should not operate separately from the community. Our school, indeed, depends on the policy and nonprofit community to operate our innovative public policy curriculum. We rely on more than 60 organizations to sponsor our 11th-grade fellows, conduct 10th-grade community action projects, and serve as panelists for senior thesis presentations. Without our volunteer corps of nearly 70 community members, we would not be able to provide so many students with tutors and mentors. We have also created supportive partnerships with organizations like College Bound and the 100 Black Men of Washington, D.C. As a charter school, we are eligible to apply for funding from foundations and corporations as well as to cultivate individual donors. We have been fortunate to receive much needed funding from Citigroup, Fannie Mae, Freddie Mac, General Electric, Washington Gas, BB&T, the Price Family Foundation, Riggs Bank, Capital One, as well as a large donation from an anonymous family foundation.

9. Parent Satisfaction and Involvement

Parent involvement at Chavez has grown stronger every year; in the last three years we have increased the average number of parents

172

attending conferences from roughly 15 to 60. We have a Parent Teacher Student Association dedicated to fund-raising, public relations, staff appreciation, facility search, and scholarships. Our parents reported at the end of the 2002 school year that they are overwhelmingly satisfied with the quality of education and instruction offered by Chavez. Parents also say they feel welcome at the school and informed about their children's progress. And, there is a strong perception among parents that Chavez will help their children get into college.

10. Student Satisfaction

Perhaps the most telling statistic about student satisfaction is our growing re-enrollment rate from around 70 percent in year one to more than 80 percent this year. (Also, the Chavez School is in demand, with a current waiting list of more than 50 students.) The school used an extensive end-of-the year questionnaire to assess student satisfaction, administered in June 2002. The questionnaire included general questions as well as more specific questions pertaining to specific programs and services. Overall, Chavez students are satisfied with the education that they are receiving, and believe that the school is preparing them for college. Students also say they are learning about problems in their community, and acquiring the skills they will need to make positive changes.

The Future of Chavez

As we began our fifth year in September 2002, the Board of Chavez gathered groups of students, staff, community members, and funders to begin a strategic planning process for the next five years of Chavez. We began by identifying what we believe to be four defining characteristics, namely, (1) Innovative Public Policy Curriculum, (2) Demanding Standards, (3) Supportive Learning Environment, and (4) Inclusive Program. In a sense, these are our values—the heart of our school—and we have made and will continue to make critical decisions to preserve these qualities.

Now that we know what our four-year program looks like and even a little bit about how well our 2002 graduates are doing at their respective colleges, we have a picture of the Chavez graduate. We think it's important to keep this idea in our minds as we work everyday to make graduation and college acceptance a reality for every student.

The Chavez Graduate

At a minimum, Chavez graduates will leave Chavez with excellent writing and analytical skills, which will be realized as they complete the culminating project, the Senior Public Policy Thesis. A typical Chavez student will graduate having scored at least "basic" on Stanford-9 math and reading tests and with positive NCE gains over his or her four years at the school. In addition, the Chavez graduate will graduate with clear skills in and knowledge about the discipline of public policy. All Chavez graduates will enroll in two- or four-year colleges and universities.

Every student that attends Chavez receives a college preparatory curriculum, can only pass courses with a grade of C or above, attends summer school, completes SAT classes, receives some kind of one-on-one tutoring and/or mentoring, receives mental health and social services if needed, adheres to very strict discipline and attendance standards, completes a semester-long community action project, completes a three-week full-time fellowship at a public policy institution, writes a 10–15 page public policy thesis, and applies to a two- or four-year college.

With five solid years behind us, we are still faced with many challenges, most notably the need to find a permanent and suitable facility. Other challenges include revamping our English curriculum, aligning our public policy curriculum, and evaluating our programs comprehensively.

Facility

Our facility is overcrowded; we do not have enough classrooms for every course that we offer; teachers have very little planning space (none have their own classroom); administrators are tightly packed into small offices (if they are lucky enough to have an office); and students do not have the comfort or opportunities associated with a gymnasium, field space, a theater, a large computer lab, or even adequate cafeteria space. The political landscape in Washington, D.C., has not afforded charter schools much support in the way of facilities. Many D.C. public school buildings sit empty or tremendously below capacity while charter school students are cramped into nontraditional buildings.

Curriculum

The curriculum is still a work in progress. At the end of the fourth year we decided we needed to first commit to literacy across the curriculum, the most distinct feature of which involves requiring most 9th- and 10th-graders to take an extra English class by the year 2004. (We will begin with an extra class for all 9th graders next year.) As a staff we are in agreement: the average level of literacy of our students is not high enough to carry them through four years of our rigorous curriculum. The hope is to place more resources at the 9th- and 10th-grade level and to see more growth.

Public Policy

The four-year public policy curriculum is in place, but we still need to integrate the learning outcomes, goals, and standards present into the academic curriculum. Essentially, we would like to add depth to the Public Policy Program by connecting it more comprehensively to the academic curriculum. The challenge is not only that the Public Policy Program is currently a one-person department but also that teachers need to accomplish the enormous task of bringing students up to grade level and beyond while also integrating new standards.

Evaluation

At Chavez we have evaluated many of our programs over the years, but we have not yet standardized our evaluation procedures. Lack of resources—both financial and in terms of personnel—is the main reason. However, we are committing funds for year six to building internal data management systems and conducting rigorous on-site research of our programs and their effects on our students.

Conclusion

Chavez is fortunate to have many compelling opportunities ahead of us—especially because of our unique mission. Experts from academia, the charter schools movement, and the business community often approach Chavez to learn more about everything from school-to-careers programs to civic education. With the popularity of small, individualized schools growing, Chavez is interested in exploring options around replication and the dissemination of our experiences to assist school leaders interested in improving public education around the country.

We are proud of what we have accomplished as a school community, and will eagerly continue our work to improve education for D.C.'s public school students. We hope and believe that our efforts will reap future greatness for the District of Columbia—as young people invest and engage in this great city as active, well-educated citizens who can make a difference in their communities.

Notes

1. U.S. Census Bureau, 2001 Supplementary Survey. See http://www.census.gov/acs/www/Products/Ranking/SS01/R11T040.htm.

2. D.C. Kids Count, *Every KID COUNTS in the District of Columbia: Seventh Annual Fact Book, 2000,* (Washington: D.C. KIDS COUNT Collaborative for Children and Families, 2000). Available at http://www.dcctf.org/downloads/2000factbook.pdf.

3. Richard Fry, "Hispanic Youth Dropping Out of U.S. Schools: Measuring the Challenge," *Pew Hispanic Center,* June 2003, p. 4. Available at http://www.pewhispanic.org/site/docs/pdf/high percent20school_percent20dropout percent20report—final.pdf.

4. Marc Fisher, "Chavez Seniors Find Hard Work Very Rewarding," *Washington Post,* June 4, 2002.

5. Nathan Lee, "Charter School Success," *Washington Post,* June 9, 2002, p. B6.

10. The Politics of School Choice: African-Americans and Vouchers

David A. Bositis

Introduction

Since 1996, the Joint Center for Political and Economic Studies has conducted six national surveys of African-Americans and the mostly white general population to ask about education issues, including support for school vouchers. During this period, more African-Americans supported school vouchers than opposed them, and they consistently supported school vouchers more than non-Hispanic whites. In our most recent survey, conducted during September and October 2002, 57 percent of African-Americans supported school vouchers, while 52 percent of non-Hispanic whites supported them; Hispanics supported school vouchers more than either group with 60 percent endorsing school vouchers.

African-Americans care very deeply about the education of their children because their future depends on schooling. As Joint Center Vice President Margaret Simms explains—

> Going to college clearly pays off. People age 25 and over who had at least a college degree had median earnings of $45,273 in 2001, compared with $24,655 for high school graduates, and $17,159 for those workers who did not complete high school.[1]

Black parents care because what parent of any race aspires to have their children earn the near-poverty income of $17,159—or even the mediocre income of $24,655?

Since 1996, Joint Center surveys have been cited by both supporters and opponents of vouchers—including members of Congress—because during that time, African-Americans have been at the center of the school vouchers debate. Black Americans have been at the center of that debate largely because black children disproportionately attend poor schools—and parents know when their children's schools are not working. Because of this dissatisfaction, much of black public opinion will favor any alternative to the status quo, including vouchers. Further, those advocates who favor vouchers for economic, philosophical, or partisan reasons—conservatives and Republicans—believe black public support for vouchers is advantageous in advancing the cause of school vouchers.

For most black Americans, support for school vouchers is not so much an endorsement of vouchers but a rejection of the status quo, that is, poorly performing or mediocre schools. In the Joint Center's most recent survey, conducted in the fall of 2002, 35.2 percent of African-Americans rated their local public schools as excellent or good. In Joint Center surveys conducted over the past six years, an average of 37.3 percent of African-Americans rated their local public schools as excellent or good. These surveys represent interviews with 4,900 African-Americans. In contrast, in 2002, 53.7 percent of the respondents in our surveys of the mostly white general population rated their local public schools as excellent or good, and over the previous six years, 56.6 percent of general population respondents rated their local schools as excellent or good.

The ratio of respondents rating their local public schools favorably or very unfavorably (i.e., "poor") highlights the different levels of satisfaction between whites and blacks. In our research over the past six years, there were only 1.6 black respondents rating their schools favorably for every one rating them very unfavorably. Among whites, that ratio was 4.1 to one. This difference explains quite clearly why African-Americans are dissatisfied with the status quo.

There are other twists to this interesting story. Three-quarters of African-Americans younger than age 35 supported vouchers as did 62 percent of black baby boomers. However, blacks older than age 50 oppose vouchers 48 to 44 percent. Politically this is important because older people vote while younger people do not. So, because most African-Americans are reluctant to vote for Republicans anyway, elected officials who oppose vouchers have nothing to fear from black voters on this issue.

Whites have a somewhat different take than blacks on this issue. First, older whites also don't like vouchers—even more so than older blacks. Politically what is true for blacks is also true for whites with respect to age and voting. White suburbanites bring a very different perspective to the voucher debate than do African-Americans—white suburbanites generally like their local public schools. Although a plurality of whites favor school vouchers, 49 to 46 percent, that support is based more on partisanship, ideology, and self-interest than a rejection of the education status quo.

In sum, here is how I read the politics: Younger African-Americans support vouchers, and people over age 50—white and black—as well as white suburbanites are generally cool on school vouchers. With that juxtaposition, if you were to call Las Vegas for the line on this issue, I don't think there would be much question on the odds they would quote you. The fact is that whenever school vouchers have appeared as a ballot issue, the public has said "no."

It is important not to limit an analysis of the school voucher issue to these matters. There are some other issues that are just as important. First, virtually all black leaders oppose school vouchers. Conservatives suggest they are out of touch with the black public—probably not—but certainly not with black voters, a much older group. They also suggest that black leaders are in thrall to the National Education Association. It is certainly true that black elected officials have close ties with organized labor, including the National Education Association. However, I think that is a comparatively small part of their opposition. If conservatives are pushing school vouchers, then black leaders are generally going to be pretty suspicious, because more often than not they view those conservatives at best with suspicion and at worst with enmity. Does any politically astute observer believe that black leaders are going to think that white conservatives are truly concerned about poor black children and that that is why they are such strong advocates for school vouchers? They believe, not surprisingly, that this argument is a Trojan horse, and that the conservatives are hiding their support for vouchers for mostly white and mostly "unpoor" children. After the U.S. Supreme Court ordered the desegregation of American schools in the *Brown v. Board of Education* decision, southern whites responded by creating "segregation academies"—all-white (and usually Christian) private schools—to avoid having their children going to school with African-Americans. Concomitantly, support, namely financial support, for the increasingly black public schools diminished dramatically. In consequence, desegregation did not provide the advantages its advocates hoped for. Many southern whites still send their children to private schools for that same reason. To many black leaders, school vouchers would represent a significant tax break—or a transfer of public money to private schools and mostly white citizens—so that white parents could avoid sending their children to school with black children.

With the preceding as background, the rest of this chapter reports the results of national surveys of African-Americans, non-Hispanic whites, and Hispanics (in 2002 only) on education issues that were conducted at the Joint Center for Political and Economic Studies. The political context of the findings from those surveys are then examined. And finally, the future prospects for school choice are then considered.

Education Issues and School Choice

The 2002 Joint Center for Political and Economic Studies National Opinion Poll is a national survey of 2,463 adults, conducted between September 17 and October 21, 2002. The survey has three components: a national general population sample of 850 adults, a national sample of 850 adult African-Americans, and a national sample of 850 Hispanic adults. There are 53 African-American and 34 Hispanic respondents in the general population sample who are also part of the samples of African-Americans and Hispanics. Thus, in total, there are 2,463 adults, 18 years of age or older, who are included in this study. The survey methodology is described in an accompanying appendix.

During the 2000 presidential campaign and the 2002 midterm elections, respondents in most of the major public opinion polls conducted in the United States identified education as one of the most important issues in the country. There are many elements to education and education policy as issues, with the quality of education being foremost. Within this overall focus on educational quality has been a particular concern about failing urban schools and the quality of education received by African-American and other minority students.

For the past six years, the Joint Center for Political and Economic Studies National Opinion Poll has tracked the attitudes of African-Americans and the general public in the area of education. This analysis is based on those surveys.[2] As in the earlier surveys, this analysis examines issues of school quality, safety, support for spending on education, and school vouchers. This analysis also includes (for the first time) survey data from a national sample of Hispanics that was part of the Joint Center's 2002 National Opinion Poll.[3] Although both black and white Americans rank education as one of the most important national problems, their views on many education issues differ—sometimes considerably. These racial differences exist alongside of and are related to other factors that influence individual views on education, including age and ideology. Older and younger adults, and liberals and conservatives frequently differ in their views on educational issues and education policy.

The Joint Center's 2002 National Opinion Poll shows that African-Americans generally had more positive views of their local public schools than they did in 2000, and reveals flattening support for school vouchers. The findings of the survey also show several areas in which there is significant continuity over the 1996–2002 period. There continues to be large and significant public support for increased school funding across all groups. Support for school vouchers among blacks has fluctuated over the past six years, but blacks have consistently been more supportive of vouchers than whites. The gap between the two populations, however, is at its narrowest over that time frame. Further, although there has been a certain volatility in African-Americans' ratings of their local public schools over this period, a significantly smaller proportion of blacks than whites rated their local schools as excellent or good. Except for 1998, the gap between black and white ratings has been approximately 20 percentage points.

Other previously seen patterns and trends that were replicated in the 2002 survey were especially related to generational differences—with adults under the age of 50, black and white, having significantly different views than their elders. Also seen before and apparent in the 2002 survey is the "money" divergence in education, with Republicans and conservatives showing significantly less support for spending more money on education than Democrats or political liberals and moderates.

It is important to keep public opinion on education issues in perspective because on many education issues there is a considerable degree of natural volatility in the public's opinions. Some of this volatility is attributable to the fact that a significant proportion of the black, Hispanic, and white populations do not possess solid firsthand knowledge of what is going on in the schools.[4] As a result, political campaigns and media coverage of certain issues and events can often cause substantive shifts in public opinion.

President Bush's "No Child Left Behind" initiative passed with modifications but also with genuine bipartisan support in 2001. The current partisan debate in Washington on education has two main fronts: education spending (especially as related to the 2001 legislation) and school vouchers. Although both Republicans and Democrats generally support higher levels of education spending, budget constraints due to rising deficits and the Iraq war have contributed to keeping the increases modest. From the states' point of view, however, the 2001 legislation is beginning to be viewed as another unfunded mandate from Washington. While both sides acknowledge the recession's (and subsequent weak economic growth) and the war's impact on the budget, the Democrats are emphasizing the role of tax cuts in limiting Washington's contribution to education spending. Most state and local governments are experiencing massive budget problems, and since most K–12 school funding comes from those sources, education spending has naturally been affected. The Bush administration and the Republicans in Washington are generally opposed to helping the states with their budget problems and, hence, education programs—including No Child Left Behind— are likely to remain inadequately financed. Among the problems frequently mentioned are large class sizes; the cuts in education and sports programs, after-school initiatives, and teacher pay; and the looming standardized test requirements from the 2001 legislation.

With respect to school vouchers, the current debate is mostly a continuation of the previous battles between supporters and opponents with one exception: The U.S. Supreme Court has removed the "separation of church and state" argument from the debate when it sanctioned Cleveland's school voucher program in *Zelman v. Simmons-Harris*. As in previous sessions, Republicans in the Congress are pushing for vouchers in the District of Columbia. Most Democrats oppose the move, but Washington's mayor and school board president support it. Because of the time provisions for failing schools to improve, the voucher provisions from the 2001 No Child Left Behind legislation have not yet been implemented.

In the Joint Center's National Opinion Poll, the gap between black and white satisfaction with their local public schools narrowed somewhat between 2000 and 2002; between 1999 and 2000 the gap had increased. In 2002, most whites (53.7 percent) rated their local public schools as excellent or good, while 35.2 percent of blacks did so (see Table 10-1). This 18.5 percentage point gap (on excellent or good ratings) is 3.1 percentage points smaller than the gap between blacks and whites observed in the Joint Center's 2000 survey. This decrease in the evaluation gap between blacks and whites is mainly attributable to the larger proportion of blacks rating their local public schools as excellent or good. With the exception of the 1998 National Opinion Poll when African-Americans rated their local public schools unusually favorably, the gap between black and white evaluations of their schools in 2002 is smaller than in any Joint Center survey since 1996.

Among African-Americans surveyed, there was also a corresponding large decline in those rating their local public schools as poor—from 32.8 percent to 25.4 percent (a 22.6 percent decline); 14.3 percent of whites rated their local public schools as poor.

Hispanic ratings of their local public schools fell between blacks and whites, with 42.9 percent rating their local public schools as excellent or good, 31.4 percent rating them as fair, and 23.5 percent rating them as poor.

There were subgroup differences among blacks in rating their local public schools, but not based on generational differences. Black Christian conservatives (44.1 percent excellent or good), those without a high school diploma (43.4 percent), Independents (40.2 percent), and Republicans (40.7 percent) rated their local public schools somewhat more favorably. A majority of every black subgroup rated their local schools fair or poor.

Among the subgroups of the general population, Christian conservatives (63.8 percent excellent or good) and Republicans (58.7 percent) rated their local public schools more favorably than members of other subgroups; secular conservatives (45.9 percent excellent or good), political independents (48.1 percent), and liberals (49.2 percent) rated their local public schools less positively than other subgroups. Secular conservatives were the only subgroup in which a plurality rated their local public schools only fair or poor.

A majority or plurality of every Hispanic subgroup rated their local schools as fair or poor. Hispanic liberals (48.9 percent excellent

Table 10-1
RATINGS OF LOCAL PUBLIC SCHOOLS (BLACKS AND GENERAL POPULATION)

Year	Black Population			General Population		
	Excellent/Good %	Fair %	Poor %	Excellent/Good %	Fair %	Poor %
1996	41.0	37.0	16.5	63.7	22.7	7.4
1997	34.3	37.7	23.3	56.9	26.2	13.3
1998	45.8	30.4	16.8	54.4	25.3	16.1
1999	39.7	35.2	22.9	59.0	26.5	11.2
2000	30.4	33.9	32.8	52.0	23.3	20.4
2002	35.2	37.3	25.4	53.7	27.3	14.3

or good), those without a high school diploma (48.6 percent), and baby boomers (48.3 percent) rated their local schools more favorably than other Hispanic subgroups. The youngest (18 to 25 years) age cohort of Hispanics rated the local public schools least favorably (39.2 percent excellent or good vs. 60.9 percent fair or poor).

Another important aspect of how people feel about their local schools is whether they believe they are improving or not. Roughly equal proportions of blacks believed that schools in their community were getting better, staying the same, and getting worse (see Table 10-2). The proportions were not statistically different from the responses seen in the 2000 Joint Center survey. Significant pluralities of the youngest black respondents (43.1 percent), black seniors (39.8 percent), and those without a high school diploma (38.2 percent) believed the schools were getting better; only 9.7 percent of black secular conservatives thought this. In contrast, a plurality of black baby boomers (39.5 percent) thought their local schools were getting worse; baby boomers represent the largest age cohort in the population.

A plurality of whites (36.1 percent) believed their schools were staying the same, and slightly more believed they were getting better (29.5 percent) than worse (26.5 percent). In contrast to the 2000 Joint Center survey results, the better and worse categories each increased by five percentage points (approximately a 20 percent increase in those categories). As in the black population, the youngest age cohort in the general population was more positive on the changes in the schools (41.5 percent better), while a plurality of liberals (33.8 percent) and respondents from households with children (33.1 percent) believed the schools were getting worse; conservatives in the general population—both secular and Christian—were much more positive in their views on changes in the schools.

Respondents in the Hispanic population were more likely than blacks or non-Hispanic whites to believe that schools were improving. A plurality of Hispanic respondents (36.5 percent) believed their communities' schools were getting better, while only 22 percent thought they were getting worse. Hispanic men (42.2 percent) were more likely than Hispanic women (31.7 percent) to view changes in the schools favorably. The youngest age cohort of Hispanics (46.4 percent) and Hispanics from households with children (41.6 percent) were more likely than others to believe that the schools were improving. Hispanic seniors (38.3 percent worse) were the only subgroup

Table 10-2
OVER THE PAST FIVE YEARS, DO YOU THINK THAT THE SCHOOLS IN YOUR COMMUNITY HAVE GOTTEN BETTER, STAYED ABOUT THE SAME, OR GOTTEN WORSE?

	Black Population					General Population					Hispanic Population				
	Better %	Same %	Worse %	DK %	(N)	Better %	Same %	Worse %	DK %	(N)	Better %	Same %	Worse %	DK %	(N)
Total	31.6	30.7	31.9	5.8	850	31.1	34.9	26.9	7.1	850	36.5	35.6	22.0	5.9	850
non-Hispanic White	—	—	—	—	—	29.5	36.1	26.5	7.9	714	—	—	—	—	—
18–25	43.1	30.2	25.0	1.7	116	41.5	27.8	25.8	4.8	73	46.4	33.2	18.3	2.1	235
26–35	26.0	34.3	32.4	7.1	169	26.8	28.9	31.9	12.4	116	35.7	38.9	17.8	7.6	185
36–50	37.0	26.6	39.5	6.9	233	24.1	41.3	29.9	4.8	234	35.9	38.0	23.1	3.0	234
51–64	35.7	36.4	25.3	2.6	154	31.9	34.5	25.1	8.5	214	32.7	35.5	24.5	7.3	110
65+	39.8	23.6	30.1	6.5	123	37.1	38.4	19.6	4.9	174	20.0	18.3	38.3	23.3	60

in the population in which a plurality believed that the schools were getting worse.

The school spending debate in Washington and elsewhere is not surprising because large majorities of African-Americans, Hispanics, and non-Hispanic whites think too little is being spent on education (see Table 10-3). In the black population, 80.9 percent of respondents believe the government is spending too little on education, while 78.5 percent of Hispanics and 62 percent of non-Hispanic whites think likewise. For blacks, support is unchanged from the 2000 Joint Center survey, and for whites it represents a 10 percent decrease in those believing too little is being spent on schools.

In the black population, large majorities of all subgroups think too little is being spent on education. In the general population, respondents in the youngest age cohort (86.3 percent), Generation Xers (79.5 percent), liberals (78.3 percent), moderates (74.6 percent), and Democrats (76.2 percent) were those more likely to think too little is being spent on education; also, women (68.8 percent) were more likely than men (59.5 percent) to think that too little was being spent. Senior citizens (44.3 percent), secular (44.5 percent) and Christian (50.7 percent) conservatives, and Republicans (48.3 percent) were less likely to believe that too little was being spent on education; one in five seniors believed too much was being spent on education.

Very large majorities of all Hispanic subgroups surveyed thought too little was being spent on education. Hispanic seniors (61.7 percent) were the subgroup with the smallest percentage of respondents who thought too little was being spent on education.

The respondents in the survey were asked how much they think the average private school charges for tuition (see Table 10-4). They were offered four categories: $2,500, $3,500, $5,000, and $10,000 or more. The modal (i.e., most common) response for blacks was $3,500, while the modal category for Hispanics and non-Hispanic whites was $5,000. Approximately one in five respondents in each sample gave "don't know" responses; more than 30 percent of seniors in all three samples responded "don't know." Respondents from households with children in both the black and mostly white general populations gave comparatively similar responses to the question, offering monotonically increasing and decreasing responses around the modal response ($5,000), and with fewer than average "don't know" responses.[5]

Table 10-3
Do You Think that the Government Is Spending Too Much, Too Little, or Just the Right Amount of Money on Education?

	Black Population					General Population					Hispanic Population				
	Too Much %	Too Little %	Just Right %	DK %	(N)	Too Much %	Too Little %	Just Right %	DK %	(N)	Too Much %	Too Little %	Just Right %	DK %	(N)
Total	6.6	80.9	10.1	2.4	850	10.2	64.4	19.2	6.2	850	3.1	78.5	15.1	3.4	850
non-Hispanic White	—	—	—	—	850	10.9	62.0	20.6	9.8	714	—	—	—	—	—
18–25	1.7	84.5	12.1	1.7	116	1.2	86.3	11.3	1.2	73	0.4	77.9	20.0	1.7	235
26–35	9.5	79.3	7.7	3.6	169	6.1	79.5	11.4	3.1	116	3.2	85.4	8.6	2.7	185
36–50	8.6	83.7	6.9	0.9	233	8.3	64.5	20.5	6.8	234	3.8	76.5	16.2	3.7	234
51–64	4.5	83.1	9.7	2.6	154	10.7	64.3	20.6	4.4	214	7.3	79.1	10.0	3.6	110
65+	4.9	72.4	21.1	1.6	123	20.1	44.3	24.3	11.2	175	3.3	61.7	21.7	13.3	60

Table 10-4
How Much Do You Think the Average Private School Charges for Tuition?

(× $1000)	Black Population						General Population						Hispanic Population					
	2.5 %	3.5 %	5 %	10+ %	DK %	(N)	2.5 %	3.5 %	5 %	10+ %	DK %	(N)	2.5 %	3.5 %	5 %	10+ %	DK %	(N)
Total	16.8	22.8	20.8	21.3	18.2	850	11.4	18.9	29.8	20.2	19.7	850	16.1	20.9	25.9	15.2	21.9	850
non-Hispanic White	—	—	—	—	—	—	9.6	19.1	31.1	20.8	19.4	714	—	—	—	—	—	—
18–25	19.8	20.7	23.3	22.4	13.8	116	21.0	18.9	35.9	17.3	6.9	73	19.6	21.7	26.0	16.6	16.2	234
26–35	13.0	39.1	17.2	20.7	10.1	169	18.2	20.5	31.4	20.2	9.6	116	16.2	22.2	29.7	10.8	21.1	185
36–50	15.9	19.7	29.2	22.3	12.9	223	6.9	17.7	35.8	23.5	16.2	234	17.9	16.7	23.1	17.5	24.8	234
51–64	20.8	18.8	16.2	18.8	25.3	154	8.9	20.0	34.6	18.4	18.0	214	9.1	21.8	26.4	16.4	26.4	110
65+	13.0	16.3	13.8	24.4	32.5	123	10.1	17.3	15.1	20.3	37.2	175	13.3	28.3	16.7	10.0	31.7	60

Table 10-5
SUPPORT FOR VOUCHERS (BLACKS VS. GENERAL POPULATION)

	Black Population		General Population	
	Support Vouchers	Oppose Vouchers	Support Vouchers	Oppose Vouchers
Year	%	%	%	%
1996	48	44	43	50
1997	57	38	48	46
1998	48	40	42	50
1999	60	33	53	40
2000	57	37	49	44
2002	57	43	52	48

The responses to this question follow an almost random pattern largely suggesting ignorance of private school tuition rates. With five categories (including "don't know"), a random distribution would lead to an expectation of 20 percent of respondents (and subgroup respondents) in each category. The pattern responses—within the margin of error—with few exceptions generally follow this expectation.

Among African-Americans, support for school vouchers in the Joint Center's 2002 survey (57.4 percent) shows no change from the previous survey (see Table 10-5). White support for school vouchers increased slightly from 49 percent support in the Joint Center's 2000 National Opinion Poll to 52 percent in 2002. Hispanics supported school vouchers (60.8 percent) more than either blacks or non-Hispanic whites (see Table 10-6).

Although a solid majority of the black respondents (57.4 percent) supported school vouchers, opposition to vouchers increased from the last survey from 37 to 43 percent (a 16 percent increase in opposition). White opposition to vouchers also increased from 44 to 48 percent. The gap between blacks and whites on school vouchers narrowed considerably from the 2000 survey, and is now at its narrowest point since the Joint Center began asking this question, with only 10 percentage points separating blacks and whites.

It is clear in evaluating the results from Joint Center surveys between 1996 and 2002 that both black and white views on the school voucher issue are still somewhat in flux; blacks continue to

Table 10-6
WOULD YOU SUPPORT A VOUCHER SYSTEM WHERE PARENTS WOULD GET MONEY FROM THE GOVERNMENT TO SEND THEIR CHILDREN TO THE PUBLIC, PRIVATE, OR PAROCHIAL SCHOOL OF THEIR CHOICE?

	Black Population			General Population			Hispanic Population		
	Yes %	No %	(N)	Yes %	No %	(N)	Yes %	No %	(N)
Total	57.4	42.6	850	51.7	48.3	850	60.8	39.2	850
non-Hispanic White	—	—	—	51.4	48.6	714	—	—	—
18–25	66.4	33.6	116	60.5	39.5	73	67.2	32.8	235
26–35	70.4	29.6	169	62.5	37.5	116	57.8	42.2	185
36–50	58.8	41.2	233	51.9	48.1	234	60.7	39.3	234
51–64	43.5	56.5	154	48.5	51.5	214	58.2	41.8	110
65+	47.2	52.8	123	45.5	54.5	175	48.3	51.7	60

favor school vouchers more than whites, but as noted earlier, to a lesser degree. This volatility is not surprising since public knowledge of school vouchers is scant, principally because so few in the public have experience with vouchers or nonpublic schools.[6] As previously noted, respondents in all three samples not only expressed a great deal of uncertainty when asked about private school tuition, but also gave highly variable, almost random answers.

Despite the insufficient level of public knowledge of vouchers, they seem to have three main attractions for various people: for some, vouchers represent an alternative to a status quo (e.g., poor schools) they dislike; others are attracted to vouchers because of the choice vouchers offer; for others, whose children attend nonpublic schools, vouchers would represent a new financial advantage.

Except for black seniors (52.8 percent opposed) and blacks between the ages of 51 and 64 (56.5 percent opposed), a majority of all subgroups of the black population support vouchers. Generational differences were considerable: Blacks over the age of 50 oppose vouchers, more than two in three blacks under the age of 35 support vouchers, and a solid majority (58.8 percent) of black baby boomers support vouchers.[7]

Apart from age and generation, the greatest subgroup differences on school vouchers are between respondents from households with children (67 percent support) and those from households without children (52.1 percent).

As was the case for the black population, in the general population, solid majorities of the under-the-age-of-50 cohorts supported vouchers, while a majority of those between the ages of 51 and 64 (51.5 percent) and a majority of seniors (54.5 percent) opposed school vouchers. Conservatives (56–57 percent), persons without a high school degree (65 percent), Republicans (59 percent), and persons from households with children (56 percent) were the subgroups of the general population most supportive of vouchers. General population respondents with a postgraduate education (54.8 percent), liberals (54.7 percent), and Democrats (52.8 percent) opposed vouchers. Several subgroups of the general population were essentially evenly divided in their views on vouchers.

Among Hispanics, as with blacks and non-Hispanic whites, younger respondents were more supportive of school vouchers. Hispanic seniors and those with a postgraduate education were the only subgroups with majority opposition to vouchers. Hispanic conservatives (67.9 percent), Republicans (69.7 percent), and those from households with children (66.8 percent) were the strongest voucher supporters.

School voucher supporters were asked whether they would consider sending their children to nonpublic schools if vouchers were available. Exactly three in four voucher supporters in all three samples responded affirmatively to this question. Those who responded affirmatively were then asked how much would they be willing to spend to supplement a voucher if they did receive one and it was insufficient to send their child to the school of their choice. (See Table 10-7). Almost half (46.2) of African-Americans responded "don't know" as did 37.8 percent of non-Hispanic whites and 37.1 percent of Hispanics. A negligible number of blacks (1.1 percent) and non-Hispanic whites (4.3 percent), and slightly more Hispanics (6.6 percent) said they would be willing to spend $5,000 or more; 17.9 percent of blacks, 19.8 percent of whites, and 14.1 percent of Hispanics said they would be willing to spend $1,000 or less. The modal response for blacks was between $1,000 and $2,000; for Hispanics and non-Hispanic whites it was between $2,000 and $5,000. The modal response from respondents from households with children in the black population was between $1,000 and $2,000; for whites the modal response was less than $1,000; for Hispanics, it was between $2,000 and $5,000.[8]

The Political Context of School Choice: Age and Voting

African-Americans under the age of 35 differ considerably in their partisanship from older blacks. In the Joint Center's 2002 National Opinion Poll, only 55 percent of blacks under the age of 35 were self-identified Democrats.[9] Among those between the ages of 18 and 25, 34 percent were self-identified independents; of those between the ages of 26 and 35 years, 26 percent were self-identified independents. In contrast, 75 percent of black senior citizens were self-identified Democrats and only 16 percent were self-identified independents; African-Americans between the ages of 50 and 64 were slightly less Democratic and slightly more independent.

This diminishing identification with the Democratic party has led many Republican party leaders to fashion strategies to attempt to reach out to these—from their view—potential supporters. Since

Table 10-7

IF YOU RECEIVED A SCHOOL VOUCHER FOR YOUR CHILD, AND IT WAS NOT ENOUGH TO SEND YOUR CHILD TO THE SCHOOL YOU WANTED, HOW MUCH MONEY WOULD YOU BE WILLING TO SPEND IN ORDER TO SEND YOUR CHILD TO A SCHOOL OF YOUR CHOICE? [RESPONDENTS WHO WOULD CONSIDER PRIVATE OR PAROCHIAL SCHOOL WITH VOUCHER]

(× $1000)	Black Population						General Population						Hispanic Population					
	<1 %	<1-2 %	2-5 %	5+ %	DK %	(N)	<1 %	<1-2 %	2-5 %	5+ %	DK %	(N)	<1 %	<1-2 %	2-5 %	5+ %	DK %	(N)
Total	17.9	18.1	16.7	1.1	46.2	364	18.5	17.2	19.5	4.5	40.4	330	14.1	16.1	26.1	6.6	37.1	391
non-Hispanic White	—	—	—	—	—	—	19.8	16.8	21.2	4.3	37.9	284	—	—	—	—	—	—
18–25	21.7	17.4	19.6	0.0	41.3	46	11.8	12.8	11.8	11.0	52.7	32	7.4	11.1	27.8	3.7	50.0	108
26–35	19.5	23.9	17.4	2.2	37.0	92	26.9	22.1	20.8	1.4	28.7	62	21.3	22.3	27.7	5.3	23.4	94
36–50	21.3	15.7	17.6	0.9	44.4	108	20.4	20.1	22.6	5.3	31.6	95	7.9	16.7	25.5	10.8	39.2	102
51-64	17.0	17.0	19.1	0.0	46.8	47	15.4	18.6	24.6	5.7	35.9	73	27.8	13.0	18.5	9.3	31.5	54
65+	10.2	10.2	14.3	0.0	65.3	49	17.4	11.7	11.1	2.1	57.7	56	14.4	14.3	33.4	0.0	38.1	21

the early 1990s, school vouchers has been the issue that they have believed would be most effective in attracting that support. However, there has been no evidence since that time of any movement of the black vote toward the Republican column. In fact, in 2000, the share of the black vote received by Bush and Cheney was the lowest of any Republican ticket since 1964. In the 2002 midterms, the GOP's U.S. House vote from blacks fell from 11 to 9 percent. Leaving aside the question of partisanship and whether the GOP can lure more black support using vouchers, there is another more important reason why vouchers have less political traction than might be expected (given poll support). The fact that younger adults of all races express more support for school vouchers in public opinion surveys has less political impact because their rates of political participation are low—and sometimes abysmally low.

In the 11 national elections held between 1980 and 2000, black senior citizens have consistently voted at twice the rate as blacks between 18 and 24 years (see Table 10-8). In the six presidential elections held during that time span, young blacks have averaged a 34.8 percent turnout rate; in the five midterm elections during that period, turnout averaged 20.8 percent. In contrast black seniors averaged a 62.8 percent turnout rate in presidential election years (1.8 times the rate of young blacks), and a 52.6 percent rate in midterm years (or 2.5 times the rate of young blacks). White voters were similarly arrayed. Young white voters turned out at slightly higher rates than young blacks: 38.7 percent in presidential elections and 21.1 percent in midterm years. However, white senior citizens turned out at higher rates than black seniors as well: 68.8 percent in presidential elections and 61.6 percent in midterm elections. In fact, young whites did not fare proportionally as well compared with their same-race seniors as did young blacks.

In the white voting-age population, senior citizens are 18.4 percent of the total; 18–24-year-old whites represent 11.7 percent of the white voting-age population. In the black voting-age population, black seniors only represent 11.7 percent of the total, while young black adults are 16.2 percent of the total. If the black senior and young adult populations are weighed by their relative levels of voting participation, the ratio of black senior voters to young adult voters becomes 21.1 to 16.2 (i.e., 11.7 percent times 1.8 to 16.2 percent times 1) for presidential elections, and 29.3 to 16.2 for midterm years. If

Table 10-8
VOTER TURNOUT BY RACE, 1980–2000, SELECTED AGE COHORTS

	1980 %	1982 %	1984 %	1986 %	1988 %	1990 %	1992 %	1994 %	1996 %	1998 %	2000 %
Black											
18–24	30.1	25.5	40.6	25.1	35.0	20.2	36.6	17.4	32.4	15.6	33.9
65+	59.4	50.8	61.5	53.3	63.5	51.3	64.1	51.6	63.7	56.2	64.7
Difference	29.3	25.3	21.1	28.2	28.5	31.1	27.5	34.2	31.3	40.6	30.8
White											
18–24	41.8	25.0	41.6	21.6	37.0	20.8	45.4	21.1	33.3	17.2	33.0
65+	66.0	61.1	68.7	61.9	69.8	61.7	71.5	62.8	68.1	60.5	68.8
Difference	24.2	36.1	27.1	40.3	32.8	40.9	26.1	41.7	34.8	43.3	35.8

SOURCE: U.S. Census Bureau, Current Population Report, November 2000 and earlier reports.

the white senior and young adult populations are weighed by their relative levels of voting participation, the ratio of white senior voters to young adult voters becomes 33.1 to 11.7 (i.e., 18.4 percent times 1.8 to 11.7 percent times 1) for presidential elections, and 53.4 to 16.2 for midterm years.

The biggest age cohorts in both the black and white populations are the baby boomers. However, white baby boomers are evenly split on vouchers (51.9 percent for and 48.1 percent against, and a majority of whites over the age of 50 oppose school vouchers. Thus, at the polls, white voucher supporters are outnumbered by voucher opponents, especially seniors.

Black generation Xers (26 to 35 years of age) strongly support school vouchers, and black baby boomers voice moderate support (58.8 percent for and 41.2 percent against). However, blacks over the age of 50, like black seniors, oppose vouchers. Blacks between the ages of 26 and 35, and younger black baby boomers (under the age of 44) vote at lower rates than blacks over the age of 45; in presidential elections their (older nonsenior blacks) margins are 1.3 to 1 greater than generation Xers and younger baby boomers, and in midterm elections they vote at a 1.4 times greater rate.

In sum, black majorities—and white pluralities—favoring vouchers in public opinion polls do not translate into effective political support because a solid majority of voters, who are significantly older than the total adult population (whose weight is greater in polls, but not at the polls) are opposed to school vouchers. However, in the not-too-distant future, the politics of school choice could easily change.

Demographics and the Future of School Vouchers

As noted earlier, the strong support for school vouchers expressed by younger black and Hispanic adults, does not—at the present time—translate into strong political support for school vouchers. However, the longer term prospects for school choice supporters may be better. The U.S. Education Department report, "A Nation at Risk," was released 20 years ago during the Reagan administration. Many people on both sides of the political spectrum argue that the problems identified in that report have not been resolved. If that status quo does not change, 20 years from now, demographic changes will certainly change the playing field in the school-choice debate.

The future demographics of the United States suggest great changes in the not-too-distant future. In the 2000 Census, African-Americans numbered about 35 million (35.7 million black-only and 37.1 million black-only or in combination with another or other race(s)). In the 2002 Census Bureau estimates, the black-only population was 36.7 million (38.3 million, including two or more races); this represents a 2.9 percent increase in population over two years. The African-American fertility rate (middle series) estimate for 2000 was 2,122 births per 1,000 women. The Census Bureau project the black population to grow to 42.4 million by 2015.

In the 2000 Census, 35.3 million people were identified as Hispanic, and the Census Bureau's 2002 population estimates show 38.8 million Hispanics in the United States. In two years, the Hispanic population has grown by 9.8 percent according to the Census Bureau. One-half the U.S. population growth between 2000 and 2002 was from persons of Hispanic origin. The Hispanic fertility rate suggests strong growth with the middle series estimates for 2000 at 2,921 births per 1,000 women. Further, the preponderance of immigrants to the United States—both sanctioned and unsanctioned—are of Hispanic origin. The Census Bureau projects the Hispanic population will be 50 million by 2015, and the Census Bureau has systematically and substantially underestimated the Hispanic population in its estimates and projections in the past.

In the 2000 Census, non-Hispanic whites numbered 195.6 million. In the 2002 Census Bureau estimates, the non-Hispanic white population was 196.8 million, an increase of only six-tenths of one percent. The non-Hispanic white fertility rate (middle series) estimate for 2000 was 1,833 births per 1,000 women—well below the population replacement rate. The Census Bureau projects the non-Hispanic white population to grow to 204.6 million by 2015.

These demographic projections suggest that in the medium term (say, 2015), the non-Hispanic white population's share of the total U.S. population will markedly decline. At the time of the 2000 Census, the non-Hispanic white population represented 69.5 percent of the total population. The Census projections for 2015 suggest that share will decline to 65.5 percent—a dramatic decline considering the time frame. Further, given non-Hispanic white fertility rates, continued high rates of Hispanic migration, and the Census Bureau's historic underestimation of the size of the Hispanic population, those 2015 estimates are likely to exaggerate the proportion of non-Hispanic whites in the population.

The main reason why these changes are so politically significant is that the Hispanic and African-American populations are not homogeneously distributed across the United States. Half the Hispanic population resides in the two largest states, California and Texas, while the black population is concentrated in the south, northeast, and midwest. Non-Hispanic whites are already a minority in California, and in the not-too-distant future, they will be a minority in the other largest states, including Texas, and possibly Florida and New York. Many other states in the sunbelt also have proportionally large black and Hispanic populations. The states with the proportionally largest non-Hispanic white populations, that is, the "white belt" (those states in the northern noncoastal west, and those near to Canada—save New York), are declining in political influence due to declining populations (not in absolute terms, but relative to other, especially sunbelt, states).

Politically, these demographic changes are important because the Republican party is primarily a non-Hispanic white party, and demographic trends are working against them. African-Americans regularly give the Democrats about 90 percent of their votes, and about two in three Hispanics do likewise. However, if problems in minority schools persist, minority voters would become more attracted to the GOP or, more likely, increasing numbers of Democratic politicians would begin to support school vouchers. D.C. Mayor Anthony Williams, and D.C. School Board President Peggy Cooper Cafritz—both Democrats—now support a pilot program for school vouchers.

In the near term, the political influence of Hispanics and African-Americans is limited by two major factors. First, the black and Hispanic populations are extraordinarily young compared with the non-Hispanic white population. The median age for the non-Hispanic white population (2003 estimate) is 40. The median age of the African-American population is 31, and it is 27 for the Hispanic population. This difference is important because while the non-Hispanic white population is currently 69.5 percent of the total population, it is 73.1 percent of the voting-age population. Further, younger voter turnout rates are dwarfed by those of older voters, as noted earlier.

The second reason for near-term diminished influence, principally for Hispanics, is citizenship status. At the time of the last census, 1.6 percent of non-Hispanic whites were not citizens, and 3.4 percent of blacks were not citizens. In contrast, 30 percent of the Hispanic population fall in the noncitizen category. This factor for Hispanics will diminish in importance with time (in 1990 the comparable figure was about 40 percent), but for the near term, this is a limiting factor for the voting power of Hispanics. Thus, in the short term, the political support for school vouchers voiced by African-Americans and Hispanics (especially younger adults) is limited.

Notes

1. Margaret Simms, "Education Gains Produce Mixed Economic Impact" *FOCUS* 31, no. 3, Washington, D.C., Joint Center for Political and Economic Studies (May/June 2003): 7.

2. See the Joint Center's 1996 National Opinion Poll: Social Policy; the Joint Center's 1997 National Opinion Poll: Children's Issues; the Joint Center's 1998 National Opinion Poll: Education; the Joint Center's 1999 National Opinion Poll: Education; the Joint Center's 2000 National Opinion Poll: Politics; and the Joint Center's 2002 National Opinion Poll: Education. Available at http://jointcenter.org/publications/opinion_polls.html.

3. The Joint Center's 1997 National Opinion Poll: Children Issues included an oversample of 100 Hispanics. Available at http://jointcenter.org/publications/opinion_polls.html.

4. For example, the Joint Center's 1999 National Opinion Poll was fielded shortly after the killings at Columbine High School in Littleton, Colorado. The images of deaths and violence in a well-to-do suburban high school that were featured so prominently in the news caused many Americans to think that schools were unsafe places. In reality, deaths and violence in schools had been declining during the 1996–1999 period; in other words, schools were safer.

5. Respondents were also asked about the average parochial school tuition. The responses were somewhat similar but with many fewer responses in the $10,000 category (in all three samples) and with many more responses in the "don't know" category (at least 50 percent higher).

6. There is one group of people who do have firsthand knowledge of the array of issues surrounding school vouchers, namely, people with children in private or parochial schools. For them, school vouchers would represent a very significant and tangible financial benefit.

7. On the issue of the government providing school vouchers for public, private, or parochial schools, the same generational differences seen in the 2002 Joint Center National Public Opinion Polls of the black population are seen among black elected officials. According to a 1999 Joint Center national survey of black elected officials, a large majority (69 percent) of them oppose vouchers (see "Changing of the Guard: Generational Differences Among Black Elected Officials," Joint Center for Political and Economic Studies, 2001). More than any other factor, the age cohorts among the BEOs, as in the black population, define cleavages on vouchers. There was only a

single subgroup of black elected officials who favored vouchers—the youngest age cohort—with a plurality in support (49 to 44 percent); outside of this age cohort, the remaining BEOs average more than 70 percent opposition to school vouchers.

8. Respondents were asked whether they were aware of any incidents of school violence near their residences, and the responses from the three population groups were roughly similar. Among blacks, 32.9 percent said violent incidents had occurred at schools near their residences; 60.1 percent said there were no such incidents. Among Hispanics, 33.8 percent reported school violence, while 61.8 percent indicated none. Among non-Hispanic whites, 25.2 percent reported violent incidents at nearby schools, while 66.4 percent said there were none. There was no change in the black and non-Hispanic white responses to this question from the last time it was asked in the Joint Center's 1999 National Opinion Poll. African-Americans, Hispanics, and non-Hispanic whites also responded somewhat similarly to a question about whether there should be more all-boys and all-girls schools. More same-sex education was endorsed by 26.4 percent of blacks, 21 percent of non-Hispanic whites, and 28.7 percent of Hispanics. The only subgroup in any of the populations that endorsed same-sex education was Hispanic seniors, among whom half endorsed the idea.

9. See the Joint Center's 2002 National Opinion Poll: Politics. Available at http:// jointcenter.org/publications/opinion_polls.html.

10. A random sample is a random subset of a population. One makes observations on suitable units of a random sample in order to make statements about the population and to estimate the error associated with such statements. A common misconception regarding surveys and associated statistical theory is that "population" (or population size) is a factor in margin of error. This is not true. Population does not appear in the statistical formulation for margin of error.

Appendix: Methodology

The survey was designed and the questionnaire developed at the Joint Center for Political and Economic Studies. The overall study design consisted of three groups: a national general population sample of 850, a national sample of 850 African-Americans, and a national sample of 850 Hispanics. There are 53 African-American and 34 Hispanic respondents in the general population sample who are also part of the national samples of African-Americans and Hispanics. Thus, in total, there are 2,463 adults, 18 years of age or older, who are included in this study.

The survey results are based on (random digit dialing) telephone interviews with 2,463 adults that were conducted between September 17, 2002, and October 21, 2002. The field work was done by Research America of Philadelphia, Pennsylvania. Randomized procedures were used to select respondents within each household reached by telephone, and after the initial call, there were at least eight callbacks if no interview was completed.

The results of this survey for the three populations should be interpreted with a statistical margin of error of ±3.5 percentage points. That is, one can say with 95 percent confidence that the statements made based on the procedures employed have a random error (sampling error, random measurement error, etc.) component of ±3.5 percentage points. Actually, this "survey" like all surveys does not have a margin of error. The individual items in the survey have margins of error; the margin of error for a question is based on its sample variance, the level of confidence desired (e.g., 95 percent), and upon sample size.[10] The ±3.5 percentage points is a conservative estimate of margin of error; that is, many items—especially those for which large majorities of each sample hold similar positions—have a margin of error much smaller than ±3.5 percentage points.

In addition to the random error component in surveys, there are potentially nonrandom errors that may be present. Although this survey is based on random digit-dialing techniques that effectively deal with potential problems in telephone surveys such as unlisted numbers, new numbers, and so on, nonresponse in telephone surveys produces a variety of known (and probably some unknown) biases. Further, a telephone survey by definition defines its population as those individuals with some reasonable expectation of being reached by telephone. Such a definition, of course, eliminates certain populations. For example, most homeless people and others living in poverty who are unreachable by phone are not part of the sample population. Thus, the statements made based on this survey are most likely not generalizable to homeless people, black or white.

During the field work phase of the survey, an effort was made to maximize the use of same-race interviewers, and most of the interviews were conducted with same-race interviewers (i.e., black interviewers for black respondents and white interviewers for white respondents). The Hispanic interviews were conducted by bilingual interviewers.

The sample data from the overall survey are weighted in the analyses to population parameters for a variety of demographic factors. The parameters used in this weighting are from the U.S. Bureau of the Census, the 2000 Census, and prior Joint Center surveys.

11. What Does a Voucher Buy? The Cost of Private Schools in Six Cities

David Salisbury

School vouchers are increasingly being implemented in large cities as a means to instill healthy competition and choice into stagnant urban school systems. Ohio, Wisconsin, and Florida have had voucher programs for several years. In Ohio and Wisconsin the voucher program is focused on single cities (Cleveland and Milwaukee), while in Florida the voucher program applies to children living in the worst performing schools, most of which tend to be located in urban areas. Colorado recently passed legislation implementing vouchers for students in failing school districts. In January 2004, Congress passed legislation to implement vouchers in Washington, D.C.

Impetus for vouchers as a means to reform urban public schools came most recently from a massive survey of public and private schools published by John Chubb and Terry Moe in 1990 showing that centralization and bureaucracy were the main causes of inefficiency in urban schools.[1] As evidence that America's government schools are overcentralized and bureaucratized, Chubb, Moe, and other scholars pointed to the marked difference between America's private schools and government schools in terms of administrative overhead. It was noted, for example, that New York City had 6,000 administrators in the government schools and only 25 in the Catholic schools even though the city's Catholic schools served nearly one-fourth as many students.[2] Other scholars noted the consistent trend over the last several decades toward larger, centralized school districts.[3] Although there were more than 100,000 school districts in the United States in 1945, that number had fallen to 14,881 by 1993 (see Figure 11-1). During this same period, the number of students enrolled in public schools increased from about 25 million to more than 46 million, so the number of students in each district rose dramatically.[4]

Figure 11-1
NUMBER OF PUBLIC SCHOOL DISTRICTS, 1945–96

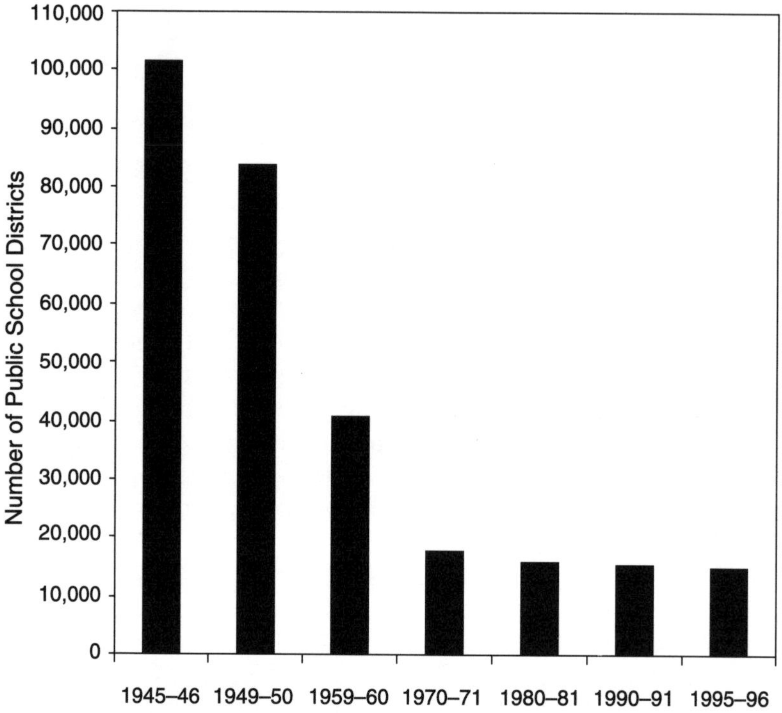

SOURCE: National Center for Education Statistics, *Digest of Education Statistics*, 2001, Table 89.

As school districts became larger, school bureaucracies increased in proportion to the number of teachers in school classrooms. Today, only 51.6 percent of school employees are teachers. In 1950, nearly 70 percent were teachers.[5] In 2000, 62 percent of public school spending went for instruction. School and district administration consumed 15 percent, or nearly a fourth of what schools spend on instruction.[6]

During this time, centralized control over school districts also increased and school administrators had to deal with an increasing number of bureaucratic rules and mandates. By the mid-1990s, the California school code had grown to more than 6,000 pages, detailing procedures on everything from infant care to use of microcomputers to paper recycling.[7] The 1995 U.S. Department of Education's Paper Reduction Act estimated that department requirements alone necessitated 49.1 million hours of paper work, the equivalent of 25,000 full-time employees.[8] Lisa Graham Keegan, Arizona's former chief school officer, noted that it took 165 of her staff (45% of the total) to manage federal programs, which make up only 6 percent of her budget.[9]

In 1989, Albert Shanker, president of the American Federation of Teachers, also pointed to centralization and bureaucracy as the core malady in public schools:

> Public education operates like a planned economy, a bureaucratic system in which everybody's role is spelled out in advance and there are few incentives for innovation and productivity. It's no surprise that our school system doesn't improve: It more resembles the communist economy than our own market economy.[10]

In addition to causing massive inefficiencies and waste, monopoly institutions tend to serve many or most of their clients poorly, especially in a large and diverse society. As economist Walter Williams has written—

> A state monopoly in the production of a good or service enhances the potential for conflict, through requiring uniformity; that is, its production requires a collective decision on many attributes of the product, and once produced, everybody has to consume the identical product whether he agrees with all the attributes or not. State monopolies in the production of education enhance the potential for conflict by requiring conformity on issues of importance to many people.[11]

Progress toward Reform

During the past 20 years, an increasing number of activists and policymakers have fought for reforms that would break the government monopoly in K–12 education. To date, 11 states have implemented school choice programs that allow families to choose between public and private schools.[12] These programs have been especially helpful to minority children living in urban areas. Recent studies by Harvard researchers Paul Peterson and William Howell have shown that scores on academic achievement tests increased for African-American students who participated in school voucher programs.[13]

School choice programs have helped to reduce the monopoly position of government schools over K–12 education in those locations where they have been implemented, but they have by no means created a level playing field between government and privately operated schools. This is because all of the programs are limited in a number of ways that have prevented a truly competitive education market from emerging.[14] Virtually all programs place limitations on the number of students who can participate or restrict participation to children from the community's poorest families or schools. Such restrictions dilute the potential benefits that would arise from a fully competitive education market. Although limited school choice programs such as these provide help to some children, they are not large enough to unleash the market forces necessary to create a revolution in educational quality.[15]

An ideal school choice program would give *every* child a voucher or tax credit to be spent on educational services at any public or private school in the state. The amount of the voucher or tax credit should be nearly equivalent to the amount of tax funds already being spent per student in the government schools.

In 2000 (the most recent year for which data are available) average private elementary school tuition in America was less than $3,500 (see Table 11-1). Average tuition at private secondary schools was $6,052. Since the average tuition for all private schools, elementary and secondary, is $4,689, a voucher amount of $5,000 would probably be adequate to cover the tuition cost at most private schools. Since the average per-pupil spending for public schools is now at $9,354, most states could propose an even higher voucher amount and still realize substantial savings.[16]

Government figures also indicate that in 1999–2000 some 41 percent of all private elementary and secondary schools—more than 27,000 nationwide—charged less than $2,500 for tuition (see Table 11-2). Seventy-nine percent of American private elementary schools and secondary schools charged less than $5,000.

The figures just cited probably underestimate the actual real costs of both public and private schools because public school cost figures typically omit such real costs as capital outlays and pension liabilities.[17] Likewise, private school tuition is often supplemented by contributions from philanthropists, fund-raising events, and in-kind

Table 11-1
PRIVATE SCHOOL TUITION BY TYPE OF SCHOOL AND LEVEL:
1999–2000

Type of School	Average Tuition
All private schools	$4,689
Elementary	$3,267
Secondary	$6,052
Combined	$6,779
Catholic schools	$3,263
Elementary	$2,451
Secondary	$4,845
Combined	$6,780
Other religious schools	$4,063
Elementary	$3,503
Secondary	$6,536
Combined	$4,260
Nonsectarian schools	$10,992
Elementary	$7,884
Secondary	$14,638
Combined	$12,363

SOURCE: Based on National Center for Education Statistics, Digest of Education Statistics, 2002, Table 61 (1999–2000). Elementary schools have grades six or lower and no grade higher than eight. Secondary schools have no grade lower than seven. Combined schools have grades lower than seven and higher than eight. Excludes pre-kindergarten students.

Table 11-2
U.S. PRIVATE SCHOOLS BY TUITION: 1999–2000

Tuition	Number of Schools	Percent
Less than $2,500	10,242	41%
$2,500–$4,999	9,645	38%
$5,000 or more	5,251	21%

SOURCE: Based on National Center for Education Statistics, Digest of Education Statistics, 2002, Table 61 (1999–2000).

contributions by parents, and below-market labor costs, especially in Catholic schools.[18]

Survey of Private School Costs

Critics of school choice often report erroneous or misleading information about the cost of private schools in various cities.[19] To evaluate the usefulness of a voucher or tax credit in a variety of urban environments, the Cato Institute surveyed all private schools in six disparate American cities.[20] Five of the six cities surveyed (New Orleans, Houston, Denver, Charleston, and Philadelphia) are in states where school choice legislation has recently passed or is currently being considered. The federal government is considering school choice legislation for Washington, D.C., the sixth city. The survey results indicate that for the 2002–03 school year, in each of those cities, most private elementary schools charged $5,000 or less. Although they were not as prevalent, each city had private secondary schools that charged $5,000 or less. Tuition rates for the six cities are reported below.

New Orleans

The New Orleans public school district spent $5,797 per pupil, according to the Louisiana Department of Education.[21] At private elementary schools, the median tuition was $2,386. One hundred-nineteen of the city's 127 private elementary schools charge less than the public schools' per-pupil expenditure and 118 of those charge less than $5,000.

Thirty-six of the 40 private secondary schools in New Orleans charge less than $5,797 per student spent by the city, and 34 of those charge less than $5,000. The median tuition at New Orleans private secondary schools is $3,895.

Houston

Annual per-pupil spending in the Houston school district was $7,089.[22] By contrast, 119 of Houston's 144 private elementary schools charged less than that amount and 90 of those charged $5,000 or less. The median tuition for Houston private primary schools was $4,325.

Twenty-four of Houston's 38 private secondary schools charged less than the city spends. Seventeen charged $5,000 or less. The median tuition for private secondary schools in Houston was $6,150.

Denver

The Denver public schools spent $9,919 per pupil[23] even though there are plenty of low-cost private schools available. Only 6 of the city's 91 private elementary schools charged as much as the government schools spent, and 62 charged $5,000 or less. The median tuition was $3,528.

In addition, only 6 of Denver's 46 private secondary schools charged as much as the government schools spend, and 20 charged $5,000 or less. The median tuition at Denver's private secondary schools was $5,995.

Charleston

The Charleston school district spent $6,701 per pupil.[24] Only 6 of the city's 31 private elementary schools charged that much and 25 charged $5,000 or less. The median tuition was $3,153.

All but four of Charleston's 18 private secondary schools charged less than the government schools spent, and 13 charged $5,000 or less. The median tuition was $4,056.

Washington, D.C.

According to the U.S. Department of Education, public schools in the District of Columbia spent $11,009 per pupil.[25] In contrast, 45 of the District's 62 private elementary schools charged less than that amount and 39 charged $5,000 or less. The median tuition for Washington's private elementary schools was $4,500.

Seven of the District's 22 private secondary schools charged less than the city spends, but only two charged $5,000 or less. The median tuition for private secondary schools in Washington, D.C., the most expensive of the six cities surveyed, is $16,075. Lower-cost private secondary schools are available in neighboring counties of Maryland and Virginia where the median tuition is $6,920.[26]

Philadelphia

Per-pupil expenditures in the Philadelphia public schools were $8,303.[27] Yet 189 of Philadelphia's 200 private elementary schools charge less than that amount and 177 of those charge less than $5,000. The median tuition for Philadelphia's private elementary schools was $2,504.

Of the city's 54 private secondary schools, 43 charge less than the public schools' per-pupil expenditure, and 37 charge no more than $5,000. The median tuition is $4,310.

Designing School Choice Programs

Currently, the majority of low-cost private schools are religiously affiliated and are subsidized in part by the affiliated church. In most cities, the Catholic church offers the largest number of schools in the low-cost price range. New start-up schools cannot be expected to match the cost of local Catholic schools. Therefore, states should not target school choice programs toward the cost of Catholic schools. However, a voucher amount of $5,000 or more would give students access to most private schools, religious and nonreligious.[28]

In addition, the ideal school choice plan would allow parents to add their own money to the amount of the voucher or tax credit, if they desired. The ability of some families to supplement the amount of tuition paid is what would drive innovation and progress in educational methods and practices. Although new innovations may first be tried in more expensive schools, those innovations would eventually be adopted by schools generally. As in all economic sectors, wealthy people provide the initial capital to finance experimentation and innovation. Those innovations that are found to be most useful are soon expanded. The price of the new innovation comes down, and the product is made available to everyone at less cost. A school choice program that prohibits families, who wish to, from adding onto their tuition produces a market that is far less attractive to new capital and new entry than a program in which entrepreneurs can attract consumers from all income levels. Without the interest and investment of wealthy and middle-income families, a real educational revolution will probably not occur.

Some school choice programs restrict the participation of for-profit schools.[29] That is a serious mistake. Since the purpose of school choice is to focus market forces and capital on the problem of education, the profit motive is an important part of educational reform. Without the benefit of the profit motive, there is less motivation for schools to expand or improve their services.

Historically, most private schools have operated as nonprofit entities. Although private schools have been shown generally to do a better job than public schools, the independent nonprofit education sector has performed very poorly when compared with economic sectors in which the profit motive is present.[30] For example, improvement and innovation in the computer, medical, and automobile industries have advanced rapidly. In contrast, schools and classrooms look basically the same as they did a generation ago, and educational costs have increased without any additional advances or improvements. Even the best and most successful private schools have generally failed to expand, and instructional innovations that have been shown to be effective on the basis of empirical evidence have been outnumbered by ill-conceived educational fads.

Economists who look at the lack of progress in educational improvement often cite the absence of the profit motive as a major factor. This absence of the profit motive has dissuaded entrepreneurs from investing substantial time and financial resources into schooling. If school choice programs exclude the possibility for profit making, entrepreneurs will continue to turn their attention to other types of activities, and schools and children will lose the benefit of the innovative products, services, and efficiencies that creative people would have brought to the education enterprise.[31]

Unfortunately, many politicians and members of the public think that the profit motive has no place in education. There's no reason that should be so. For-profit day care and preschools are thriving industries in the United States, giving quality childcare and early childhood educational services to children every day. The same would be true in K–12 education. For-profit schools like Sylvan Learning Systems and Kaplan Inc. have been providing quality educational programs to thousands of satisfied children and parents for years. The profit motive, in education as in any other enterprise, is a necessary ingredient in the generation of new ideas, innovations, and efficiencies.[32]

Vouchers or Tax Credits

Access to private schools can be achieved through vouchers or tax credits. Under a voucher program, a state would issue a voucher to the parent or guardian of every child, to be spent on tuition at the private or government school of the parent's choosing. Government schools should be required to honor the voucher or tax credit as full payment, but private schools should be free to charge an additional amount if they choose to do so—this will allow more variety in the educational system.

Under a tax credit approach, parents who choose a private school for their child would be required to pay tuition out of their own pockets, then claim a dollar-for-dollar credit off of their state income tax each year at tax time. For a tax credit approach to be successful, the program would have to include both parental tax credits and scholarship tax credits. Parental tax credits allow parents to receive a dollar-for-dollar credit off of their own state income tax in exchange for paying tuition at a private school. Scholarship tax credits allow other taxpayers (either individuals or businesses) to receive a dollar-for-dollar credit off of their individual or corporate income tax for contributions made to scholarship-granting organizations within the state. Scholarship tax credits make funds available to low-income children whose parents pay little or no state income tax and who therefore cannot claim the credit themselves.

One disadvantage of credits over vouchers is that credits make less money available for private school tuition since most parents don't pay enough in state income tax to cover the cost of tuition even if they receive a full credit. This disadvantage can be overcome by allowing taxpayers to, in addition, claim a credit against property taxes paid for public schools. Parents who pay private school tuition could receive a certificate that could be used as full or partial payment of property taxes. Likewise, parents who rent rather than own property could pass the certificate along to their landlord as partial rent payment. The landlord could then use the certificate toward payment of real estate tax.[33]

Avoiding Regulations on Private Schools

For the maximum benefits of school choice to be realized, it is important that private schools remain independent and free of regulations that would prohibit specialization, innovation, and creativity. Private schools should not be required to administer state-sanctioned tests or adopt state curriculum guidelines or "standards."

Requiring private schools to give state-selected achievement tests would have deleterious effects on the participating private schools. Some private schools would have to give up the curriculum they have designed for their own students and teach the state-sanctioned curriculum instead. That would be a drastic blow to the diversity and vitality of the private education sector. Many state tests emphasize "new math" over traditional math and stress the use of modern "culturally diverse texts" over traditional literature, a staple of many effective private schools.[34]

Most private schools already administer standardized tests as a way to measure student academic progress, but there is wide variation among private schools in terms of test preference.[35] Some prefer the Iowa Test of Basic Skills because they think it tests for a more traditional coverage of the curriculum; others prefer the Stanford-9 or the CAT. Some private schools shun standardized tests altogether, choosing to rely instead on more holistic measures of student progress. The fact that many private schools don't want to administer state tests doesn't mean that they are not serious academic institutions with rigorous standards of excellence. It simply means that their curriculum and standards are different from those of government schools. Most state standards have no empirical basis. Rather, state standards and tests are typically the product of an awkward compromise between disparate factions of the professional education community, many of which are influenced by educational fads and politically popular thinking.[36]

Rules requiring private schools to accept all applicants severely jeopardize the ability of private schools to specialize by focusing on specific types of students. Consumers have diverse preferences and producers have unique skills, talents, and interests. The purpose of school choice is to give parents choices among schools of differing specializations, ideologies, and practices. It defeats this purpose to make private schools into one-size-fits-all carbon copies of public schools. There is value in allowing schools to specialize in helping students with special needs, students with an interest in the performing arts, students with particular religious preferences or allowing schools to admit only boys or only girls. Requiring schools that participate in school choice programs to admit all students dilutes the positive benefits that can be derived from specialization.

There is reason to believe that many private schools will not participate in school choice programs if those programs require that they give up their curriculum, religious environment, or their ability to admit students on the basis of the school's unique specialization or mission.[37] Imposing state standards or admission policies on private schools would create an institutional rigidity and uniformity that would limit the diversity of standards, school practices, curricula, and educational philosophies that exist in the private school market. States that enact school choice programs should therefore avoid imposing regulations on private schools that would only dilute the positive effects of competition and choice.

Conclusion

A new Gallup poll, released in 2003, showed that of parents with children in public school, 59 percent would choose a private school if given a full-tuition voucher and 44 percent would choose a private school if half-tuition vouchers were offered.[38] This may be due to the drop in parent's high regard for public schools reported by the same poll. The percentage of public school parents in 2003 who said they would choose to keep their children in public school when offered a full-tuition voucher was 39 percent, down from 56 percent in 1999. Opponents of school choice claim that vouchers would harm students whose parents opted to leave them in public schools, but American parents do not share that view. According to the same Gallup poll, only 12 percent of parents thought the academic achievement of students remaining in the public schools would get worse; 29 percent thought it would be better, and 59 percent thought it would stay the same.

Our survey of private school costs shows that private schools can be an option for inner-city low-income families as well as higher-income families. In all six cities surveyed, low-cost alternatives to public schools exist today. Even a poor child, armed with a voucher of $5,000, could obtain a quality private education in any of these cities and the prices of private schools in these municipalities are representative of private school costs around the country. Even if the amount of the voucher or tax credit were limited to two-thirds of the per-pupil cost of public schools, the value would exceed $5,000 in many urban communities.

Lower-income cities included in our survey—New Orleans and Philadelphia—have greater proportions of low-cost schools than high-cost schools, with 93 percent of elementary schools in New Orleans and 89 percent of elementary schools in Philadelphia charging less than $5,000. This fact demonstrates that the creation of private schools follows basic principles of supply and demand. Education entrepreneurs in those two cities cater to a clientele that, for the most part, cannot spend more than several thousand dollars for private schools so they create schools to cater to parents who will look for a school in that price range.

In some cities, only a relatively small number of students could be accommodated immediately in private schools once a voucher or tax credit program is implemented. Available seating capacity in private schools is particularly scarce for high school students. Yet the benefits of choice go beyond what would be available the day after a choice plan is put into place, and the benefits would increase each year. Choice sets in motion a dynamic process of growth and change that would result in an ever-increasing number of private school options for students.

Existing school choice programs have already provided evidence that increased benefits and options become available to students after choice is implemented. In Florida, for example, where students are able to attend private schools under several choice programs, the number of private schools in the state has increased as school choice has become more widespread.[39] Private entrepreneurs and philanthropic foundations have poured more than $76 million into Milwaukee's private schools since school choice was implemented there. Sixty-five schools in Milwaukee have completed capital expansion projects, indicating that educational entrepreneurs do respond to increased market demands.[40]

It's time to release children living in America's big cities from failing urban public schools. Not only would a program of school choice give these children access to a better education today, it will unleash the power of constructive competition that will lead to dramatically improved outcomes in the future. Armed with a voucher or tax credit of $5,000 or more per student, urban families would be able to pick from among the best schools in their area. They would use the power of the consumer to force schools to improve. Good schools will thrive because parents will choose them. Likewise, bad schools will disappear as they lose students. Our survey of private schools shows that there are already many affordable high-quality private schools available on the market and, once they are allowed to compete on a level playing field with government schools, many more will come into operation. School choice is the best way to give urban children the schools they deserve.

Notes

1. John E. Chubb and Terry M. Moe, *Politics, Markets, and America's Schools* (Washington: Brookings Institution, 1990).

2. John Chubb, "Making Schools Better," Manhattan Institute, Center for Educational Innovation, New York, 1989, pp. 10–11. Comparisons of private and government school systems in other cities showed similar disparities. For example, see Mike Bowler, "Catholic Schools: More for Less," *Baltimore Sun*, October 8, 1995, p. 2C. David Boaz, "The Public School Monopoly: America's Berlin Wall," in *Liberating Schools: Education in the Inner City*, ed. David Boaz (Washington: Cato Institute, 1991). Also see David W. Kirkpatrick, *Choice in Schooling: The Case for Tuition Vouchers* (Chicago: Loyola University Press, 1990); and H. J. Walberg, M. J. Bakalis, J. L. Bast,

and S. Baer, *We Can Rescue Our Children: The Cure for Chicago's Public School Crisis* (Chicago: Heartland Institute, 1988).

3. See David Boaz, ed., *Liberating Schools: Education in the Inner City* (Washington: Cato Institute, 1991), pp. 14–17.

4. For enrollment figures see U.S. Department of Education, *Digest of Education Statistics 2002* (Washington: National Center for Education Statistics, 2002), Table 36.

5. *Digest of Education Statistics 2002,* Table 80. The 1970 figure listed in Table 80 is 70.3 percent. However, this figure included instructional aids, librarians, and counselors so the actual number of teachers would be somewhat less than 70.3 percent.

6. *Digest of Education Statistics 2002,* Table 162. The 62 percent figure includes expenditures given under "instruction." The 15 percent figure includes "general administration," "school administration," "student support," and "other support." For a discussion of the bureaucratic nature of public school governance, see John E. Chubb, "The System" in *A Primer on America's Schools,* ed. Terry M. Moe (Stanford: Hoover Institution Press, 2001), pp. 39–40.

7. California Education Code. See http://www.leginfo.ca.gov/cgi-bin/calawquery? codesection = edc&codebody = &hits = 20.

8. Office of Management and Budget, Reports to Congress, Under the Paperwork Reduction Act of 1995, Table 3. See http://www.whitehouse.gov/omb/inforeg/ prarep2.html#burden.

9. *USA Today,* editorial, March 5, 1999.

10. Quoted in "Reding, Writing & Erithmatic," editorial, *Wall Street Journal,* October 2, 1989.

11. Walter E. Williams, "Tuition Tax Credits: Other Benefits," *Policy Review* (Spring 1978): p. 85.

12. Florida, Maine, Ohio, Vermont, and Wisconsin have school voucher programs. Arizona, Florida, Illinois, Iowa, Minnesota, and Pennsylvania offer tax credits or deductions for private school tuition or contributions to private school scholarship programs.

13. See William G. Howell and Paul E. Peterson, *The Education Gap: Vouchers and Urban Schools* (Washington: Brookings Institution, 2002).

14. For example, Arizona's tax credit program is limited to $500 per individual taxpayer ($650 for couples). Businesses and corporations cannot participate. In Pennsylvania and Florida, businesses can claim tax credits for contributions to private scholarship organizations but individual taxpayers or parents cannot. The cities of Cleveland and Milwaukee have voucher programs that are limited to children living within the city's school districts and are focused primarily on low-income students. In Florida, almost 24,000 children use vouchers to attend private schools, but these are limited to children in low-performing public schools or to children with disabilities.

15. To date, two states (California and Michigan) have proposed statewide voucher programs through ballot initiatives. Although these initiatives failed to be approved by a majority of voters in either state, polls indicate that the percentage of Americans who support allowing parents to spend their education tax dollars at the public or private school of their choice continues to increase. According to the 2001 Annual Phi Delta Kappa/Gallup Poll, 52 percent of Americans were supportive of school choice (up from 44 percent in the previous year). From 1996 to 2000, support levels were 43, 49, 51, 51, and 45 percent, respectively. See George Clowes, "What Does America Think? Attitudes About School Choice, Education, and Related Issues," *School Reform News,* April 2003, p, 16. Also, according to a poll conducted by the Joint Center for Political and Economic Studies, 60 percent of black adults favor

allowing families to use their education tax dollars at a private or public school. Of blacks in the 18–25 age range, 71 percent favor school choice. See *2002 National Opinion Poll*, Joint Center for Political and Economic Studies, Washington, D.C.

16. National Center for Education Statistics, *Digest of Education Statistics 2002*, Table 166. See http://nces.ed.gov/pubs2003/2003060b.pdf. The $9,354 figure is the total per-pupil expenditure based on average daily attendance.

17. Myron Lieberman and Charlene K. Haar, *Public Education as a Business: Real Costs and Accountability* (Lanham, Md.: Scarecrow Education Press, 2003). According to Lieberman's analysis, the omission of capital outlays and financial liabilities such as debt service and pensions results in a 15 percent or more underestimate of the cost per pupil in public schools. See also Myron Lieberman, *Privatization and Educational Choice* (New York: St. Martin's, 1989), pp. 65–73, 220–28; and Myron Lieberman, *Public Education: An Autopsy* (Cambridge, Mass.: Harvard University Press, 1993), pp. 114–42.

18. According to a 1998 survey of Catholic and other religious schools, tuition covers approximately 82 percent of operating costs. The rest is made up through church subsidies. See Lana Muraskin and Stephanie Stullich, "Barriers, Benefits and Costs of Using Private Schools to Alleviate Overcrowding in Public Schools," U.S. Department of Education, Office of the Undersecretary, November 1998, p. 13.

19. For example, a recent report on the use of vouchers in Florida by the anti-voucher People for the American Way Foundation reported only the high-end costs of Florida private schools. See People for the American Way, "Jeopardizing a Legacy: A Closer Look at IDEA and Florida's Disability Voucher Program," Washington, March 6, 2003. See www.pfaw.org/pfaw/general/default.aspx?oid=9063. Anthony Williams, mayor of Washington, D.C., and a supporter of vouchers, stated that "most private school tuitions run in the five figures—far beyond what is contemplated for the voucher program." (In reality, only 39 percent of D.C. private schools have tuitions of $10,000 or more.)

20. Tuition data were obtained from the Children's Scholarship Fund and through direct contact with the private schools. CSF provided tuition data on private schools in which there were CSF students enrolled. Other private schools were contacted by telephone. Since tuition often varies by grade level, tuition may be reported as the average tuition paid by students at the school. The author wishes to thank Puja Ahluwalia and the Children's Scholarship Fund for their assistance in obtaining these data.

21. See Louisiana Department of Education, *152nd Annual Financial and Statistical Report 2000–2001*, p. 148. Available at www.doe.state.la.us/DOE/PDFs/AFSR01.pdf.

22. National Center for Education Statistics, *Digest of Education Statistics* 2002, Table 93.

23. See Colorado Department of Education, Fiscal Year 2000–01 District Revenue and Expenditures. See www.cde.state.co.us/cdefinance/download/spreadsheet/AllExp01.xls.

24. South Carolina Department of Education, Fiscal Year '01 In$ite, Charleston County. See www.sde.state.sc.us/offices/finance/01InSite1.xls.

25. National Center for Educational Statistics, "Early Estimates of Public Elementary and Secondary Education Statistics: School Year 2001–2002." See http://nces.ed.gov/pubs2002/2002311.pdf.

26. Cato telephone survey of private high schools in Fairfax County, Virginia, and Montgomery County, Maryland.

27. Pennsylvania Department of Education. Selected Expenditure Data for Pennsylvania Public Schools 2000–01, Table 5. See www.pde.state.pa.us/k12_finances/lib/k12_finances/2000-01Table5Exp.pdf.

28. In all six cities surveyed, there were a number of nonparochial schools that charged less than $5,000. Washington, D.C., the most expensive of the six cities surveyed, has 10 nonparochial private schools that charge $5,000 or less.

29. Most states prohibit for-profit companies from creating charter schools. See Center for Education Reform, *Charter School Laws Across the States* (Washington: Center for Education Reform, 2003). See http://www.edreform.com/press/2003/charterlaws.htm. Other states, such as Michigan, have attempted to ban for-profit companies from managing public or charter schools. See http://www.csdc.org/bulletin/archive/stateLeg/w00state.html.

30. For an overview of U.S. private school performance compared with public schools, see Andrew Coulson, *Market Education: The Unknown History* (New Brunswick: Transaction, 1999), pp. 259–290. In addition, a new report from the National Center for Education Statistics shows that parents of children in private schools are more satisfied with their schools than parents of children in public schools. See National Center for Education Statistics, "Trends in the Use of School Choice 1993–1999," May 2003.

31. For a review of the literature on the importance of the profit motive in education, see Andrew Coulson, *Market Education: The Unknown History* (New Brunswick: Transaction, 1999), p. 287.

32. Many of the most promising and innovative developments in education are taking place in the private for-profit sector. Software companies have developed some of the most effective and innovative learning programs available. Online high schools and universities are increasingly providing services to regular, home-schooled, and special education students. Kaplan "Score" learning centers have established a firm track record of teaching reading and math to children who failed to learn in the public schools. See Gregory Fossedal, "Ed-biz: Where Business and Education Meet," UPI, March 31, 2003. See also Carrie Lips, " 'Edupreneurs': A Survey of For-Profit Education," Cato Institute Policy Analysis no. 386, Washington, November 20, 2000.

33. Lawmakers in New York and Texas have proposed property tax credits for private school tuition. Sample legislation can be found at http://www.capitol.state.tx.us/cgi-bin/tlo/textframe.cmd?LEG=76&SESS=R&CHAMBER=H&BILLTYPE=B&BILLSUFFIX=03701&VERSION=1&TYPE=B.

34. For example, the California Learning Assessment System or CLAS, focused on "new math," "whole-language," and "natural spelling." In the words of Gov. Pete Wilson's education secretary, the CLAS, "Gave no individual scores, tested no basic skills, was related to a scale no one could explain, and never used the expertise of professional measurement experts." See Maureen DiMarco, "Measurement and Reform," in *What's Gone Wrong in America's Classrooms?*, ed. William Evers (Stanford, Calif.: Hoover Press, 1998).

35. In Florida, where private schools are largely unregulated, 95 percent of private schools already administer commercially designed standardized tests according to a recent survey. See Jay P. Greene and Marcus A. Winters, "Forcing the FCAT on Voucher Schools Is a Bad Idea," *Tallahassee Democrat*, March 31, 2003.

36. For a review of the strengths and weakness of state tests, see Williamson M. Evers, "Standards and Accountability" in *A Primer on America's Schools*, ed. Terry M.

Moe (Stanford, Calif.: Hoover Press, 2001). See also Paul T. Hill, "Getting Standards Right," *Hoover Digest*, no. 2 (2002), at www.hoover.stanford.edu/publications/digest/022/toc022.html; and Matthew Carolan and Raymond Keating, "Private Schools Should Flee State Testing Requirements," *Newsday*, June 4, 2002, at http://pqasb.pqarchiver.com/newsday/122570811.html?did = 122570811&FMT = ABS& FMTS = FT&PMID = 33538&desc = Private + Schools + Should + Flee + State + Testing + Requirements.

37. According to a 1998 U.S. Department of Education survey, at least half of all private schools would decline to participate in a school choice program if voucher students are randomly assigned to participating private schools (rather than allowing the schools to exercise control over which students they admit). And 89 percent of religious schools said they would not participate in a school choice program if students were allowed to opt out of religious instruction. See Lana Muraskin, "Barriers, Benefits, and Costs of Using Private Schools to Alleviate Overcrowding in Public Schools," U.S. Department of Education, Planning and Evaluation Services, Washington, 1998.

38. The 35th Annual Phi Delta Kappa/Gallup Poll of the Public's Attitudes Toward Public Schools. Available at http://www.pdkintl.org/kappan/k0309pol.pdf.

39. The percentage of school-age children in Florida's private schools has risen from 9.31 percent in 1992 to 12.5 percent in 2000–01. See "Distribution of Students Over a Ten-Year Period," June 28, 2001, available from the Florida Department of Education at http://www.firn.edu/doe/choice/tencomp.htm. According to the Department's Choice Office, 353 new private schools registered with the Department between May 2000 and December 2002.

40. American Education Reform Council, *Schools That Choice Built* (Milwaukee: American Education Reform Council, 2003).

Appendix
TUITION FOR PRIVATE ELEMENTARY AND HIGH SCHOOLS IN SIX U.S. CITIES (in dollars)

New Orleans (Elementary Schools)

One In Christ Academy	$975
St. George's Episcopal School	1,055
Solid Rock Academy	1,400
Sister Clara Muhammad School	1,400
St. Alphonsus School	1,654
Ephesus Adventist Junior Academy	1,700
St. Jude School	1,700
St. Mark School	1,721
St. Benilde School	1,750
Mt. Carmel Christian Faith Academy	1,800
Visitation of Our Lady School	1,837
St. Mary of the Angels	1,875
Sacred Heart of Jesus	1,926
St. Peter Chanel School	1,930
Westbank Christian Center Academy	1,931
St. Louis Cathedral School	1,950
Lake Castle Private School	2,000
Light City Christian Academy	2,000
St. Raymond School	2,000
Our Lady of Perpetual Help School—Belle Chasse	2,050
St. Joan of Arc Catholic School	2,056
Corpus Christi School	2,065
St. Rita School—New Orleans	2,090
First Baptist Christian School	2,100
Myrtle Magee Christian Academy	2,100
St. Edward the Confessor	2,100
St. Monica Catholic School	2,100
St. Peter Claver School	2,100
Concordia Lutheran	2,116
St. Elizabeth Ann Seton School	2,170
Holy Ghost Catholic School	2,190
Our Lady of Divine Providence	2,195
Chalmette Christian Academy	2,200
St. David Catholic School	2,200
St. Paul the Apostle School	2,200
St. Simon Peter	2,200

222

New Orleans (Elementary Schools) (cont.)

Victory Christian Academy	$2,208
St. Frances Cabrini Elementary School	2,227
The Primary School	2,230
Our Lady of Grace School	2,250
St. Louis King of France	2,270
St. Andrew the Apostle School	2,275
St. Angela Merici School	2,275
Bishop McManus Academy	2,295
Grace Baptist Academy	2,300
St. Rita School—Harahan	2,300
Strong Faith Christian Academy	2,300
St. Joseph the Worker School	2,308
St. Stephen Catholic School	2,310
St. Peter School—Covington	2,320
St. Agnes School	2,324
St. Catherine of Siena School	2,329
Faith Academy	2,330
St. Mary Magdalene	2,335
Our Lady of Perpetual Help School—Kenner	2,340
The Upper Room Bible Church Academy	2,340
Reserve Christian School	2,350
Word of Life Academy	2,350
St. Cletus School	2,374
St. Louise de Marillac School	2,375
St. Philip Neri	2,375
Riverside Academy	2,385
St. Paul Lutheran	2,385
Terrytown Academy	2,386*
Calvary Baptist School	2,400
Providence 2 Christian Academy	2,400
River Ridge Christian Academy	2,400
St. Peter School—Reserve	2,409
Christ the King Parish School	2,425
Immaculate Heart of Mary	2,440
Our Lady of Prompt Succor School—Chalmette	2,450
St. Rosalie School	2,450
St. Francis Xavier	2,470
St. Anthony School	2,479
St. Margaret Mary	2,490

New Orleans (Elementary Schools) (cont.)

All Saints Catholic School	$2,500
New Orleans Christian Academy	2,500
Primary School	2,500
Prince of Peace Lutheran School	2,500
Our Lady of Prompt Succor School—Westwego	2,525
St. Pius X School	2,525
Immaculate Conception School	2,540
Believer's Life Christian Academy	2,550
St. Robert Bellarmine	2,550
St. Anthony of Padua	2,560
St. Joseph Central	2,575
St. Leo the Great	2,620
Walden Academy	2,675
Ascension of Our Lord	2,676
St. Joseph Major School	2,695
First Baptist Christian School-Kenner	2,700
Salem Lutheran School	2,700
St. Joan of Arc School—LaPlace	2,728
Westbank Cathedral Academy	2,760
Elmwood Park Academy	2,790
Lynn Oaks School	2,800
St. John Lutheran School	2,880
Crescent City Baptist School	2,900
Faith Christian Academy	2,900
Memorial Baptist Christian	2,900
Resurrection of Our Lord	2,900
Our Lady of the Lake	2,920
St. Michael Special School	2,925
St. Dominic School	2,956
Kuumba Academy	2,985
Holy Name of Mary	2,990
Northlake Christian School	3,023
Marrero Christian Academy	3,270
John Curtis Christian	3,300
Our Lady of Lourdes Catholic School	3,445
Ecole Classique	3,700
Ridgewood Preparatory School	3,990
Crescent Academy	4,000
Arden Cahill Academy	4,100

New Orleans (Elementary Schools) (cont.)

Ursuline Academy	$4,315
Holy Name of Jesus School	4,383
Perrault's Kiddy Kollege	4,400
Kehoe—France	4,986
Christ Episcopal School	5,350
Holy Rosary Academy	6,100
Saint Andrew's Episcopal School	7,090
Academy of the Sacred Heart	7,350
Trinity Episcopal School	10,510
St. Paul's Episcopal School	10,750
St. Martin's Episcopal	10,850
Isidore Newman School	10,865
Louise S. McGehee School	11,100

*Median cost.

New Orleans (High Schools)

Grace Baptist Academy	2,300
Word of Life Academy	2,552
Bishop McManus Academy	2,595
St. Mary's Academy	2,735
Riverside Academy	2,790
Marian Central Catholic Middle School	2,793
St. Michael Special School	2,925
Zina Christian Academy	3,000
Redeemer-Seton Senior High School	3,237
Life of Christ Christian Academy	3,400
St. Augustine High School	3,450
Crescent City Baptist High School	3,500
Xavier Preparatory School	3,500
St. Paul's High School	3,650
St. Mary's Dominican High School	3,735
St. Charles Catholic High School	3,775
Immaculata High School	3,800
Archbishop Hannan High School	3,850
Archbishop Chapelle High School	3,875
Ridgewood Preparatory School	3,890*
Ecole Classique	3,900*
Archbishop Shaw High School	4,000
Archbishop Blenk High School	4,100

New Orleans (High Schools) (cont.)

Archbishop Rummel High School	$4,175
Christian Brothers School	4,200
Lutheran High School	4,300
Ursuline Academy	4,315
Northlake Christian School	4,350
Cabrini High School	4,365
Marrero Christian Academy	4,440
Pope John Paul II Sr. High School	4,500
De La Salle High School	4,600
Jesuit High School	4,625
Mt. Carmel Academy	5,000
Holy Cross School	5,025
Brother Martin High School	5,090
Louise S. McGehee School	11,100
Isidore Newman School	12,355
St. Martin's Episcopal	12,375
St. Stanislaus College	14,500

*Median cost, $3,895, falls between these two values.

Houston (Elementary Schools)

Walden School	1,320
Childrens Garden Montessori	1,440
Christ the Lord School	1,440
Helmers Street Christian	1,750
Finney Christian Academy	1,850
New Covenant Christian Academy	1,950
Holy Name Catholic School	2,000
Christian Academy	2,080
Shady Acres Christian School	2,100
Smaller Scholars Too	2,100
St. Francis of Assisi Catholic School	2,100
McGee Chapel Rainbow Academy	2,180
Pecan Street Christian Academy	2,250
Sacred Heart School	2,300
St. Cecilia School	2,350
Channelview Christian School	2,400
A and B Nursery	2,500
Central Christian	2,500
Houston Church Christian Academy	2,500

Houston (Elementary Schools) (cont.)

Southeast Academy	$2,500
St. Peter the Apostle	2,500
Woodward Acres	2,500
Encourager Christian Academy	2,600
Irvington Pentacostal Church	2,600
St. Philip Neri Catholic School	2,600
Our Lady of Mt. Carmel	2,629
Restoration Outreach Christian	2,700
Robindell Private School	2,788
Holy Trinity Methodist	2,850
Humble Christian School	2,975
Darul Arqam School	3,000
Excel Adventist Academy	3,000
Virgie-Lu Children's Center for Cognitive Growth	3,000
St. Jerome Catholic School	3,100
St. Agnes Christian Academy	3,150
St. Ambrose School	3,150
W. Houston Adventist School	3,150
St. Chris Catholic	3,170
R. Christian Academy	3,250
Beth Yeshurun Day School	3,300
St. Jerome School	3,300
Texas Christian School	3,300
Royal Christian Academy	3,350
St. Rose of Lima Academy	3,350
All God's Children	3,360
Baytown Christian Academy	3,391
Grace School	3,400
St. Claire's	3,400
St. Clare of Assi Catholic School	3,440
Academies of Houston School	3,500
St. Anne Catholic School	3,500
St. Augustine Catholic School	3,500
St. Mary of the Purification Montessori	3,500
Tower Christian	3,500
Al-Hadi School	3,540
Abiding Word Lutheran School	3,600
Crestmont Kiddie College	3,600
Mission Christian Academy	3,600

Houston (Elementary Schools) (cont.)

Seatob Catholic Junior High	$3,650
Incarnate Word Academy	3,780
Inwood Oaks Christian School	3,780
Grace Christian School	3,880
Adapt Learning System and School	4,000
Banff School	4,000
Southwest Christian Academy	4,000
Your University	4,000
St. James Epsicopal School	4,050
John Paul II Catholic School	4,100
Immaculate Heart of Mary School	4,250
St. James Episcopal Day School	4,250
American Montessori School	4,300
The Fay School	4,300*
Champions Christian Academy Day	4,350*
St. Vincent's	4,380
Classical School	4,420
Westbury Christian School	4,450
Our Savior Lutheran School	4,485
Holy Ghost	4,500
Mackes Private School	4,500
St. Michael Catholic School	4,500
Ma Montissori	4,535
Northwest Montessori	4,550
West Houston Christian Academy	4,750
Trinity Lutheran Academy	4,900
Memorial Hall School	4,950
Rainard School	4,950
St. Mark Lutheran School	4,950
Phoenix Academy	4,961
Woods School	4,961
The Alphabet Club	5,000
St. Catherines Montessori	5,150
Redd School	5,200
St. Thomas	5,200
Christian School of Kingwood	5,220
Jesus Center Academy	5,280
Sherwood Forest Montessori School	5,308
Broadway Christian School	5,400

Houston (Elementary Schools) (cont.)

Cypruss Community Christian School	$5,400
Montessori Country Day	5,450
Carethers Academy SDA School	5,490
Fort Bend Baptist Academy and Middle School	5,520
Banff School	5,652
Ambassador	5,750
American Preparatory School	5,950
Galloway School	5,960
Lutheran Academy	6,250
Melrose Baptist School	6,265
Sherwood Montessori	6,300
Cornerstone Christian Academy	6,350
St. Nicholas School	6,500
St. Agnes Academy School	6,600
Ascension Episcopal School	6,630
Ascension School	6,630
Northland Christian	6,650
Wesley Academy	6,720
St. Theresa's School	6,800
Mission Bend Methodist Day School	7,000
Queen of Peace	7,000
St. Thomas Episcopal	7,000
Branch School	7,250
The Walden School	7,300
First Baptist Academy	7,350
Small S. Montessori School	7,600
First Baptist Academy	7,875
Aston Academy	8,100
Renard Academy	8,200
River Oaks	8,250
St. Mark Lutheran School	8,250
The Village School	8,253
West Oaks Private School	8,300
Annunciation Orthodox School	8,405
School of the Woods	8,500
St. Elizabeth Ann Seton	9,100
Fay School	9,200
Kinkaid School	9,355
School of the Woods	9,936

Houston (Elementary Schools) (cont.)

Cottage School	$10,000
St. Jerome School	10,925
St. Johns School	10,925
Presbyterian School	11,030
Duchesne Academy of the Sacred Heart	11,940
River Oaks Baptist School	13,280
Alexander Smith Academy	19,200
Early Montessori	22,500

*Median cost, $4,325, falls between these two values.

Houston (High Schools)

New Covenant Christian Academy	1,950
Montessori School	2,000
Christian Academy	2,080
Southeast Academy	2,500
Woodward Acres	2,500
Irvington Pentecostal Church	2,600
Central Christian	2,750
Seton Catholic Jr. High School	2,950
Excel Adventist Academy	3,000
W. Houston Adventist School	3,150
R. Christian Academy	3,250
Academies of Houston School	3,500
Darul Arqam School	3,500
Abiding Word Lutheran School	3,800
Texas Christian School	3,900
Grace Christian School	4,875
Mount Carmel High School	5,000
Houston Jr. Academy	5,400
St. Pius X High School	5,950*
Cornerstone Christian Academy	6,350*
Melrose Baptist School	6,415
Cypruss Community Christian School	6,790
Lutheran High North	6,800
St. Theresa's School	6,800
Tower Christian Academy	7,200
Lutheran Academy	7,250
St. Thomas Episcopal	7,775
St. Thomas High School	7,900

Houston (High Schools) (cont.)

River Oaks	$8,250
Northland Christian	8,400
Strake Jesuit College Prep	8,500
School of the Woods	9,936
Duchesne Academy of the Sacred Heart	11,940
Kinkaid School	12,715
St. John's School	13,775
Episcopal High School	14,380
Tenney School	16,000
Alexander Smith Academy	19,200

*Median cost, $6,150, falls between these two values.

Denver (Elementary Schools)

Messiah Baptist Schools	1,800
Zion Lutheran	2,225
Arvada SDA Christian School	2,250
Mile High Baptist School	2,250
Cedarwood Christian Academy	2,280
Our Lady Help of Christians Academy	2,400
Emmaus Lutheran School	2,430
St. Andrew Lutheran School	2,475
Union Baptist Excel Institute	2,475
Calvert Christian	2,500
Colorado State Academy of Arvada	2,660
St. Frances De Sales	2,700
Peace with Christ	2,800
Presentation of Our Lady School	2,800
Colorado Christian School	2,830
Redeemer Lutheran School	2,850
St. Catherine of Sienna School	2,871
Guardian Angels	2,900
Our Lady of the Rosary Academy	2,917
Beth Eden Baptist School	2,950
St. Pius Catholic School	2,950
St. Bernadette School	2,988
Assumption Catholic School	2,990
Loyola Catholic Grade School	3,000
Belleview Christian School	3,050
Shrine of St. Anne	3,050

Denver (Elementary Schools) (cont.)

Annunciation Catholic School	$3,200
Colorado Christian School	3,200
Westland Christian Academy	3,200
Silver State Baptist School	3,225
Change Christian Academy	3,249
Most Precious Blood Parish School	3,250
Sts. Peter and Paul's Christian School	3,250
Christ the King Catholic School	3,300
St. Mary's School	3,300
St. Therese School	3,300
St. Thomas Moore School	3,300
Our Lady of Lourdes School	3,400
Notre Dame Catholic School	3,475
Aurora Christian Academy	3,487
Escuela de Guadalupe	3,500
Faith Christian Academy	3,500
Mile High Adventist Academy	3,500
St. Rose of Lima School	3,500
Good Shepherd Catholic School	3,528*
Riverview Christian Academy	3,528*
Christian Fellowship School	3,600
Holy Family Grade School	3,680
University Hills Lutheran	3,700
St. James Catholic School	3,780
St. John's Lutheran	3,800
St. Louis Catholic School	3,811
American Christian Academy	4,000
Institute of Global Scholarship	4,000
Love Christian Fellowship	4,000
St. Vincent de Paul School	4,000
Watch Care Academy	4,000
Blessed Sacrament School	4,200
Bethany Christian Academy	4,500
Jim Elliot School	4,750
Denver Christian Schools	4,990
Van Dellen Christian School	5,000
Dove Christian Academy	5,200
Escuela Tlatelolco	5,890
Denver Academy	6,000

Denver (Elementary Schools) (cont.)

Montessori School of Denver	$6,244
Denver Waldorf School	6,400
Hillel Academy	6,550
Tetra Academy	6,550
Inner-City Christian School	6,780
Denver Academy of Torah	7,300
Mount St. Vincent School	7,500
Denver International School	7,860
Herzl Jewish Day School	7,940
Rocky Mountain Hebrew Academy	7,941
Stanley British Primary School	7,954
St. Mary's Academy	8,800
Montclair Academy	8,925
Kent Denver School	9,000
Beacon Country Day School	9,200
Logan School for Creative Learning	9,320
Calvary Apostolic Academy	9,700
St. Anne's Episcopal School	9,800
MacIntosh Academy	9,814
Graland Country Day	11,102
Rick's Center for Gifted Children	11,400
Havern Center	12,250
Colorado Academy	13,225
Alexander Dawson	13,575
Accelerated Schools Found #1	13,850

*Median cost.

Denver (High Schools)

Messiah Baptist Schools	1,800
Our Lady Help of Christians Academy	2,400
Emmaus Lutheran School	2,430
Calvert Christian	2,500
El Dorado Academy	2,525
Colorado State Academy of Arvada	2,660
Colorado Catholic Academy	3,000
Belleview Christian School	3,250
Westwood Academy	3,400
Mile High Adventist Academy	3,500
Silver State Baptist School	3,644

Denver (High Schools) (cont.)

CHANGE Christian Academy	$3,753
Christian Fellowship School	3,780
Aurora Christian Academy	3,795
Wood Adventist	3,800
La Academia	4,000
Riverview Christian Academy	4,095
Bethany Christian Academy	4,500
Jim Elliot School	4,750
Lutheran H.S. of the Rockies	5,000
Dove Christian Academy	5,200
Denver Christian Middle School	5,540
Denver Lutheran High School	5,990*
Denver Academy	6,000*
Love Christian Fellowship	6,000
Lutheran High School	6,000
Bishop Machebeuf High School	6,100
Yeshiva Toras Chaim	6,250
Mullen High School	6,300
Denver Waldorf School	6,400
Denver Christian High	6,470
Denver Street School	6,600
Regis Jesuit High School	6,750
Holy Family High School	7,000
Denver Academy of Torah	7,300
Escuela Tlatelolco	7,500
Beth Jacob High School	7,700
Rocky Mountain Hebrew Academy	8,694
St. Mary's Academy	8,800
Kent Denver School	9,000
Calvary Apostolic Academy	9,700
University of Denver High School	11,970
Humanex Academy	12,000
Alexander Dawson	13,575
Colorado Academy	13,990
Accelerated Schools Found #1	17,750

*Median cost, $5,995, falls between these two values.

Charleston (Elementary Schools)

First Baptist Church School	2,160
Christ our King—Stella Maris	2,360

Charleston (Elementary Schools) (cont.)

Ferndale Baptist School	$2,400
Abundant Life Christian Academy	2,500
Divine Redeemer School	2,600
Charleston SDA Jr. Academy	2,700
Blessed Sacrament School	2,800
St. John's Christian Academy	2,840
Archibald Rutiledge Academy	3,000
Summerville Catholic School	3,000
New Israel Christian School	3,024
Northwood Academy	3,036
Evangel Christian School	3,048
Harvest Baptist School	3,058
Northside Christian School	3,058
St. John's Catholic School	3,100
Nativity Elementary School	3,150*
Northwood Christian School	3,156*
Cathedral Academy	3,200
West Ashley Christian Academy	3,704
Charleston Catholic School	3,742
St. Paul's Country Day School	3,828
Charleston Christian School	3,838
James Island Christian School	3,908
First Baptist School of Mt. Pleasant	4,100
Pinewood Preparatory School	5,100
Mason Preparatory School	6,390
Charleston Collegiate School	6,553
Addlestone Hebrew Academy	6,950
Charleston Day School	9,550
Porter-Gaud School	10,795
Ashley Hall	11,055
North Charleston Academy	17,000
Trident Academy	18,200

*Median cost, $3,153, falls between these two values.

Charleston (High Schools)

Ferndale Baptist School	2,500
First Baptist Church School	2,500
Archibald Rutiledge Academy	3,000
St. John's Christian Academy	3,325

Charleston (High Schools) (cont.)

Harvest Baptist School	$3,355
Northside Christian School	3,553
Cathedral Academy	3,595
Palmetto Academy	3,750
Northwood Academy	3,912*
James Island Christian School	4,200*
St. Paul's Country Day School	4,323
First Baptist School of Mt. Pleasant	4,500
Bishop England High School	4,650
Pinewood Preparatory School	6,200
Charleston Collegiate School	7,683
Ashley Hall	11,055
Porter-Gaud School	12,390
Trident Academy	18,350

*Median cost, $4,056, falls between these two values.

Washington, D.C. (Elementary Schools)

Immaculate Conception School	$3,000
Rhema Christian Center School	3,000
Holy Comforter/St. Cyprian School	3,100
Holy Name School	3,100
Our Lady of Perpetual Help	3,100
Our Lady Queen of Peace School	3,100
Sacred Heart Elementary School	3,100
St. Augustine School	3,100
St. Francis de Sales School	3,100
St. Francis Xavier School	3,100
St. Thomas More Elementary School	3,100
St. Thomas More School	3,100
Holy Temple Christian Academy	3,108
Nativity Catholic Academy	3,245
St. Thomas More Cathedral School	3,245
St. Benedict the Moor School	3,255
Assumption School	3,265
Anacostia Bible Church Christian	3,300
Cornerstone Bible Church School	3,300
First Rock Baptist Church Christian	3,300
St. Gabriel School	3,400
Cornerstone Community School	3,500

Washington, D.C. (Elementary Schools) (cont.)

St. Anthony Catholic School	$3,535
Dupont Park Seventh Day Adventist	3,746
A-T Seban Mesut	3,750
Sankofa Fie	3,750
Holy Redeemer Catholic School	3,833
Nannie Helen Burroughs School, Inc.	3,942
Muhammad University of Islam	4,307
Calvary Christian Academy	4,400
Bridges Academy	4,483
Sister Clara Muhammad School	4,500
Washington Science and Technology Academy, Inc.	4,500*
Blessed Sacrament Elementary School	4,560
Roots Activity Learning Center	4,670
Annunciation School	4,770
Ideal Academy	4,800
Naylor Road School	4,940
St. Peter's Interparish School	4,942
Academy for Ideal Education	5,000
St. Ann's Academy	5,114
Our Lady of Victory School	5,550
Metropolitan Day School	6,200
Preparatory School of D.C.	8,000
Beauvoir the National Cathedral	8,583
Holy Trinity School	8,640
British School of Washington	12,000
Aidan Montessori School	13,075
Owl School	13,900
Capitol Hill Day School	14,650
National Presbyterian School	14,945
Georgetown Day School	15,218
Lowell School	15,990
Rock Creek International School	16,975
Sidwell Friends School	17,600
Washington International School	17,655
St. Patrick's Episcopal Day School	17,800
Sheridan School	17,980
Lab School of Washington	18,000
Maret School	18,360
National Cathedral School	20,225

Washington, D.C. (Elementary Schools) (cont.)

Kingsbury Day School	$21,200
St. Albans School for Boys	21,837

*Median cost.

Washington, D.C. (High Schools)

Washington Middle School for Girls	4,000
Ideal Academy	4,500
Archbishop Carroll High School	6,300
Sankofa Fie	7,500
San Miguel Middle School	9,000
St. John's College High School	9,470
Gonzaga College High School	10,150
Georgetown Visitation Prep School	13,100
St. Anselm's Abbey School	14,800
British School of Washington	14,900
Emerson Preparatory School	16,000*
Nora School	16,150*
Parkmont School	18,200
Edmund Burke School	18,400
Washington International School	19,670
Sidwell Friends School	19,990
National Cathedral School	20,225
Field School	20,580
Lab School of Washington	21,000
Maret School	21,140
Georgetown Day High School	21,327
St. Albans School for Boys	21,837

*Median cost, $16,075, falls between these two values.

Philadelphia (Elementary Schools)

Mt. Airy Christian Day School	1,050
Jubilee School	1,100
St. Malachy Elementary School	1,150
Celestial Christian Community	1,170
Hunting Park Christian Academy	1,200
All Saints Elementary School	1,221
St. John the Baptist School	1,442
Nativity B.V.M.	1,450

Philadelphia (Elementary Schools) (cont.)

Our Lady of Consolation	$1,525
Annunciation B.V.M. School	1,561
St. Anne School	1,575
Holy Name of Jesus School	1,595
Holy Redeemer Chinese Catholic School	1,600
Presentation B.V.M. Elementary School	1,600
St. Leo Elementary School	1,600
St. Matthew	1,600
Mother of Divine Grace	1,700
St. Thomas Aquinas School	1,700
St. Timothy Elementary	1,700
Our Lady of Mt. Carmel School	1,725
St. Martin De Porres School	1,735
St. Hugh School	1,745
Our Lady Star of the Sea	1,750
St. Adalbert Elementary School	1,750
Martin De Porres	1,800
Muhammad Islamic Academy	1,800
St. Anselm Elementary School	1,800
Gesu Catholic School	1,820
St. Mary of the Assumption School	1,835
Resurrection of Our Lord	1,845
Holy Family Elementary School	1,850
St. Richard	1,850
Visitation B.V.M. School	1,850
St. Albert the Great School	1,875
St. Raymond	1,875
St. Veronica Elementary School	1,890
Nativity B.V.M.	1,900
Our Lady Help of Christians	1,900
Our Mother of Sorrows School	1,900
St. Boniface Elementary School	1,900
St. Hilary of Poitiers School	1,900
St. Ignatius of Loyola School	1,900
St. Helena School	1,920
Stella Maris School	1,925
St. Casimir Elementary School	1,940
St. Martin De Porres Interparochial School	1,950
St. Rose of Lima Elementary School	1,950

Philadelphia (Elementary Schools) (cont.)

Al-Aqsa Islamic School	$1,952
Our Lady of Victory School	2,000
Our Mother of Sorrows School	2,000
Salafiyah Soc Islamic Day School	2,000
School of Moorish Science Temple	2,000
St. Bernard School	2,000
St. Charles Borromeo Catholic School	2,000
St. Cyprian	2,000
St. Francis de Sales School of Philadelphia	2,000
St. Josaphat Elementary School	2,000
Christ the King Elementary School	2,025
St. Cyril of Alexandria School	2,025
Our Lady of Hope Catholic School	2,080
Our Lady of Lourdes School	2,080
Holy Spirit Elementary School	2,095
Our Lady of Calvary School	2,100
Our Lady of Ransom School	2,100
Presentation B.V.M. Sch-Penn Wyne	2,100
St. Martin of Tours School	2,100
St. Nicholas of Tolentine	2,140
Epiphany of Our Lord School	2,150
Incarnation of Our Lord School	2,150
St. Bartholomew Elementary School	2,165
Ascension of Our Lord School	2,200
St. George School	2,200
St. Jerome Elementary School	2,200
St. Josaphat's Ukranian Catholic School	2,200
St. Laurentius School	2,200
St. Barnabas Elementary School	2,210
St. Bridget Parish School	2,227
Mater Dolorosa Elementary School	2,230
Bethel Baptist Academy	2,250
Cockrell Christian School	2,250
St. Joachim	2,250
St. Martha Elementary School	2,250
Holy Cross Elementary School	2,296
Our Lady of Angels	2,300
St. Joan of Arc Elementary School	2,300
Holy Innocents	2,325

Philadelphia (Elementary Schools) (cont.)

St. Cecilia Elementary School	$2,325
Our Lady of the Rosary School	2,350
St. Therese Parochial School	2,350
St. Katherine of Siena School	2,400
St. Peter the Apostle School	2,400
St. Athanasius/Immaculate Conception	2,453
St. Lucy School	2,475
Evelyn Graves Christian Academy	2,480
Trinity Christian School	2,485
Chalutzim Academy	2,500
Immaculate Heart of Mary	2,500
St. Aloysius Elementary School	2,500
St. Gabriel Elementary School	2,500
St. Joseph Elementary School	2,500*
St. William School	2,508*
Beulah Baptist Christian Day School	2,520
Fresh Fire Christian Academy of Learning	2,520
St. Christopher Elementary School	2,550
Montessori Genesis 2 School	2,555
St. Francis Xavier School	2,600
St. Philip Neri Elementary School	2,600
St. Mary's Interparochial	2,625
Broad Street Academy	2,630
St. Thomas Good Counsel School	2,650
Crusaders for Christ	2,700
Our Lady of Confidence Day School	2,700
Saints Clement-Irenaeus	2,700
St. Helena Elementary School	2,700
St. Katherine Day School	2,700
St. Monica Elementary School	2,700
The Islamic Education School	2,700
Maria Gardner Christian Academy	2,750
Crooked Places Made Straight Christian Academy	2,775
Holmesburg Baptist Christ School	2,776
Philadelphia Christian Academy	2,800
Saints Tabernacle Day School Christian Academy	2,800
Christ Academy	2,850
St. David School	2,850
Huntingdon Valley Christian Academy	2,860

Philadelphia (Elementary Schools) (cont.)

Eagle's Nest Christian Academy	$2,870
Quba Institute	2,900
Sojouner Truth SDA School	2,900
St. Ambrose School	2,904
Our Mother of Consolation School	2,910
American Christian School	2,921
St. Ambrose Elementary School	2,968
Al Mosheh Schule Pos. Ed	3,000
Christian Stronghold Academy	3,000
Christ's Christian Academy	3,000
Grace Temple Christian Academy	3,000
Growing Light Day School	3,000
Harold O. Davis Christian School	3,000
Marcus Garvey Shule Pos. Ed	3,000
New Testament Christian Academy	3,000
Triumph Christian School	3,000
St. Dominic	3,010
Our Lady of Fatima School	3,025
Calvary Christian Academy	3,100
Gospel of Grace Christian School	3,100
High St. Christian Academy	3,200
High St. Christian Academy	3,200
St. Benedict Elementary School	3,200
Sacred Heart of Jesus School	3,264
Larchwood School Inc.	3,290
Lehigh Christian Academy	3,300
Wynfield Primary Academy	3,300
Cedar Grove Christian Academy Lower School	3,319
Calvary Temple Christian Academy	3,408
West Oak Lane Christian Academy	3,410
Philadelphia Children's School—Waldorf Inspired Education	3,445
Ivy Leaf School (Lower School)	3,450
Messiah Early Childhood Center	3,500
Sanctuary Christian Academy	3,500
Deliverance Evangelistic Christian Academy & Daycare	3,536
Cornerstone Christian Academy	3,583
Immanuel Lutheran School	3,600
Abdul Hakim Family Day Care School	3,625
Redeemer Lutheran School	3,665

Philadelphia (Elementary Schools) (cont.)

Lotus Academy	$3,690
Valley Christian School	3,700
Timothy Academy	3,721
Hope Church School	3,750
Spruce Hill Christian School	3,775
St. Donato Elementary School	3,800
Cecilian Academy	4,000
St. James School	4,250
Woodbine Academy	4,300
Blair Christian Academy	4,400
St. Barnabas Episcopal School	4,750
Christian Tabernacle Academy	5,000
Direct Connection Institute for Learning	5,000
Direct Connection Institute for Learning	5,200
Federation Day Care Services	5,280
Phil-Mont Christian School-Roxborough	5,400
Politz Hebrew Academy	5,416
Fern Rock	5,500
Frankford Friends School	5,700
Project Learn School	6,675
Norwood-Fontbonne Academy	6,985
Waldron Mercy	7,100
Germantown Montessori School	7,500
Holy Child Academy	7,725
Greene Street Friends School	8,066
Sister Clara Muhammad School	8,750
Germantown Friends School	10,565
Philadelphia School	10,645
Maternity B.V.M.	11,000
St. Peter's School	12,215
Torah Academy	12,300
Friends Central School	12,975
Chestnut Hill Academy	13,700
Friends Select School	14,225
Abington Friends School	14,600
Stratford Friends School	19,350

*Median cost, $2,504, falls between these two values.

Philadelphia (High Schools)

Muhammad Islamic Academy	$1,800
Berean Bible Christian School	2,145
Evelyn Graves Christian Academy	2,480
Eagle's Nest Christian Academy	2,870
Calvary Christian Acad.	3,100
Gospel of Grace Christian School	3,100
Quba Institute	3,200
Cardinal Dougherty High School	3,500
Archbishop Carroll High School	3,520
Archbishop Prendergast High School	3,520
Father Judge High School	3,520
Northeast Catholic High School	3,520
St. Hubert's Catholic High School For Girls	3,520
Archbishop Ryan High School	3,651
Archbishop Ryan High School	3,700
John W. Hallahan High School	3,700
Roman Catholic High School	3,705
City Center Academy	3,800
Little Flower Catholic High School for Girls	3,872
City Center Academy	3,900
Mercy Vocational High School	3,910
Grace Temple Christian Academy	4,000
Huntingdon Valley Christian Academy	4,147
International Christian High School	4,250
Delaware Valley High School	4,300
Bishop McDevitt High School	4,310*
John W. Hallahan High School	4,310
Monsignor Bonnor High School	4,310
St. John Neumann High School	4,310
St. Maria Goretti High School	4,310
American Christian School	4,400
Philadelphia Christian Academy (Cottman Ave.)	4,500
Rittenhouse Academy	4,500
Student Ed Ct & Del Vly High School	4,640
West Catholic High School	4,705
Hope Church School	4,750
Blair Christian Academy	4,950
Nazareth Academy	5,700
St. Basil Academy	5,900

Philadelphia (High Schools) (cont.)

Nazareth Academy High School	$6,000
Yeshiva Bircnas Chaim	6,400
Philadelphia Mennonite High School	6,500
Phil-Mont Christian School-Roxborough	6,721
Sister Clara Muhammad School	8,750
Merion Mercy Academy	9,400
Lasalle College High School	9,600
Talmudical Yeshiva Of Philadelphia	10,500
St. Joseph's Preparatory School	11,700
Torah Academy	12,300
Germantown Friends School	15,585
Friends Select School	16,070
Springside School	16,900
Chestnut Hill Academy	17,100
Crefeld School	17,550

*Median cost.

SOURCE: Tuition data were obtained from the Children's Scholarship Fund and through direct contact with the private schools. Since tuition often varies by grade level, tuition indicated may be the average tuition paid by students at the school.

12. Markets and Urban Schooling: What Choice-Driven Competition Is Doing, and How to Make It Do More

Frederick M. Hess

For decades there has been widespread agreement that America's urban school systems are in crisis. Paralyzed by bureaucracy, politics, teachers unions, and racial conflict, three decades worth of urban educational leaders have made precious little progress in combating horrendous drop-out rates, abysmal test scores, or school safety.

Efforts to improve urban schooling through reforms targeting pedagogy, curriculum, evaluation, teacher preparation, and school governance have consistently failed to produce the desired results. During the 1990s, frustration with the inability of such efforts to produce the desired results led to the consideration of increasingly radical remedies. The most visible and consequential of these has been choice-based reform.

Choice-based reform has been received most warmly in urban areas where polling shows that school vouchers are now supported by significant majorities of African-Americans and the urban poor. Most of the choice-based activity has taken place in urban systems, both because of frustration with the condition of these systems and because they provide a dense enough network of private schools, buildings, educators, students, and transportation to make an education market feasible.

Proponents argue that educational competition sparked by choice-based reform will provide the same kind of benefits for America's schools that competition has provided in auto manufacturing, banking, or telecommunications. The claim is particularly appealing in those urban school districts where success through more conventional reforms has proved so elusive.

247

Of course, some extremist critics respond by arguing that schools are so fundamentally different from most sectors that competition will not work as intended. More thoughtful critics highlight the problems that can result from half-baked efforts at marketization, as in the case of California's energy deregulation, or when market structures are introduced without careful thought as to the dynamics and context of a sector, as in the case of HMOs or the nascent market economies of Russia or Eastern Europe. In truth, education does pose some particular challenges as a market good, but we won't be pursuing that point in this particular chapter.[1]

Despite its significance, this dispute has received surprisingly little scholarly attention in the American context. The fact is that we just don't know very much about how public schools actually respond to market competition. Some researchers have sought to consider the effect of various measures of educational competition on student performance and have suggested they improve overall efficacy, though some have challenged their conclusions.[2] Regardless of one's thoughts on these sophisticated and important efforts, they cannot shed light on the question of how educators, school officials, or communities respond to educational competition—or what that portends for the educational enterprise in both the short and long term. I have been engaged in some of this work, along with various colleagues, in a number of locales.[3]

Will competition reshape urban schooling as proponents hope, or is public schooling a sector somehow immune to market forces? Part of the answer is simple. The radical naysayers are wrong when they declare that competition cannot bring dramatic and positive change to urban schooling. However, and this critical point is too often overlooked, such change will require significant complementary reforms that serve to unleash the full power of market pressures so as to create meaningful competition, to permit educators to respond as real competitors, and to foster a productive market environment. Until such steps are taken, the primary changes from choice-induced pressure will be limited and driven in large part by political dynamics. Many of these changes will prove beneficial and will mark an incremental improvement in urban schooling, but they are likely to fall far short of the radical promise of transformative market-driven change.

248

The Promise of Markets

Markets have the ability to address these structural problems in a systemic fashion that is beyond the purview of the kind of "capacity building" and pedagogical tinkering favored by most conventional education reformers. Market competition both compels officials and managers to make hard choices and strengthens their resolve when they confront employees or external constituencies unhappy with the requisite action. The risk of being driven out of business, of losing one's position and perks, is a wonderful device for keeping decisionmakers focused.

A hard look at the promise and limits of competition is imperative. It makes clear that anemic choice programs are unlikely to drive the kind of transformative change that urban schooling requires. Let's not fool ourselves and pretend half-measures are satisfactory. Those who suggest that a smattering of charter schools, that a handful of school vouchers, or that the public choice provision of No Child Left Behind are sufficient to force systemic improvement are allowing their enthusiasm to get the best of them.

Because market competition is normally observed in the context of a private sector dominated by for-profit firms, it is natural to assume that markets always operate in such a fashion. However, such an assumption may be mistaken. If the self-interest of producers does not compel them to satisfy consumer desires or if they lack the tools to respond to competitors, then markets may not produce the anticipated results short of more fundamental change.

Markets work to the degree that they hurt. Painless markets are ineffective markets. The kinds of changes we've seen in places like Milwaukee and Mesa and Dayton are generally positive and constructive, but they are not sufficient to stem the ongoing failure that is urban schooling or to drive the kind of systemic improvement that will ensure every child is educated in an effective school. The ability of markets to compel constructive behavior is limited by a number of institutional constraints that shape the impact of educational competition in urban systems. Until these are addressed, even efforts to enhance the actual threat posed by choice-based reform will enjoy only limited success.

Political Incentives

Public school systems are governed by public officials guided by the dictates of public opinion and the pressures of concentrated constituencies. Such officials have little incentive to force wrenching changes that may upset constituencies or resistant subordinates. Leaders of public and private firms are motivated by very different incentive structures. Private-sector leaders are ultimately held responsible for profitability, with executives rewarded by boards of directors and shareholders for bottom-line performance. In the public sector, there are no owners with an analogous investment. Rather, systems are led by public officials who are accountable to voters, who may disagree about how to measure organizational performance, or who may even have some concerns they rate more highly than measured outcomes. Moreover, as schools are public bodies funded by public dollars, effective political leaders can blunt a competitive threat simply by a successful appeal to the legislature.

Of course, a loss of students or of funding can present a real black eye, giving public officials a strong incentive to respond. However, we need to understand that they're acting to blunt an embarrassment—rather than to maximize organizational productivity, timeliness, or quality—which also means they're likely to bring a halt to their efforts as soon as the public appears satisfied or when the complaints of irate constituencies grow too loud. Because public systems are governed by webs of regulations and civil service restrictions intended to protect the vulnerable and guard against the misuse of authority, it is very difficult for officials to pursue structural change. Especially given incentives to avoid antagonizing the politically active unions and advocacy groups invested in existing rules and procedures, leadership will generally choose to produce change by working around the edges of the existing system rather than by tackling fundamental restructuring.

In particular, it is important to recognize that officials in traditional school districts govern schools with a culture premised upon intrinsic motivation, in which extrinsic incentives are often viewed as alien and in which current high performers are willing to exert tremendous effort despite the lack of selective rewards. In such an environment, it is tempting to rely upon creating opportunities for the committed few, rather than seeking to demand fundamental change from the resistant many.

A key result is that school systems are likely to respond to competition by allowing individual teachers and principals to do new things rather than by overhauling current practice. The political dynamic makes it much more palatable to tack on new programs or to open new, specialized schools than to pursue wrenching change. Consequently, competition is likely to produce add-ons and efforts to satisfy particular demands rather than the kind of renewed focus on core competency that is typically thought to mark firms that respond effectively to competition.

Urban School Systems

A second key question is how leaders are able to respond when the pinch of competition is sufficiently intense. Even those board members or administrators who wish to reengineer an urban system have a limited capacity to do so. They confront strong and alert political constituencies that can use state or federal legislation and courtrooms to trump district efforts; have uneven monitoring systems; have few tools with which to reward or sanction employees; have little ability to hire their own personnel; have little or no usable information on cost structures or district productivity; and they rely on a primitive, patchwork infrastructure in which both personnel systems and information technology seem as if they were designed to frustrate efforts at effective management.

The crucial point is that many of the constraints on urban school systems are *not controlled by district officials or educators*. Bureaucratic hiring guidelines, licensure provisions limiting their ability to hire teachers or administrators, mandated salary schedules, mandates on serving particular populations, class-size mandates—each of these constraints is generally set at the state level, meaning that even motivated officials seeking to address competitive pressures cannot alter them. Of course, it is true that district officials will have renewed incentive to lobby state officials to alter archaic rules and to provide new flexibility, but this is a rather pathetic response to meaningful pressure.

The Importance of Individual Incentives

Finally, harnessing the power of markets requires that we not delude ourselves as to how and why competitive pressure works. A moment's reflection on urban education suggests some glaring problems in casually assuming that voucher or charter competition will encourage traditional district educators to struggle to maintain or add enrollment. The problem is that public school teachers and

251

principals claim little or no benefit from working to attract more students. Benefits to the system will be diffused over thousands of teachers, while the costs of any efforts will be borne solely by the teacher.

Take an elementary teacher who responds to competition by working an extra 10 hours a week on developing lesson plans and grading. If the teacher wanted to spend the 10 extra hours on teaching, there was previously nothing stopping him from doing so. So the additional personal sacrifice is made under duress, not by choice. The theory is that the teacher's exertions will improve student satisfaction and performance, boosting the attractiveness of the school, increasing its enrollment, and thereby enhancing his job security. In truth, the teacher's efforts are unlikely to impact the decision of more than a few families, and the decision of a few extra families to remain in the public schools rather than switch to other schools is highly unlikely to have a significant impact on the fiscal health of the district, and has only the tiniest chance of impacting the position of this particular teacher. Consequently, there is little rational incentive to alter one's behavior.

The same challenge holds everywhere, but most nonprofits and private firms address it by rewarding employees individually. An accountant at Gillette does not work hard because she thinks her effort will significantly affect the company's annual performance, but because she will be selectively sanctioned or rewarded on the basis of her personal efforts. It is those selective incentives that drive self-interest in large organizations—not vague links between organizational performance and individual prospects.

Charter Schooling and School Vouchers

Various kinds of choice-based arrangements can produce competition, with the two most common proposals being school vouchers and charter schooling. Although the details vary dramatically from one state or locale to the next, both plans are thought to potentially foster competitive pressure by redirecting educational resources from traditional district schools.

In an unregulated voucher system, the state simply provides an amount of funding for each child that each family is then free to spend on the school of its choice. In practice, as enacted—most dramatically in Milwaukee, and later in Cleveland and Florida and

Colorado—publicly funded voucher programs include an array of restrictions on participating students and schools. Programs have limited availability of vouchers only to low-income children or to students who attend low-performing schools, have only made vouchers worth a portion of the amount spent on each pupil in the public school system, have restricted the kinds of private schools permitted to accept vouchers, have required that schools accepting voucher students not selectively admit applicants, and so on.

Whereas voucher programs theoretically reduce the state to nothing more than a funder of education, the aims of charter schooling are less revolutionary. Charter schooling challenges the traditional practice of having school boards oversee all public schools in a geographic district. Instead, the state legislature designates a body (or bodies) that can grant school operators a "charter" to run a particular school. Because their existence depends on this grant from the state, charter schools are regarded as "public" schools subject to conventional regulations and constraints. Therefore, unlike private schools, charter schools must abide by the same restrictions on religion as public schools, cannot charge tuition, cannot selectively admit students, and are potentially subject to a host of regulations on matters ranging from curriculum to teacher salaries. Due largely to the appeal of these safeguards, charter schooling has grown by leaps and bounds, though it shows some signs of slowing.

In theory, school vouchers are likely to produce the most profound competitive effects, by creating the opportunity for the greatest expansion in potential providers and minimizing regulation on providers, while charter schooling is limited in the number of potential providers and in their operational flexibility. In practice, programs do not necessarily fit this neat continuum. For instance, Arizona and Michigan currently operate charter programs that represent a far more radical shift than the circumscribed voucher programs in Florida and Cleveland. The uncertain legal status of voucher schooling and the fact that per-pupil funding tended to be significantly lower than for students in charter schooling retarded the expansion of potential suppliers, while the more stable support for charter schooling and more generous funding levels led to a dramatic expansion of charter school providers and the entrance of large-scale, for-profit ventures like Edison Schools and National Heritage Academies.

Effects of Competition Thus Far

What have been the results of educational competition in urban communities? While choice proponents parse every change in policy or behavior for evidence that districts are responding to competition, there is little evidence that districts are restructuring or are being pushed by market pressures to overhaul their operations in a way familiar to observers of the private sector. There is widespread evidence of more narrowly cast activity—such as offering new programs to match the services of charter schools or increasing public outreach—but these efforts tend to be additions superimposed atop existing inefficiencies. These behaviors are becoming more common, as districts learn from one another and as entrepreurial behavior is—however slowly—sporadically taking root.

Meanwhile, though critics worry that school choice is "siphoning money from the communities and public schools that need it the most," there is little evidence that public educators have been given much to worry about so far. In fact, given that many urban districts were coping with growing enrollments, faculty shortages, and facilities constraints, a number of public school officials termed choice programs a useful "safety valve" that helped alleviate overcrowding.

Competition is often imagined as a mighty bulldozer, flattening ineffective firms and compelling others to become more efficient and effective. In the vast majority of urban locales where charters or vouchers have emerged, little of note has occurred. Even in the districts where the response has been greatest, in locales like Milwaukee, Dayton, Mesa, and Philadelphia there has been little evidence of such change. Competition has produced changes in both the political environment and in district behaviors, but there's precious little evidence of districts or schools substantially altering governance, management, or operations or of leaders pushing to increase organizational productivity or efficiency in systematic ways. Competitive effects have been more muted and more oriented to public opinion than the market metaphor might anticipate, but it suggests how limited markets might yield more significant results—and it highlights the steps we need to contemplate if we are serious about using markets as an engine to fundamentally reshape urban education.

When confronted with competition, districts do tend to launch popular programs, advertise themselves and their services, and lash out at their competitors. In some districts, most noticeably the case of

Milwaukee, a political counterweight to the teacher union emerged. When caught in the glare of public frustration, Milwaukee's union demonstrated some willingness to help rehabilitate its standing by agreeing to relax procedural handcuffs. Under duress, officials seek to bolster their political position by enhancing public relations and offering more appealing services, while district defenders also lashed out at system critics in an effort to undermine their legitimacy.

To date, most district change has been driven by politically motivated officials wrestling with balky systems. The largest effects of choice—the ones that have occasioned much notice in the case of Milwaukee or Dayton or Philadelphia—are the ability to change the political context. In these locales, the publicity produced by choice programs and student flight ratcheted up the pressure on political officials and the district leadership, strengthened the hand of radical reformers, and enabled officials to take firm action in the face of continued resistance. There's a real irony here—the advocates of choice-based reform like to use the language of the market, but they've been most effective to driving improvement when the political pressures unleashed by choice have helped to create new opportunities for healthy reform or to empower reformist public officials. Seeking to offer some response, but unwilling to frontally challenge the status quo, elected officials and administrators often react to empowering individual entrepreneurs to exploit new opportunities. There is little evidence that competition has led officials to bulldoze away inefficiencies or push systematic efforts to reform policy or improve practice. After all, even in these districts, there is little evidence that district officials have the incentive or the ability to mount aggressive assaults on organizational culture or procedure. However, under sufficient duress, district leadership has taken steps to chip away at the system's bureaucracy, creating holes for a handful of intrinsically motivated educators.

The response of district schools to choice-induced competition, to date, has generally taken several forms. Although each of these changes is significant, none promises the relentless commitment to organizational improvement that we generally presume when thinking about the promise that markets will "raise all boats."

First, individual schools, when subjected to particularly intense pressure, will focus more sharply on improving assessed outcomes. Public embarrassment and self-preservation will make it easier for principals and teachers to demand increased effort and performance from their peers.

Second, systems and schools also increase their focus on public outreach, on advertising their services, and on customer service. For anyone who has experience with urban school systems, even small improvements in this area are most welcome.

Third, when faced with sufficient pressure, district officials create new opportunities for entrepreneurial educators to launch new schools and programs, such as Montessori or language schools. They do this both to forestall defection and to reassure the community that the district is committed to delivering quality. This is a significant change. Entrepreneurial public educators have long been regarded as "difficult" or "disruptive," which is why many have been attracted to charter schooling. Therefore, it is significant that the need to attract families or demonstrate district energy has pressed some district leaders to focus on the strengths of these educators rather than on the headaches that their energy or disregard for standard procedure may generate. In many districts, far-sighted board members or superintendents have served as the patrons of entrepreneurial principals and helped to engineer the necessary agreements.

Fourth, when competition generates sufficient notice or pressure, the teachers' union leadership can feel pressed to agree to compromises that it had previously deemed unacceptable. To date, in districts like Boston and Milwaukee, unions have generally done this through individual memoranda of understanding (MOUs) rather than by agreeing to alter the collective bargaining agreement. The significance, of course, is that it is relatively easy for unions to back away from MOUs once the immediate crisis has cleared. In most industries, union concessions are written directly into the contract, so that they cannot be readily yanked away and so that they form the new status quo for subsequent negotiations.

Finally, local educational politics can gain new clarity and urgency. Embarrassing enrollment losses or the attention garnered by choice-related news coverage can create a sense of crisis that opens a window for aggressive reformers. Market pressures prompted the emergence of political coalitions in Milwaukee and Dayton that enhanced the sense of local educational "crisis" and spurred efforts to respond appropriately. Such pressure can produce district and union decisions that ease the way for entrepreneurs to provide new schools, new services, and even radical new leadership. The political developments can also clarify the educational debate and create a clear impetus for a reform coalition to confront the conventional interests.

There is also a type of response that probably deserves to be regarded as destructive: the tendency of system supporters to focus more on lashing out at choice proponents than on pursuing system change. Competition proponents tend to dismiss this reaction as expected and irrelevant. That is a mistake. Because education is funded with public monies, which may follow students to varying degrees at the whim of state legislators, efforts to delegitimize choice proponents or to curry favor with legislators can serve to blunt the need to mount a more constructive response to competitive pressure. The issue is precisely that which arises when the automotive or steel sectors plead for protection against foreign competition. To the extent that they can win governmental action that reduces the threat or protects their revenue stream, the pressure to improve performance or cut costs is alleviated. This is exactly what happens in schooling when traditional district schools win legislative action that caps the number of potential choice students, reduces the financial hit from lost students, alters funding formulae to cushion schools, or otherwise reduces the urgency of responding to competition.

The effects evident to date are not the substantive changes anticipated by those who overpromised what choice would yield and breezily suggested that competition would compel public systems to get "better." If one takes as a guide how quickly and devastatingly competition struck the radio industry in the 1920s, the electronics industry in the 1960s, the airline industry in the 1980s, or the financial services and telecommunications industries in the 1990s, the disparity between these cases and those of competition becomes stark indeed. At the same time, there is evidence that even limited competition has the potential to provoke significant reactions from public school systems.

Understanding the Effects of Education Competition

Why have we not generally seen a more substantial competitive response? First, it's vital to keep in mind that the competition bred by even these widely hailed experiments was rather minimal. A limited number of students were involved, potential districts losses were generally modest, and legal and political forces helped to moderate the threat and constrict the development of new competitors. Political and legal uncertainty also helped to deter entrepreneurs. All of this served to limit the actual and potential threat posed by choice programs.

257

In particular, state legislators and education officials have taken a number of actions that have blunted the competitive threat and alleviated the pressure on choice schools to respond. Many states have adopted program caps on charter school or voucher programs, which have served to limit the potential loss of enrollment. States have funding rules that generally smooth out the funding losses associated with lost enrollment over a multiyear period and that generally provide for districts to retain between 20 percent and 70 percent of per-pupil funding for each student they lose to a charter or voucher school. Third, states have generally provided little or no funding for the start-up expenses or capital needs of charter or voucher schools, limiting the development of potential competition. Fourth, some states, such as Wisconsin, have even modified their funding formulas so that students lost to choice schools no longer produce a one-for-one reduction in state aid to the district the child exits. While each of these actions can be justified and understood on its own merits, it is important that all concerned realize how they have served to reduce the pressure on districts or schools to respond to nascent markets.

Although some observers might suggest that these kinds of limits alone are to blame for the minimal effects of competition, the truth is that many choice proponents have argued that even limited programs would spur radical improvement. Consequently, acknowledging the significance of these constraints is an important and useful caution. The results should provide a useful caution to choice proponents. Although districts were prompted to take some actions, short of larger changes, it is unlikely that competition will deliver on its full promise. Why?

Imagine if CEOs of firms like Dell Computer or General Electric faced a market in which their revenues barely depended on attracting or losing customers, if the pressure of competition could always be trumped by successful efforts to glean subsidies from the government, if they possessed only sparse information on the performance of personnel, if they lacked the ability to fire or demote most employees, and if they knew potential competitors were being deterred or stamped out by political and legal forces.

Insulated School Systems

Organizational protections and routines insulate system officials and educators from competition. As an *anti*-voucher Milwaukee school board member argued in 1999, "The bureaucrats who come out of the schools of education don't intend to be affected by competition. They are going to concede 5,000 students, or even 25,000 students, simply because they are insulated within the walls of a bureaucracy that need not respond to competition." The claim is not outrageous. Given the rules, regulations, contracts, and statutes governing competition, educators may very well try to ride out even increasing levels of competitive pressure for years to come.

Unfortunately, for all their theoretical elegance, market analyses of educational competition have been hobbled by a lack of understanding for the political and organizational arrangements that govern schooling and dictate the market context. In the case of choice-based proposals, where most of the market threat is anticipatory rather than existent, it matters that insulation from sanctions leaves educators able and willing to ignore such pressure. Educator hostility is significant because public educators have substantial resources of legitimacy and goodwill on which to draw. If public educators answer competition by marshaling public opinion or mounting legal challenges, they may win statutory or judicial protections that insulate the schools from the threat posed by choice programs. This notion of political response should be disconcerting to those who see markets as irresistible and as a means for bypassing the frustrations of educational politics.

A decade-long surge in enrollment and continuing increases in education spending have also buffered urban school systems from the effects of competition. Meanwhile, annual teacher turnover of 10 percent or more and a desperate need for teachers in a number of critical shortage areas has ensured that the jobs of urban teachers have been well-protected even when competition has affected enrollments. Finally, crumbling facilities and crowded classrooms have prompted more than one district official to deem choice schools as helpful by alleviating classroom crowding or the need for capital expenditures.

Making Markets Matter

Our present course does not produce the relentless, insatiable pressure of a market characterized by avaricious executives, interpretable consumer criteria, managerial tools, and a significant competitive threat. Instead, what we have created is more of a political market. Heightened competitive pressure puts public officials in harm's way, creating new room for reform activity, serving as a circuit breaker when student flight becomes severe enough, and providing political cover to agents of change.

This is not a bad thing. It presents real advantages when compared with the status quo and I don't mean to suggest otherwise. However, it will not summon the market's invisible hand to steadily, relentlessly push schools to improve. Rather, once crisis is abated, matters are likely to settle back to business as usual—albeit with more children able to use choice-based alternatives.

Don't misunderstand me. This is a reasonable course, but one unlikely to deliver the radical transformation that many desire competition to deliver. We ought not imagine that piecemeal competition will magically transform those schools and districts that today ill-serve too many urban students. If we want competition to force systematic change, we must contemplate additional measures. The most effective way to do this is by responding to the absence of competitive pressure and by answering the political and organizational constraints discussed earlier. How might we do this?

Increasing Competitive Pressure

The scope of district response will depend in large part on how much competitive pressure exists. Increasing pressure generally means increasing the number of students able to leave the public schools or the amount of money that schools may lose if students leave. The threat posed by choice plans has generally been mild. We can accelerate competition by increasing the number of choice schools, the size of these schools, or the financial loss that public systems suffer when they lose enrollment. Eliminating caps on voucher program enrollment or the number of permitted charter schools, or providing generous financing or support for start-up costs, is likely to foster significant supply-side expansion. However, losing students will only give district schools pause if the financial losses are commensurate; if the district loses students but comes out financially even or ahead, it is easy for district educators to shrug off any losses. Having 100 percent of per-pupil spending immediately follow a student to her new school, while it poses real concerns about logistics and the welfare of students who remain behind, clearly ramps up the incentives for educators to respond.

Early efforts to launch choice schools benefited from the ability to draw on a large supply of frustrated educators and an array of funders eager to demonstrate viability of school choice or fund new models of schooling. Although philanthropies are happy to seed models or promote new initiatives, they are generally much less willing to support ongoing operations. Meanwhile, existing charter schools have taken advantage of the "low-hanging fruit," those frustrated teachers and principals who were looking to escape their traditional public schools. Continuing efforts will have to draw on new sources of support. Increasing competitive pressure demands a substantial increase in either the number of new schools or their size. Requirements that raise barriers to entry—by making entrepreneurship more costly or problematic—will serve to limit capacity expansion. One key to expanding private-sector capacity is likely to be the role of for-profit operators. It is the for-profit educators who have the most straightforward interest in adding capacity. They are educators most likely to open big schools and establish chains of schools, because their bottom-line concern with profitability will press them to seek to minimize costs and increase their customer base. For-profit educators have a major advantage in seeking to open or expand schools because they can access the capital markets for necessary support.

Empowering Districts to Respond

Competitive response requires that decisionmakers be motivated to worry more about outcomes and less about the political consequences of their decisions. One possible avenue to doing this is to enhance the role of for-profit or other nonstate providers of educational services. Within the conventional public sector, however, simply placing such officials in a market or quasi-market does not change the fact that they have strong incentives to move cautiously and to adopt procedures that minimize controversy and do not upset vocal constituencies. Effective competition needs to link the personal and professional self-interest of officials and managers to their competitive performance. We need to begin rewarding and sanctioning executives and managers on the basis of competitive performance. If the job security, the salaries, and the prospects of central administrators and principals were linked more tightly to changes in enrollment, self-interest would induce them to compete for students. Of

261

course, such systems must be crafted with care and attention to unintended side effects. For instance, some students are more troublesome or more expensive than others—and will therefore be pursued more or less avidly—and appropriate adjustments would be necessary.

In many ways, addressing the constraints on urban school systems overlaps with the steps that will help to address the lack of individual incentives that hamper the ability even of motivated superintendents and principals to drive an effective competitive response. After all, urban school systems are a managerial nightmare, ossified under the weight of rules, procedures, contractual language, and local politicking. Whatever threat an organization faces, leaders cannot respond unless they have the ability to do so. Administrative energy can be focused more tightly on productivity and performance by making available more sophisticated and more accessible information systems. Particularly effective will be mechanisms that effectively track student enrollment and school market performance, especially if they are linked to incentives that prompt administrators to treat the data seriously. Once administrators have information on market performance and have incentives to care, they can act more effectively if they are empowered to fire, promote, reward, pay, and monitor teachers. The more discretion administrators have, the larger the impact of such changes will be. Reform in this area requires changes in collective bargaining agreements at the district and state level as well as changes to state statutes governing hiring, firing, compensation, and operations. Absent such tools, administrators must rely on personal charm and informal agreements to drive organizational improvement. Relaxing certification requirements, recruiting nontraditional educators more aggressively, and permitting administrators to readily reward teachers for performance will help attract more entrepreneurial personnel into the profession. An increase in the number of potential teachers will also give educators more reason to fear for their jobs, making them more receptive to administrative direction.

Conclusion

Truly using competition to transform urban schooling requires creating a market characterized by substantial competition, harnessing the self-interest of individuals to their performance, and giving individuals the tools necessary to act effectively. Schools in such a world will be more effective, productive, focused, and responsive than are today's oft-troubled urban schools. It is not that competition alone will magically make schools better, which is the derisive formulation that conventional education reformers sometimes use when critiquing choice-based reform. It is that market forces will ruthlessly focus educators on what needs to be done and will empower them to make the unpopular decisions that real improvement requires.

Of course, the changes required for meaningful competition do risk alienating many educators traditionally regarded as inspirational and selfless icons and fostering a school culture alien to our educational heritage. Betting on markets is a decision to trade an uneven system marked by the ministrations of the well-intentioned for the more reliable efforts of those guided by self-interest and market signals. This is not simply a matter of "improving" schools; it is a decision to alter the nature and culture of K–12 education. Although the trade is likely to produce real benefits, it is not a casual one.

Unleashing transformative competition will require significantly altering public education. Many market proponents finesse the inevitable tradeoffs, disavowing any interest in the harsher aspects of competition while promising that choice-induced competition will deliver systemic improvement. Proponents cannot have it both ways; they must forego claims of promoting systemic improvement or work to create real markets. This will prove immeasurably frustrating to many choice proponents, who have long viewed choice-based reform as a way to cut the Gordion knot of school reform and avoid the need to engage in prolonged conflict with the education establishment and vested interests on an issue-by-issue basis. Such an easy resolution is not to be.

The statutes, bureaucracy, and procedural routines that hamper school officials are central to the structure of urban districts. Too often the educational debate proceeds as if those discussing educational markets were in one room and those discussing the political constraints on school reform were in another. In fact, educational competition cannot be divorced from discussions about testing, teacher certification, school district governance, educational administration, or other frustrating conversations that many school choice proponents have long wished to avoid. In the end, the fate of educational markets, for good or ill, is intertwined with broader issues of schools and schooling.

Notes

1. For a discussion of those challenges, see Chapter 2 of Frederick M. Hess, *Revolution at the Margins: The Impact of Competition on Urban School Systems* (Washington: Brookings Institution, 2002).

2. The most prominent efforts to demonstrate that competition from voucher schools or charter schools leads to improvement in the performance of traditional public schools are those by Jay P. Greene, *An Evaluation of the Florida A-Plus Accountability and School Choice Program* (New York: Manhattan Institute: 2001); and Caroline M. Hoxby, "School Choice and School Productivity (Or, Could School Choice Be a Tide That Lifts All Boats?)," NBER Working Paper No. 8873, Cambridge, Mass., National Bureau of Economic Research, 2002. Hoxby has also used innovative techniques to make a compelling case that the presence of multiple local school districts creates competitive pressures that increase efficiency and performance. See Caroline M. Hoxby, "Does Competition Among Public Schools Benefit Students and Taxpayers?" *American Economic Review* 90 (2000): 1209–1238; and Caroline M. Hoxby, "Do Private Schools Provide Competition for Public Schools?" NBER Working Paper No. 4978, Cambridge, Mass., National Bureau of Economic Research, 1994. It is worth noting that other researchers have not found such effects in analyzing the data for individual states. See William L. Sander "Private Schools and Public School Achievement," *Journal of Human Resources* 34 (1999): 697–709; and Kevin B. Smith, and Kenneth J. Meier, *The Case Against School Choice: Politics, Markets, and Fools* (Armonk, N.Y.: M. E. Sharpe, 1995).

3. My previous empirical work examining how school districts respond to competition can be found in Frederick M. Hess, *Revolution at the Margins: The Impact of Competition on Urban School Systems* (Washington: Brookings Institution, 2002); Frederick M. Hess, "Hints of the Pick-axe: Competition and Public Schooling in Milwaukee," in *Charters, Vouchers, and Public Education*, ed. P. Peterson and D. Campbell (Washington: Brookings Institution, 2001); Frederick M. Hess and David L. Leal, "Quality, Race, and the Urban Education Marketplace," *Urban Affairs Review* 37, no. 2 (2001): 249–266; Frederick M. Hess, Robert Maranto, and Scott Milliman, "Little Districts in Big Trouble: How Four Arizona School Systems Responded to Charter Competition," *Teachers College Record* 103, no. 6 (2001): 1102–1124; Frederick M. Hess, Robert Maranto, and Scott Milliman, "Coping with Competition: The Impact of Charter Schooling on Public School Outreach in Arizona," *Policy Studies Journal* 29, no. 3 (2001): 388–404; Frederick M. Hess, Robert Maranto, and Scott Milliman, "Responding to Competition: School Leaders and School Culture" in *Charters, Vouchers, and Public Education*, ed. P. Peterson and D. Campbell (Washington: Brookings Institution, 2001); and Frederick M. Hess and Patrick McGuinn, "Muffled by the Din: The Competitive Noneffects of the Cleveland Voucher Program," *Teachers College Record* 104, no. 4 (2002): 727–764.

13. How Markets Affect Quality: Testing a Theory of Market Education against the International Evidence

Andrew J. Coulson

Introduction

In a previous publication, I presented a comparative analysis of education systems from classical Greece to the modern United States.[1] The purpose of that investigation was to look for patterns in the performance of alternative school management and funding mechanisms that persisted across time and place. In particular, three sorts of comparative observations were made:

- Observations of similar education systems operating in distinctly different cultural and economic settings
- Observations of different education systems operating in similar cultural and economic settings
- Observations of changes in educational conditions and outcomes as particular societies shifted from one sort of education system to another

Such a broad historical and international study did not, of course, permit the formulation of a highly elaborated or mathematically precise theory of comparative school governance. It did, however, suggest that some types of school systems are indeed better at serving the public than others. In trying to identify the critical ingredients of those superior school systems, I enumerated a short list of features that those systems tended to share. From this list, and the discussion that accompanied it, it is possible to impute rough predictions about the expected behavior of school systems (based on whether or not they share the features in question).

From that earlier work, and the predictions that follow from it, I have argued elsewhere that a particular arrangement of education tax credits should be preferred to both our current system of public schooling and to alternative market-inspired education reforms.[2]

This chapter attempts to test the validity of my earlier predictions and the argument for education tax credits by vetting them against a body of empirical findings not used in the original study.[3] The findings in question are drawn from the international econometric literature on private versus public schooling in less developed countries. This data set is particularly valuable because of the broad spectrum of governance and funding systems in place both within and among the subject countries.

Immediately following this introduction is a brief summary of the features I have alleged to be associated with superior school system performance, and a short list of predictions that follow from them. The subsequent section, which is the main body of the chapter, distills the international evidence comparing alternative forms of public and private schooling in less developed nations. Every effort was made to ensure the comprehensiveness of this research summary, but some studies of interest could not be considered because they were not obtained (or were not obtainable) within the time frame of this project, while others could simply have been missed. These omitted papers, and any new contributions to the field, may be considered in a subsequent revision of this investigation.

Following the presentation of findings is a discussion of the patterns that emerge from the literature, and an evaluation of the validity of the subject predictions. Finally, my earlier arguments in favor of education tax credits are evaluated in light of the evidence presented below.

Effective School Systems: Features and Predictions

Features

In 1999, I suggested that the historically most effective education systems tended to share most or all of the following five features: choice and direct financial responsibility for parents, and freedom, competition, and the profit motive for schools. For concision, this will be referred to simply as FFT (the Five Feature Theory) for the remainder of this chapter.

The requirement that individual parents decide what and by whom their children are taught is based on two concerns. First, it is argued that parents have historically made better decisions regarding their own children's education than appointed or elected officials have made on their behalf. Second, government school systems offering a uniform curriculum are claimed to have caused more social conflict than have parent-driven education markets.[4]

The direct payment of tuition by parents is alleged to encourage parental involvement, reduce the likelihood of school fraud, make schools more responsive to parental demands, stave off the encroachment of government regulation, and help control costs.[5]

Freedom for educators means that anyone can open a school and that schools have complete discretion over their staffing, curricula, admissions, fees, and budgets. The rationale given for these stipulations is that they are necessary to permit and foster innovation, responsiveness to families, specialization, and the expansion of popular schools.[6]

Competition among educators is advocated on the grounds that it allegedly provides a powerful incentive for schools to adopt effective instructional methods and to strive to maximize the conditions and outcomes valued by the families they served. Vigorous competition, specifically the risk of losing students to (and being forced out of business by) competitors, is also credited with compelling schools to maintain their facilities in acceptable condition.[7]

The case for the profit motive is based on the alleged need for an extra incentive capable of overcoming the risks associated with innovation and expansion. The absence of the profit motive in mainstream U.S. K–12 education, for example, is blamed for the fact that even highly popular nonprofit schools have not added substantially to their enrollments over time. Conversely, the presence of the profit motive is credited with the vigorous expansion of tutoring services in Asia and North America, and of education chains such as Brazil's Objetivo and the American University of Phoenix.

Predictions

It is not contended that possession of these characteristics guarantees the perfect operation of schools or the complete satisfaction of families, but simply that systems closely approximating this arrangement are more likely than alternative school governance and funding formulations to create the conditions and outcomes valued by parents.

Some specific predictions follow from the absence or substantial compromise of these characteristics.[8]

- When parents lack choice and control over their children's education they are likely to have greater difficulty obtaining the kind and quality of educational services they seek. To the extent that an official curriculum is imposed by the state (thus greatly limiting parental choice and control), it is expected to precipitate social conflict (at least in pluralistic societies).[9]

- Lack of competition between schools is expected to increase costs and decrease quality and efficiency while also lessening the likelihood that schools will try to do their best with each and every child. It is also expected to be associated with inferior facilities maintenance and with parents having reduced access to concrete information on their children's performance.[10]

- Government restrictions on the creation and autonomy of schools are predicted to abbreviate the range of educational services available to families, preventing schools from offering the services desired by their specific clienteles. Caps on school fees and the imposition of government budgeting rules are expected to stifle innovation and expansion by making it difficult for schools to raise and allocate the funds necessary to pay for these activities.[11] Lack of school autonomy, particularly combined with lack of parental choice, may also result in a less communal and more disruptive school and classroom atmosphere.[12]

- Reducing or eliminating direct payment of tuition by parents is predicted to erode parental control and choice (leading to the problems associated with low parental choice), and to increase corruption and fraud. Since state education funding is generally associated with comprehensive state regulation, it is also likely to decrease the level of meaningful competition among schools by homogenizing the services they offer. The extent of the damage caused is suggested to be proportional to the reduction in parental fees.[13]

- Lack of the profit motive is expected to stifle innovation and to impede the process by which more effective schools would expand and either take over or crowd out their less effective competitors. It is also argued to dull the incentive for cost-cutting and efficiency, discourage entrepreneurs from entering the profession, and discourage the most ambitious and proficient educators from remaining in the profession over the long term.[14]

The Modern International Evidence
Market, Pseudo-Market, and Bureaucratic Systems Compared

India

Conditions

There are four main categories of schools in India:

- Government schools
- Government-recognized, government-aided private schools (hereafter, "private aided")
- Government-recognized, unaided private schools (hereafter, "private unaided")
- Unrecognized, unaided private schools (hereafter, "unrecognized")

Private aided schools are in many ways indistinguishable from government schools. In the northern state of Uttar Pradesh, for example, government funding comes in the form of a block grant that is not tied to enrollment levels or performance. Expenditures are thus comparable between private aided and government schools. Private aided schools cannot charge tuition, nor can they hire, fire, or set compensation levels for their own staffs. Personnel are instead appointed by the Uttar Pradesh Education Service Commission.[15] Levels of teacher unionization are also comparable between private aided and government schools.

Unaided private schools are fully self-financed and independent. Average per-pupil expenditures are roughly half those in the aided and government sectors.[16] If an unaided school is "recognized" by the state, it is allowed to offer officially sanctioned degrees—something that unrecognized schools are not permitted to do.[17] To be recognized, however, schools must satisfy a range of requirements, including having large (1,000 sq. yard minimum) playgrounds, government-trained teachers, and a substantial minimum bank balance. These and other requirements make recognition prohibitive for most unaided schools serving the poor. In the state of Andhra Pradesh, only 40 percent of private schools are recognized.[18] In villages and rural areas, recognized schools make up an even smaller segment of the private education sector.

Detailed information on the conditions in rural public and private schools is available from a 1999 study of five Indian states,[19] known as the PROBE report.[20] Only about five percent of the private schools in this study were found to be government aided, while two-thirds or more were unrecognized.[21]

In terms of the kinds of facilities available to them, private schools were found to be roughly comparable to public schools. Private schools were more efficient in using and maintaining their facilities, however.[22] Private school buildings and equipment were generally in a much better state of repair. About three quarters of public schools were in need of major repairs of one or more kinds, and a third required completely new buildings.[23] Half of the private schools, by contrast, needed no major repair of any kind.

Even when the resources were available, the PROBE team found that public schools made little effort to "create a congenial school environment,"[24] adding that public "schoolrooms are allowed to degenerate . . . and the area around the school is often dirty and unpleasant."[25] The situation was usually different among the private schools, they noted, many of which did "manage to create some kind of learning environment with the simple means available to them."[26]

School records indicated that attendance levels were higher among private than among public school students, and private school records were found to much more accurately reflect actual attendance as observed by PROBE researchers. Public school attendance records were determined to be inflated vis-à-vis actual observed attendance levels.[27]

There is no simple correlation between class size and school type. In the rural areas studied by PROBE, the (predominantly unaided) private schools had much smaller classes than government schools.[28] In urban areas, however, there is evidence that unaided schools have considerably larger classes than aided schools and especially government schools.[29]

In the PROBE states, public school teachers had more and higher teaching credentials as well as much higher salaries than private school teachers—often more than five times higher.[30] Actual teaching activity was much less common in public schools, however. When PROBE researchers made their unannounced visits, they found that only 53 percent of public schools had any teaching activity going on in any of their classes. A third of headteachers[31] were simply absent, and only a quarter were engaged in teaching activity. Even this is an overstatement because schools that were closed on the day of the visit (which was a school day) were simply omitted from the calculations rather than being counted as having no teaching activity.[32] "Generally," the researchers observed, public school "teaching activity has been reduced to a minimum, in terms of both time and effort. And this pattern is not confined to a minority of irresponsible teachers—it has become a way of life in the profession."[33] The five states surveyed by PROBE are not unique in this respect because low-levels of teaching activity have also been observed in the government school system of Tamil Nadu.[34]

Unlike the situation in public schools, PROBE researchers found a "high level of teaching activity in private schools, even makeshift ones where the work environment is no better than in government schools."[35] Private schools "placed a visible emphasis on discipline and instruction,"[36] and their classroom activity was described as "feverish."

Apart from the higher level of teaching activity in private schools, they were also found to more closely and individually monitor their students. First-grade children, who were found to be "much neglected" in government schools, "received close attention in private schools, perhaps because private-school teachers are keen to retain their 'clients', and know that a neglected [first-grader] can easily drop out."[37] Private schools' greater and more successful efforts at maintaining order and discipline were another major difference appreciated by parents. The differing learning conditions in public and private schools were not lost on parents.

> Most parents stated that if the costs of sending a child to a government and private school were the same, they would rather send their children to a private school. The reason, almost invariably, is that they are dissatisfied with the functioning of the local government school. . . . As parents see it, the main advantage of private schools is that, being more accountable, they have higher levels of teaching activity.[38]

Not surprisingly, given the characteristics of the schools just noted, the parent/teacher relationship was found to be "more constructive" in the private sector.[39]

Total expenditure figures for the various school types were not reported by PROBE researchers, but figures are available from urban Uttar Pradesh, one of the states covered in the PROBE report. Government and aided private schools in Uttar Pradesh had comparable per-student expenditures, while unaided private schools spent roughly half as much as the other two school types.[40] Both government and aided schools spent 97.5 percent of their budgets on salary costs, while unaided schools had a 74 percent/26 percent split between salary and nonsalary costs.

Outcomes

Though the PROBE report indicates that teaching activity was substantially more common and more assiduous in rural private schools, the researchers did not test students to ascertain the comparative effectiveness or efficiency of public and private schools. Fortunately, a study of urban school performance in Uttar Pradesh was published around the time that data collection for PROBE was going on. This study controlled for student background variables as well as selection bias.[41] After controlling for these factors, Kingdon found that the average student would perform better in a private unaided school than in either a government school or an aided private school. The average student would do very slightly better in a government school than in an aided school.

Factoring in per-student expenditures, Kingdon concluded that unaided schools were twice as efficient as government schools, and almost twice as efficient as aided private schools. Aided schools were slightly more efficient than government schools because their spending levels were somewhat lower.[42]

Though Kingdon's findings are consistent with the situation observed in five Indian states by the PROBE team, conflicting results have been published for primary schools in the southern state of Tamil Nadu. After analyzing a sample of schools in that state, Sajitha Bashir found that unaided schools performed significantly better in mathematics but significantly worse in the Tamil language than government schools, and that they were vastly more expensive and thus less efficient than government schools.[43] Bashir found aided private schools to be uniformly more effective and more efficient than government schools.

The weak unaided school performance in the Tamil language is explained by the fact that all of the unaided schools in Bashir's study taught in English, not Tamil. Instructional use of the Tamil language at unaided schools was limited to a single class in that subject. If parents pay to send their children to unaided schools in part to learn English, it would seem inappropriate to judge their effectiveness by testing students' Tamil language proficiency.

272

The cost discrepancy between Bashir's findings and those of PROBE and Kingdon are striking. The average total parental expenditure on private unaided schooling found in the PROBE states was 940 rupees.[44] This is lower than the total per-pupil expenditure that Bashir reports for government and aided private schools in her Tamil Nadu sample. The unaided private schools in Bashir's sample, by contrast, cost parents a total of 1,398 rupees.

One possible explanation for these higher costs is that Bashir seems to have included only government-recognized schools in her sample.[45] Because of the costly requirements imposed by recognition, these schools have to charge substantially higher fees than unrecognized unaided schools. By itself, this fact may account for much if not all of the higher cost of Bashir's sample. School fees averaged only 296 rupees in the PROBE report, but between 646 and 771 rupees in Bashir's unaided schools. Other out-of-pocket costs, such as for clothing or school uniforms, and notebooks, also appear to have been higher in Bashir's sample, which would be consistent with higher spending on these items by the relatively wealthier patrons of more expensive recognized (versus unrecognized) schools.

Unaided schools are also far rarer in Tamil Nadu than elsewhere in India. According to a World Bank study, only one tenth of one percent of elementary schools in Tamil Nadu were unaided in the early 1990s, though Bashir puts the figure as high as 4 percent.[46] By contrast, 10 percent of all schools in rural India were found to be unaided schools in the mid-1990s, and the percentage was much higher in urban areas, reaching as high as 80 percent in urban Uttar Pradesh, and these figures are thought to undercount unrecognized unaided schools.[47] Duraisamy also found that Tamil Nadu's small cadre of unaided schools enjoyed, on average, better facilities and smaller classes than government schools.[48]

Taking all of this into account, it seems that unaided schools are a smaller and perhaps somewhat more elite sector in Tamil Nadu than elsewhere in India, and Bashir's sample appears to include only the more expensive recognized schools from among this group. Up until the mid-1990s, government restrictions existed on the creation of unaided private schools in Tamil Nadu, perhaps explaining their disproportionately small share of unaided schools when compared with the rest of India (Uttar Pradesh in particular).

The slight discrepancy between Bashir's and Kingdon's findings regarding private aided schools is likely due in part to the impact of different regulatory conditions in Tamil Nadu versus the rest of India. Private aided schools in Tamil Nadu are afforded more autonomy than those elsewhere, being permitted, for example, to hire and fire their own teachers. This autonomy could certainly have a positive impact on school efficiency if school managers select teachers who are better suited to their schools, more motivated, or more competent. Evidence from Tanzania, for example, suggests that private schools make better personnel decisions than government schools.[49]

This brings us to a methodological concern regarding Bashir's work. Fee-charging private schools are not theorized to be more efficient or effective due simply to private ownership but rather, because their greater autonomy and market incentives, are presumed to both allow them and pressure them to make better decisions in such areas as staffing, management, and curricula. Despite this fact, Bashir actually controlled for several of these factors in her model, effectively tying private school managers' hands behind their backs.

For example, Bashir's model controlled for the mathematical competence of mathematics teachers, and this vitiates any advantage that private schools might have in recruiting, training, and retaining more competent mathematics instructors through their control over personnel policy. Bashir controlled for the motivation of headteachers despite the fact that the autonomy enjoyed by market schools is claimed to lead to a more motivated workforce.[50] Bashir also controlled for the hours headteachers worked on academic tasks outside of their teaching duties and for the frequency of their meetings with teachers. Holding all of these operational details of schools constant in a study that is supposed to determine sectoral differences resulting *from* those differences would seem to be counterproductive.

Pakistan

Conditions

Officially, Pakistan is well endowed with public schools, but in practice "a combination of corruption and bureaucratic inefficiency has all but destroyed the system."[51] In Punjab, for instance, one audit revealed that a third of all state-paid teachers never showed up for work. Many schools exist only on paper, with local bureaucrats simply embezzling the government funds allocated for their creation and maintenance, without ever hiring a teacher or enrolling a student.[52]

In the public schools that do operate, "student achievement is poor because of teacher absenteeism, an inappropriate curriculum, poor textbooks, limited availability of supplementary learning materials, and weak teaching," according to the World Bank.[53] The same World Bank report notes that public-sector education management "is inefficient, and planning and budgeting capacities are weak," with unpredictable release of government funds aggravating the managerial and operational inefficiency of the schools.

The government system's organizational problems are manifested in the quality of education received by students. Appraisals of student performance generally suggest that the value added by these schools is low, and parents appear to recognize that fact. Attendance rates are low, with 20 to 30 percent of schools having few if any students.[54]

The perceived low quality of public schools led to rapid growth in private education during the 1980s and 1990s. These schools serve families at all income levels, even the poorest. In a study of Lahore, Alderman, Orazem, and Paterno found that the very poorest families (earning less than $57 per month) in the poorest neighborhoods, were almost as likely to enroll their children in private as in public schools (37 percent in private schools versus 40 percent in government schools).[55] Families in the next income category, earning between $57 and $100 per month, were substantially more likely to send their children to private than to public schools (40 percent were enrolled in government schools, 56 percent in private schools). In this sample of poor Lahore neighborhoods, only 12 percent of families earning more than $285 per month sent their children to public schools.

Total rates of school enrollment are strongly correlated with population density. Nationwide, gross urban enrollment rates are 50 percent larger than those in rural areas.[56] This urban/rural divide is more pronounced in the private than the public sector. In Punjab, for instance, urban children are two-and-a-half times more likely to attend private schools than rural children are.[57]

Outcomes

Comparisons of Pakistani public and private school student achievement are scarce, but Alderman, Orazem, and Paterno did undertake such a study in 2001. Among their findings were that "private schools have better [academic] outcomes than government schools holding fixed measured home and school inputs into the human capital production process." The measure of achievement was the aggregate of two tests, one in the Urdu language and one in mathematics.

Overall efficiency was also found to be greater in private than in government schools. After taking into account all the various costs associated with private schools (fees, books, uniforms, supplies, transportation, and tutorial services), the researchers noted that "government schools [had] much higher per-pupil expenditures,"[58] than private schools had.

Alderman, Orazem, and Paterno also examined the link between spending and achievement. When all public and private schools were taken together, they found no significant correlation between spending and achievement. However, when private schools were considered on their own, spending and achievement were found to be positively linked.

Summarizing their findings, the researchers concluded that—

> Schooling choices of poor households are very sensitive to school fees, proximity, and quality. Rather than being exploited by private schools, evidence suggests that strong demand for private schools is in response to better quality and learning opportunities offered by private schools.[59]

Indonesia

Conditions

Though virtually all elementary education in Indonesia is government run, the same is true of only about 70 percent of secondary schooling. Access to government secondary schools is rationed, with admission contingent on the test scores of applicants. Public schools also have much lower out-of-pocket costs to students and higher overall expenditures than private schools have. This combination of selectivity, lower fees, and higher spending means that public schools are highly sought after. As a corollary, private schools are often seen as a fall-back option for students unable to gain admission to public schools.[60]

Both public and private schools receive some government funding, with the level of funding varying widely both between and within sectors. Central government funding of private schools averages 7.4 percent of total school revenues in Jakarta, 42.2 percent in other parts of Java, and 80.7 percent outside of Java. Among public schools, central government funding of public schools ranges from 70 percent in Jakarta to 95.5 percent outside of Java.[61] Considerable variation exists within regions as well. The balance of school funding is local, with the vast majority coming from tuition and fees paid directly by parents.

Outcomes

Estelle James, Elizabeth King, and Ace Suryadi took advantage of the diversity in management and funding sources in Indonesian education to disentangle the effects of private funding and private management on educational efficiency. Their data set covered 68,000 public and private schools.[62]

First, for the sake of argument, they assumed that the proportion of a school's budget derived from parental financing was exogenous (i.e., that there were no unobserved factors that simultaneously influenced both the amount of parental financing and school efficiency). This represents a simple Ordinary Least Squares regression model. In doing so, they found that higher parental financing generally increased efficiency for both public and private schools. They also found that the percentage increase in efficiency was generally inversely proportional to the initial level of private financing. In other words, increasing the share of total revenues made up by private financing had a larger impact when overall/initial private financing level was low than when it was already high to begin with. They also found that, under their exogeneity assumption, that optimum school efficiency was achieved when the balance of funding was 85 percent private and 15 percent government.

Statistical tests revealed, however, that they could not reject the possibility that the share of private financing was endogenous (i.e., that unobserved factors did indeed influence both the amount of parental financing and school efficiency). That meant the simple OLS estimate was biased. To control for the endogeneity problem, they adopted a two-stage least squares (2SLS) model. The first stage was to identify the factors that determined the parental share of total school expenditures. Those factors were then used as an instrumental variable for the second stage of the regression (the stage measuring the correlation between parental share of financing and efficiency). The only significant difference of using the 2SLS model was that the effect of increasing the share of school budgets paid for by parents never became negative: "The result from the endogenous model indicates that cost per student decreases over the entire range of Locshare [local/parental share of financing], but at a diminishing rate."[63] That is to say, a higher share of parental financing always leads to greater efficiency, but its marginal benefit diminishes as that share reaches 100 percent. This meant that their OLS estimate showing an optimum budgetary breakdown that included 15 percent government funds was in fact erroneous, and that zero percent government funds was in fact optimal for school efficiency.

Separately, James and her colleagues also concluded that "private management is more efficient than public management in achieving academic quality."[64] So, for any given level of parental funding, a privately run school is apt to be more efficient than a publicly run school.

In 2000, Arjun Bedi and Ashish Garg looked beyond academic achievement and school efficiency to study the correlation between attendance at private secondary schools and later earnings. In line with what might be expected due to their selectivity and higher resources, raw data show that public schools in Indonesia do well compared with private schools. On average, their graduates enjoy higher earnings than those of private schools. Bedi and Garg did not have data to break down schools by funding source, but they did have a breakdown by type of private school. Their raw data showed that graduates of Christian private schools (which make up a small segment of the market) earn the most, followed by graduates of Islamic private schools and public schools (whose graduates' earnings are roughly comparable), followed by graduates of nonreligious private schools, who earn the least.[65]

These raw results were, of course, subject to selection bias because public school applicants were admitted on the basis of their test scores, and because selection of school type was correlated with a number of other student and family factors. After controlling for the higher ability of students accepted into selective public schools, and for such family factors as parental education, Bedi and Garg found that nonreligious private schools were by far the most effective, followed by Christian private schools, followed by public schools, with graduates of private Islamic schools earning the least. Taking private and public sectors as a whole, graduates of private-sector schools outearned those of public schools.[66] The raw earnings advantage enjoyed by selective public school graduates, the authors concluded, could "be attributed to the selective nature of the [public school] student intake and differences in student characteristics and *not* to the school-type attended."[67]

Some other findings of interest were that larger class size lowered earnings of graduates of public schools, but actually led to higher earnings for graduates of private schools. Nonreligious private schools were also found to make more efficient use of their school-term lengths than religious private schools.[68]

Philippines

Conditions

There are three broad categories of secondary education in the Philippines: national public high schools, local public high schools, and private schools (which can be either religious or secular). During the 1988/89 school year, 63 percent of secondary students attended public schools, while the remainder attended private schools.[69] At that time, the government passed a law promising free secondary public schooling for all, and authorizing subsidies to private schools in areas without access to public schools. Budgetary constraints have hindered the implementation of this plan, and many children of secondary school age are either not attending school or have to pay tuition at private schools.[70] Total secondary enrollments have nevertheless increased and stood at roughly 80 percent in 2000.[71]

To be able to award official degrees (and hence make their graduates eligible for higher education), private schools must be recognized by the government. Recognition is considered burdensome by many private school managers. Among the requirements for recognition are hiring of only government licensed teachers and allocating funds raised by any tuition increases in accordance with the government's 70-20-10 plan (70 percent of the increase must be spent on salaries, wages, and benefits for teachers; 20 percent spent on upgrading facilities, and the remainder can be considered a return on the school owner's investment.)

In a study of education in poor regions of the country, Charisse Gulosino and James Tooley (2002) reported that public schools were not present or were underserving the poor in many areas, and that fee-charging private schools were filling the gap. They noted that a few free places were usually available in these schools, indicating that the poor were subsidizing the truly destitute.

Outcomes

Emmanuel Jimenez and Marlaine Lockheed compared public and private student achievement in the mid-1980s.[72] After controlling for student background characteristics and selection bias, they determined that private school students enjoyed an overall academic achievement advantage. This overall advantage broke down into substantial advantages in both English and in Filipino, but a slight disadvantage in mathematics. These differences persisted for all SES (socioeconomic status) groups, but the magnitudes varied. For low-SES students, the disadvantage in mathematics became even smaller, the advantage in English became small, and the advantage in Filipino was unchanged. For high-SES students, the disadvantage in mathematics became slightly larger, the advantage in English became considerably larger, and the advantage in Filipino was unchanged.[73] These achievement findings led to the conclusion that private schools were more efficient than public schools given that their costs were roughly half those of government schools.[74]

It has also been noted that graduates of private schools tend to earn more than public school graduates in the Philippines, but Futoshi Yamauchi and Joy Abrenica suggest that this advantage is reduced to statistical insignificance when student characteristics are held constant.[75]

Thailand

Conditions

During the mid-1980s (when the research discussed below was conducted), private schools were tightly regulated by the central government. The core curriculum of private schools was prescribed by government guidelines, though some flexibility existed. Private schools were more likely, for instance, to offer foreign language instruction. Both public and private secondary schools administered entrance exams to applicants.

After 1977, private schools deemed by the government to be of "high quality" became eligible to receive subsidies of up to 40 percent of their operating costs, though this entailed a greater degree of government control. As a result of the extensive conditions attached to government subsidies, participation in the program dropped from 90 percent to 60 percent of eligible "high quality" private schools between 1977 and 1984.

All in all, the public system was extremely centralized during the 1980s. "All important decisions about curriculum, budget, and personnel," note Jimenez and Lockheed, "[were] taken in Bangkok, allowing for little variation at lower levels."[76]

Outcomes

After controlling for family and student characteristics as well as selection bias, Jimenez and Lockheed found that private school students did enormously better than public school students.[77] A significant portion, but not all, of this difference turned out to be correlated with student peer groups. The idea behind peer group effects is that a student with a given set of personal and family characteristics is expected to do better academically if her classmates are brighter or from wealthier or better-educated families.

To determine a pure school-type effect, Jimenez and Lockheed added additional controls for peer group effects to their model, including classroom averages of students' mothers' education level, students' (pre-test) achievement levels, and the percentage of students' fathers working in professional occupations. After controlling for all of these factors, the typical student still gained .45 of a standard deviation in achievement (generally considered a large effect size) from attending a private versus a government school.

Some other findings included—

- Public school students attending schools in richer communities did better academically, whereas community wealth had no effect on private school student achievement.
- Teaching credentials were not significantly related to achievement in public or private schools. (Sixty-one percent of all public school teachers in the sample were government certified to teach mathematics. The same was true of only 10 percent of the private school teachers.)
- Private school teachers spent 25 percent more time maintaining order in the classroom, and this appeared to pay dividends in achievement, since "more teacher time devoted to maintaining order [was] positively related to achievement in private

schools." In public schools, by contrast, additional efforts to maintain order were negatively related to achievement.

- Private school teachers were found to spend 50 percent more time quizzing and testing their students.

Interestingly, observed school characteristics accounted for the vast majority of the sectoral difference in achievement. When the researchers held teaching practices and school characteristics constant, the private school advantage was almost eliminated. In other words, if the sampled public schools could have consistently imitated the typical private school, their students would theoretically have been able to do virtually as well as private school students overall.

Finally, Jimenez and Lockheed estimated from the limited available evidence that private schools seem to have spent substantially less per student than government schools, suggesting that better academic achievement was accompanied by higher efficiency as well.

Vietnam

Conditions

According to Paul Glewwe and Harold Patrinos, private schools were historically common in Vietnam, existing in the North until 1954, and in the South until 1975.[78] With the North's victory in 1975, all private enterprises in the South, including schools, were nationalized. After *doi moi*, or "Renovation," in 1989, the establishment of private institutions was once again permitted. Since that time, public, semipublic, and private schools have existed side by side.

Public schools are operated by the state, and although they are meant to be fully state funded they, in fact, charge substantial fees. Semipublic schools, often run by local community groups, have their facilities and curricula provided by the state but are responsible for hiring and compensating their staffs, which they do by charging tuition. Private schools were autonomous and did not receive government subsidies as of 1994. Private schools accounted for between 1.2 and 2.1 percent of student enrollment in 1992/93, depending on the level of education, while semipublic schools made up between .4 and 2.5 percent. The remaining students were enrolled in public schools. The cost to parents of sending their children to public schools ranges between 52 percent and 105 percent of the cost of sending them to private schools, depending on the level of schooling (with upper secondary schooling being more expensive in the public sector). Except at the lowest (primary school) level of education, semipublic schools are more expensive than private schools, costing more than twice as much at the upper secondary level.[79]

There is no clear pattern in the family characteristics associated with student enrollment in a particular kind of school. Contrary to some other countries, higher levels of parental education reduce the probability of private school attendance. Wealthier parents are more likely to send their children to private school but less likely to send them to semipublic school. No correlation exists between private school enrollment and urban versus rural residence.

Outcomes

Glewwe and Patrinos, who studied intersectoral differences in later earning power, concluded from a simple regression that "there are probably (statistically significant at the 10 percent level) benefits to attending semipublic schools and definite benefits to attending private schools."[80] It should be noted, however, that their analysis did not control for family characteristics, presumably because correlations between family characteristics and school type were (as noted earlier) found to be small and inconsistent. Nevertheless, including these controls would have added weight to their conclusions.

Because the cost of private secondary schooling was comparable to that of public schooling, the implication was that private schools may be more efficient, with respect to generating later earnings, than public schools.

Tanzania

Conditions

Access to public secondary schooling is tightly rationed in Tanzania, being contingent on high scores on an end-of-primary-school test.[81] During the mid-1980s, public schools did not charge fees,[82] but this changed over the ensuing decade. As of the late 1990s, the cost to parents of private secondary schools was still, on average, 50 percent higher than the cost of public schools. With regard to total

283

spending, private schools have been estimated to spend between 69 and 86 percent of average public school expenditures per pupil.

Because they have lower direct costs to parents and are academically selective, public secondary school places are coveted by most families. Consequently, private secondary schools are viewed as an expensive alternative for those who fail to gain acceptance to public secondary school.[83] The bulk of secondary enrollment is in the private sector, which itself mostly comprised nonprofit religious and community schools during the mid-to-late 1980s. This pattern continues to the present, though for-profit schools began appearing in small but increasing numbers in the late 1990s.[84] Fifty-five percent of secondary students are enrolled in private schools of one type or another.[85]

Regulation of private schools is extensive. All public and private schools follow the same national curriculum and are subject to central government inspections. Private schools must hire government-certified teachers, and their fee policies are, in theory, controlled by the government, but violations of these requirements exist.[86] In keeping with the central government's significant role in education, self-reported school-level control over the educational process is limited across the board. On the basis of survey data from 1994 to 1996, only one quarter of all public schools and one half of all private schools indicated that they had any control over their own instructional practices (textbooks, curricula, schedules, etc.).[87]

Outcomes

Jimenez and Lockheed studied the relationship between school type and achievement using data from the mid-1980s. They had extensive data on student and family characteristics that allowed them to control for students' aptitudes and family backgrounds. They also controlled for selection bias, which was deemed to be a significant problem given the elite, academically selective character of public secondary schools.

After controlling for all of these factors, Jimenez and Lockheed found that the benefit of attending private school for a random student was nearly one standard deviation (or 8.25 achievement test points), a very large effect. Another effect that the researchers calculated was the expected change in test score if a typical public school student were to switch to a private school. That student, they estimated, would enjoy a gain of 6.34 achievement test points, or three quarters of a standard deviation.[88] These findings appear to be consistent with earlier research.[89]

No investigation of peer group effects was made, but the results for the public-to-private school switch perhaps shed some light on this question. Given the academically selective nature of public secondary schools, and the fact that private schools are seen chiefly as a fall-back for students who fail to gain entry to the public sector, it stands to reason that public school peer groups may have had higher aptitudes than private school peer groups. The lower gain that researchers found for a typical public school student switching to a private school, as compared with the gain expected for any student (public or private) chosen at random, would be consistent with the loss of a positive public school peer effect. Support for this theory can be found in the average mathematics and verbal aptitude scores reported for public and private school students. Both were higher for public school students, and the combined average was 51.5 for public students versus 47.6 for private students (out of a possible 100).[90]

Other interesting findings include the fact that teachers' salaries were "positively and strongly associated with achievement test scores in private schools but inversely [though negligibly] related to scores in public schools," and that private students tended to "perform better in larger classrooms while public students [performed] best in intermediate size classrooms (student-teacher ratio between 20 and 24)."[91]

Finally, though Jimenez and Lockheed lacked nationally representative expenditure figures for the school sectors, they presented local sample observations showing that no significant difference in public versus private per-pupil expenditures existed.[92]

Lassibille, Tan, and Sumra took a different approach to the question of public versus private-sector effects in their 1999 study. They used a value-added approach based on aggregated school-level data from the mid-1990s, omitting any consideration of individual student or family effects, and ignoring selection bias. They concluded that public schools had higher average test scores than private schools, and that public schools were associated with higher average test-score gains over the three-year period studied.

Their raw test-score findings are consistent with those of other researchers, and with the academic selectivity of public schools.

Given that they do not control for student factors, family background, or public school selectivity, however, these results are not likely to isolate sectoral school effects. The value-added portion of their findings is potentially more revealing, but without an analysis to demonstrate that it is not confounded with student aptitudes or family backgrounds, it too is only suggestive. Somewhat surprisingly, Lassibille et al. find academically selective public schools to be less efficient than private schools, even though they do not control for student or family variables or selection bias.

Lassibille and his colleagues also point out that the late 1980s and early 1990s were a period of "explosive" growth in the private education sector, and note that the start-up difficulties faced by new schools may have had a dampening effect on the performance of the private sector as a whole.[93] Evidence from their study on improvement trends in the public versus private sectors is consistent their view. While more than a third of private schools improved their national performance ranking over the three-year period studied, the same was true of only a quarter of public schools.[94]

Also of interest is their finding that the private schools' ability to attract and retain students was tied to their performance. Private schools that improved their national ranking between 1992 and 1995 saw their enrollments increase by 18 percent over that period, while private schools whose rankings fell lost 3 percent of their enrollments. Changes in school rank had a smaller effect on public school enrollments, with all public schools seeing their enrollments increase whether their ranking had improved or deteriorated.[95] The growth in public school enrollments regardless of performance changes may have been tied to rising national enrollment levels among lower-income families (since public schools have substantially lower out-of-pocket costs to parents).

Colombia

Conditions

Private schools formerly made up a majority of secondary schools in Colombia, but, following an expansion of government provision from the late 1950s onward, they were reduced to enrolling 40 percent of all secondary students by the late 1980s.

Admission to private schools is generally academically selective and, as a result, private schools are seen as being of higher quality than public schools.

Average per-pupil costs are roughly comparable between the sectors, with public schools spending about 10 percent more due mainly to higher teacher salaries, lower pupil/teacher ratios, and lower teacher/supervisor ratios.[96]

In 1991, Colombia introduced a voucher program known as PACES that provided more than 125,000 pupils from poor neighborhoods with vouchers covering about half the cost of private secondary school. These vouchers were renewable annually provided that students maintained a satisfactory level of school performance. In many parts of the country, the vouchers were distributed by random lottery to eligible applicants. To be eligible, students had to come from families in the bottom third of the SES distribution.[97]

Outcomes

Using data from the 1980s, Jimenez and Lockheed compared public versus private school effects on student achievement, controlling for both student/family characteristics and the selection bias caused by parental choices and the selective admissions policies common among private schools. After incorporating these controls, Jimenez and Lockheed concluded that the typical student did benefit academically from attendance at private school. They also estimated that the average public school student, had he transferred to a private school, would have benefited academically, but to a lesser degree. The biggest intersectoral academic achievement difference they estimated was for the typical private school student. In other words, students who shared the family and personal characteristics typical of private school students gained more by actually attending private schools than did students with different characteristics.[98]

A notable correlational finding was that larger classes had a negative effect on achievement in public schools but not in private schools. In fact, within the normal range of class sizes, private school students in bigger classes outperformed their peers in smaller classes.[99]

Angrist, Bettinger, Bloom, King, and Kremer used data from the PACES program to conduct a natural education voucher experiment—one of the few (if not the only) instances of a randomized field trial outside of the United States. This experiment allows for a more reliable estimation of school-type effects because randomization controls not only for observed characteristics of students but also for any unobserved characteristics that might also affect achievement.

After three years in the program, Angrist and his colleagues determined with a simple OLS model that voucher lottery winners were scoring .2 standard deviations better than students who had participated in the lottery but had not won a school voucher. Lottery winners were also 10 percent more likely to have completed the 8th grade. These gains, though nonnegligible in magnitude, were only moderately statistically significant because of small sample size.[100]

The researchers observed, however, that only 90 percent of voucher winners actually used the vouchers to attend private schools, and that 24 percent of voucher losers received scholarships from other sources. Since the relevant policy question to be tested was whether or not scholarship use (i.e., subsidized private school attendance) had a net educational benefit, they modified their model to account for these observations. Using lottery win/loss status as an instrument for actual scholarship use in a two-stage least squares (2SLS) model, they found that scholarship use actually produced gains that were 50 percent larger than the muddied gains suggested by the simple OLS estimate. This finding was true both for academic achievement and educational attainment. The actual effect of scholarship use (whether the scholarship was from the PACES lottery or from another source) was a 0.3 standard deviation gain in test scores and a 15 percent increase in the likelihood of completing the 8th grade.[101] The effect on girls was also found to be stronger than that on boys.[102]

Dominican Republic

Conditions

The Dominican Republic has three main types of schools: public, ordinary private, and elite private. Ordinary private schools are often operated for profit, tend not to have selective admissions policies, and generally spend much less per pupil than public schools. Elite private schools, called "Escuelas Con Facultad," are authorized by the Ministry of Education to administer official examinations. Almost all elite schools are nonprofits, and three quarters are affiliated with religious denominations. Fees at elite private schools are similar to average public school per-pupil expenditures. To obtain and preserve their special status, elite schools must follow state education standards.[103] Between the mid-1980s and mid-1990s, private schools enrolled roughly a third of secondary school students.[104]

Outcomes

Here again, Jimenez and Lockheed used a data set from the mid-1980s that included achievement scores along with student and family characteristics, including measures of wealth, parental education, and parental occupation. After controlling for those characteristics and for selection bias, they found that students from both kinds of private schools outperformed their public school peers. The advantage for both sectors was substantial, but for elite private schools it was very large (1.18 standard deviations).

Given the very different peer characteristics of elite private schools, however, the presence of peer effects seemed likely. After controlling for peer-group characteristics (classroom averages of family income, mother's education, father's white-collar job status), Jimenez and Lockheed concluded that ordinary private schools still had a positive effect on achievement, whereas the effect of elite private schools actually turned negative and significant.

Interestingly, it was the lower-SES students who were estimated to gain the most from attending ordinary private schools. The typical public school student (who has lower SES than students in other school types) would gain more than a quarter of a standard deviation in achievement by transferring to an ordinary private school. The typical student already enrolled in an ordinary private school does better there than he would in a public school, but only by .11 of a standard deviation. The benefit estimated for the typical elite private school student (high SES) transferring to an ordinary private school is negligible.[105]

Since ordinary private schools were found to spend roughly 1/3 less than public schools, they were significantly more efficient. Jimenez and Lockheed estimated that the cost-per-mathematics-test-score-point in ordinary private schools was roughly half that of public schools.[106]

Chilean Government Subsidy Program

Conditions

In 1981, Chile's military government drastically revised the country's public funding of education. The system it introduced allocated subsidies to both public and participating private schools on the basis of enrollment, allowing the two sectors to compete on more equal footing for the patronage of Chilean families, beginning in 1982. Following the introduction of the program, there were three types of schools in Chile: municipal public schools (MUN), private subsidized schools (PS), and private nonsubsidized schools (private paid or PP).

Though Chile's education system is usually referred to as a national voucher program, it differs from the archetypal conception of school vouchers in two ways. First, subsidies do not go to parents but rather are awarded to schools on the basis of their average daily attendance over the three preceding months. Second, the subsidies do not make up the entirety of government spending on public schools. Many MUN schools have had soft budget constraints, which is to say they have spent more than the per-pupil allotment provided by the central government. To make up the difference, they have received additional financing from their municipalities.[107] More recently, many have also received additional funds from the central government over and above the per-pupil subsidy.

Many preexisting private schools whose tuitions exceeded the per-pupil subsidy amount elected not to participate in the program, and continue to finance themselves solely through tuition. These PP schools enrolled 6 to 8 percent of students in the years before the subsidy program was introduced,[108] and have enrolled 10 or 11 percent of students in recent years.

From 1982 to 1993, the per-pupil subsidy constituted the entire budget for PS schools because they were prohibited from charging tuition. After 1993, per-pupil subsidies could be supplemented by tuition payments at private schools, with the government subsidy declining on a sliding scale based on the amount of tuition being charged. The higher the co-payment charged by PS schools, the lower the fraction of the government subsidy they were eligible to receive. About 40 percent of PS schools had adopted this new funding mechanism by 1996, comprising about 65 percent of total PS school enrollment (hence, the larger schools were the first to take advantage of the program).[109]

Subsidies to MUN and PS schools vary based on several factors, including the number of enrolled special education students, the level of education (primary versus secondary), and a variety of school-type programs based on areas of subject concentration or extension of the school day. These latter programs tend to be concentrated in MUN schools, and Sapelli and Vial point out that this means poorer families receive a lower net subsidy if they send their children to independent schools.[110]

A recent UNESCO study of high-performing schools in Chile reports that MUN schools and PS schools differ systematically in both their facilities and the degree to which they maintain those facilities.

> In the government-subsidised private schools the infrastructure is better, more modern and more spacious compared to the municipal schools visited. The private subsidised schools are in buildings made of reinforced concrete and on two levels, first and second floors. In contrast, the municipal schools are one story in groups of 4 or 5 rooms. They are temporary structures designed to last no more than 15 years, and built in the 1960s.[111]

The study notes that although schools in both sectors show concern for cleanliness, proper lighting and ventilation, and spaciousness of classrooms, MUN schools have "more limitations in these areas."[112]

In 1981, 22 percent of students were enrolled in nongovernment schools. That percentage had more than doubled to 46 percent by 1999.[113]

Raw Outcomes

Since 1988, students in MUN, PS, and PP schools have been administered tests in Spanish and mathematics under the government's SIMCE testing program. Until 1997, the available test-score data were either aggregated at the school level (rather than providing test-scores of individual students), or were unaccompanied by individual-level data on students' family backgrounds. All research based on pre-1997 data is thus apt to be less precise than research based on more recent per-pupil data.

One finding that has been consistent across all periods and all studies is that the raw test-scores break down by school type as follows: They are highest among students in PP schools, next highest among PS schools, and lowest among MUN schools. From the mid-1990s onward, as some PS schools began charging parents directly for a portion of the cost of their children's education, these schools' test scores were found to be higher than those of subsidized schools that did not require a parental co-payment.

Vegas, for example, finds that PP school students score two full standard deviations (a very large difference) above MUN school students, that Catholic subsidized schools score .80 of a standard deviation above MUN schools, and that secular private schools score .50 of a standard deviation above MUN schools. Sapelli and Vial report the following raw score averages from 1998: MUN, 238; PS (no co-pay), 248; PS (co-pay), 260.5; PP, 299.5.[114]

The rate at which students repeat grades also differs from one school type to the next. Patrick McEwan found that the percentage of students having repeated at least one grade was 29 percent in MUN schools, 23 percent at secular PS schools, 14 percent at Catholic PS schools, and 11 percent at PP schools.[115]

Because student socioeconomic status is correlated with school type, and because selection into particular school types is also correlated with many other factors, these raw figures cannot be used to draw conclusions about the relative effectiveness or efficiency of the different school types. The sections that follow describe various attempts at controlling for some or all of these factors to isolate the effects of school type on educational outcomes.

Simple OLS Regressions of Academic Outcomes by School Type

Until recently, the most common mathematical model applied to the Chilean data was an Ordinary Least Squares regression controlling for family income and parents' levels of education. Studies of this kind have shown mixed results. In 2000, using school-level data, McEwan and Carnoy found a substantial and statistically significant positive effect favoring PP schools. Two years later, however, McEwan found no significant benefit from attendance at these schools.[116] Vegas, corroborates the earlier McEwan and Carnoy result, finding a large (1.00 standard deviation) positive effect for unsubsidized schools.[117]

McEwan generally finds a small, statistically significant benefit to attendance at PS schools, but concludes that this is due entirely to the benefit of attending Catholic subsidized schools—secular PS schools, he finds, have no significant effect on student achievement. These results are similar to Vegas's, who found a .25 standard deviation effect size for Catholic subsidized schools, but no effect for secular PS schools.

292

Correcting for the Problem of Selection Bias

As noted earlier, OLS estimates assume that selection into a particular school type is exogenous, which is to say there are no unobserved variables correlated with both parents' selection of school type and student outcomes. If this assumption is wrong, then the results of OLS estimates will be biased.

Dante Contreras explored this issue in 2002, using private school availability (which differs substantially from region to region) as an instrument for school choice. The hypothesis he tested was that the availability of private schools in a given area was correlated both with the likelihood of actually choosing a private school and with test scores. His findings confirmed the hypothesis, revealing that OLS estimates were indeed biased. Under Contreras's two-stage least squares model, the benefit of attending a PS school more than doubled (compared with the biased OLS estimate). PP schools were found to have an even larger benefit than PS schools. From these findings, Contreras concluded that "the previous literature has overestimated the impact of parental education and underestimated the impact of the voucher system in providing better education."[118]

Sapelli and Vial also controlled for selection bias using variables known to be associated with test scores, including region variables that captured the effect of school availability on school selection. After all these controls, they found that a student taken at random from the entire population would not gain significantly from attendance at a private school (this scenario is known as the "Average Treatment Effect" or ATE). Separately, they compared how well the typical PS school student performed in his current school versus how well he would be expected to perform in a MUN school. In this scenario (known as "Treatment on the Treated" or TT), they did find a significant benefit to attendance at a PS school. Importantly, they noted that the TT effect persisted at all income levels. This finding is consistent with the idea that parents who chose private schools do so because they think their children will do better there, and that they are in fact correct in so thinking.[119]

What makes the Sapelli and Vial paper unique in the Chilean "voucher" literature is that it goes on to break out the effect of varying per-pupil expenditures on sectoral differences in achievement. As noted previously, many MUN schools spend more per pupil than the central government subsidy, receiving additional financing from their municipal governments. Although evidence for an overall positive relationship between expenditures and achievement in public schools is weak in rich countries, there are several studies finding such a link in less developed countries (where public school spending levels are quite low to begin with).[120]

To ascertain the effect of varying MUN school expenditures, Sapelli and Vial break MUN schools down into five quintiles, corresponding to the total amount they receive from local and national government sources over and above the basic per-pupil subsidy. In the first quintile, MUN schools spend an average of 112 percent of the per-pupil subsidy, whereas in the fifth quintile they spend an average of 171 percent of the per-pupil subsidy. MUN schools in the first quintile are thus argued to be those whose expenditure levels are most comparable to the average expenditure among PS schools.

In analyzing these expenditure-grouped results, the researchers found that the Average Treatment Effect for attending a PS school was small but positive and significant for the first three quintiles, slightly negative in the fourth quintile, and very substantially negative (1.5 standard deviations) in the fifth quintile (where MUN schools are spending 71 percent more than the per-pupil subsidy). Perhaps also accounting for some of the dramatic jump at the fifth quintile is the fact that MUN schools in this group are more likely to be academically selective in their admissions.

The effect of Treatment on the Treated (i.e., how much the typical PS school student is expected to gain from actually attending a PS school) follows a similar pattern but is much larger in the first three quintiles. In quintile one, where MUN and PS schools are asserted to have similar per-pupil spending, the TT effect is half of a standard deviation. The TT effect is still very large and negative in quintile five.

Summarizing their results, Sapelli and Vial conclude that higher-spending MUN schools have skewed the results of earlier studies, causing them to underestimate the positive impact of PS schools. There is, however, a potential problem with their analysis in that it does not also factor in any additional funds spent by those PS schools that receive parental co-payments under the *Financiamiento Compartido* program. The reason for this omission, according to one of the researchers,[121] was practical: Per-school data were not available on the amount of funds PS schools raised through parental co-payments. Concluding that the average level of co-payment funding was less than the average level of additional expenditure by MUN schools, they concluded that their analysis was fundamentally sound, but in the absence of PS per-school co-payment data, this conclusion remains an open question.

In an earlier paper, Sapelli and Vial calculated a three-way comparison of MUN, PS, and PP schools controlling for school availability and student/family characteristics. They concluded that PP schools had a moderate-to-large ATE when compared with MUN schools (.33 of a standard deviation in language and .50 in math), and that PS schools had a smaller but still statistically significant effect (.20 of a standard deviation in both subjects).[122] Interestingly, children from the poorest decile of families gained far more in mathematics (nearly .90 of a standard deviation) from attending PP schools instead of MUN schools than any other group. Given their very limited financial means, it must be surmised that these students had their tuitions underwritten by the schools.[123]

It should be noted that none of the findings reported in this section had controls for peer-group effects.

Redistribution of Students—Competition through Creaming?

In their 2002 paper, Hsieh and Urquiola assert that the Chilean subsidy program has not been responsible for any improvement in overall student achievement, having instead simply redistributed high-SES (and hence generally higher achieving) students to the private sector.[124]

To make their point, they concentrate on data from the first seven years of the subsidy program, arguing that this is the period during which it had its largest and strongest effect.[125] Specifically, the biggest shift out of MUN schools and into PS schools occurred before 1990, though it continued at a slower pace thereafter.

One of Hsieh and Urquiola's first observations is that, in 1988, public school test scores were lower in communities with higher private-sector enrollment.[126] They suggest that this is consistent with the idea that PS schools "skimmed" off the best students (the "cream") from public schools, causing MUN school test scores to fall. They also acknowledge that the direction of causality may be reversed, that is, that areas in which MUN schools performed especially poorly may have driven a greater percentage of parents to seek alternatives in the private sector.

They attempt to disambiguate between these two causal explanations by looking at trends over time, showing an association between rising PS enrollment rates and declining MUN performance. This, however, is inconclusive. Continued "skimming" could cause a continued decline in MUN scores, but continued poor MUN performance could also perpetuate a continuing out-migration from MUN to PS schools. Both causal explanations remain valid possibilities, as does some combination of the two.

Hsieh and Urquiola's next observation is that, in 1988, more established PS schools had higher average SES than recent start-ups.[127] This pattern, they point out, is consistent with the idea of the "early bird getting the worm" in the cream-skimming process, that is, that the first PS schools on the scene attracted the highest SES students, leaving fewer such students for later entrants to the market. This is certainly consistent with the notion that high SES families would likely be better informed of their educational options than low SES families, and hence more apt to be early adopters of the newly introduced PS school option. It is also consistent, however, with the fact that private schools may have opened in the most commercially viable locations first—that is, those with the highest population densities—and only then begun to expand into lower density areas as the urban markets became saturated. Since population density (urbanicity) and SES are correlated, this would not necessarily connote creaming on the part of PS schools.

The SES distribution between PS start-ups and their more established competitors is a key premise in a central argument of their paper: that PS schools and the Chilean subsidy program as a whole do not contribute to higher overall student achievement, but instead simply shuffle around the high SES students and thereby do nothing more than change which schools end up with the high test scores.[128] To bolster their argument, Hsieh and Urquiola observe that average 1988 test scores were somewhat higher in established than in recently created PS schools.[129]

To argue that average educational outcomes for all students were not improved by the introduction of the subsidy program, Hsieh and Urquiola present four other empirical findings:

- After controlling for observable school and community characteristics, communes (districts) with a higher private enrollment share do not differ significantly from other communes in math scores, repetition rates, or student attainment (i.e., years of school completed).[130]

- After controls, communes with higher growth in private enroll-ment share between 1982 and 1988 do not differ significantly in educational outcomes from communes in which private enrollment grew more modestly.
- Nationwide, "average test scores did not change," though repe-tition rates did fall somewhat and school attainment did rise somewhat. (They note though that these last two findings are consistent with national income growth during the period).[131]
- Chile dropped one place in the international ranking of coun-tries participating in the 1970 and 1999 international tests of mathematics and science.

Taking the last observation first, a comparison between the Chilean and U.S. performance trends on these international tests would be, if anything, an argument for the United States to adopt Chile's private school subsidy program. Although Chile dropped by one place, the United States dropped by three while having maintained throughout the period a 90 percent public sector education monopoly.

The first three bullet points must also be considered in light of the period examined by Hsieh and Urquiola. The years 1982 to 1988 were a period of radical change in the Chilean education system, during which a disproportionate share of PS schools were newly formed, and during which many public schools were undergoing the shock of rapidly hemorrhaging enrollments. The growing pains suffered by newly formed schools could easily have impeded their ability to improve student achievement, and the relatively unex-pected losses of students in the public sector could have temporarily depressed MUN effectiveness.

If that indeed was the case, and if the subsidy system began to function as intended as the turmoil of its early years was overcome, two predictions would follow. First, test scores in the subsidized sector should have begun to improve after 1988, as PS schools created during the early-to-mid-1980s either matured and improved or were driven out of business by those that did. Second, the test score difference between schools that predated the subsidy program and those created to take advantage of that program should have dimin-ished or even disappeared over time.

Table 13-1
AVERAGE 4TH GRADE SIMCE SCORES BY SCHOOL TYPE,
1988–1996

Type of School	1988	1990	1992	1994	1996
Municipal	49.25	56.70	63.85	64.43	68.00
Private Subsidized	56.35	58.80	70.15	70.66	73.65
Private Unsubsidized	76.15	80.05	86.05	85.07	85.85

SOURCE: Françoise Delannoy, "Education Reforms in Chile, 1980–98: A Lesson in Pragmatism," World Bank Country Studies, Education Reform and Management Publication Series I, no. 1 (June 2000): 39. Available online at http://www1.worldbank.org/education/globaleducationreform/pdf/delannoy.pdf.

Addressing the first of these predictions is difficult because the SIMCE testing system was not guaranteed to be comparable from one year to the next until 1997.[132] To whatever extent trends in SIMCE scores do happen to represent actual achievement changes over time, however, they suggest the steady improvement of all three school types between 1988 and 1996 (see Table 13-1).

In an attempt to extract more reliable conclusions from the SIMCE data, Francisco Gallego came up with the idea of examining the MUN and PS scores as a fraction of the PP scores in any given year.[133] That approach, presented in Table 13-2, shows MUN and PS schools both closing the gap with PP schools over time. This is suggestive of improvement in the subsidized school sector, at least with respect to the more elite paid private school sector.

The second prediction also appears to be borne out by the evidence. According to Sapelli and Vial—

> Pre-reform schools are significantly better than post-reform schools in 1989, but the difference halves in 1993 and disappears in 1997. In 1997 both pre- and post-reform [private] schools are significantly better than municipal schools.[134]

The evidence discussed earlier also suggests that PS schools do as well or better than MUN schools even after controlling for student SES and selection bias, and these schools would not exist were it not for the introduction of the subsidy program.

The preceding analysis suggests that Hsieh and Urquiola were correct in noting that PS schools enroll students with somewhat

Table 13-2

TRENDS IN SIMCE SCORES BY SCHOOL TYPE AS A PERCENTAGE OF THE SCORES OF UNSUBSIDIZED PRIVATE SCHOOLS

Type of School	4th Grade						8th Grade					
	1988	1990	1992	1994	1996	1999	1989	1991	1993	1995	1997	2000
Municipal	64.7	70.8	71.9	74.4	77.9	81.1	68.5	69.1	71.7	72.9	76.4	80.5
Private Subsidized	74.0	73.4	78.8	81.0	82.9	87.4	75.3	75.0	78.7	79.5	82.5	86.4

SOURCE: Gallego, "Competencia," p. 6.

higher SES. It also suggests that these researchers were mistaken in inferring from the SES difference that the subsidy program has not been associated with improved student achievement in the long term. The central flaw underlying their mistaken inference was their heavy focus on the tumultuous early years of the program.

Effects of Competition on Public and Private Schools

Performance does appear to have gone up in subsidized schools, and some positive ATEs and especially TTs are associated with PS versus MUN schools, but it remains to be seen if these effects have anything to do with market forces. Do competition and parental choice improve PS or MUN school performance? Hsieh and Urquiola present data for the early years of the program that suggest the answer may not only have been "no" in the case of MUN schools but also the growth of PS schools could actually have hurt MUN school performance.[135] Was this finding only a symptom of the developmental stage of the program, or does it persist? Are pseudo-market forces now associated with improved school effectiveness? Those questions were addressed in a recent paper by Francisco Gallego.

Using school-level data for 1994 to 1997, and controlling for average student and family characteristics and selection bias, Gallego concluded that the greater levels of competition faced by PS schools, and their greater responsiveness to competitive pressure, explains an important percentage of their superior performance with respect to MUN schools. Gallego also observed that, within the MUN sector, greater levels of competition were associated with improved performance, but to a lesser degree than is found in the PS sector.[136]

Gallego attributes the weaker MUN school response to competition to the different incentive structure that obtains in that sector, such as their greater use of government funds not tied to per-pupil attendance rates. Since the option of charging parental co-payments among PS schools was only introduced in 1993, and since only 40 percent of schools had adopted this practice by 1996, the incentive for PS schools to better serve their clients may have increased since the period analyzed by Gallego.

U.S. Privately Funded Scholarship Programs

Conditions

Over the past decade, a number of philanthropists and foundations have begun offering financial assistance (often called "scholarships," despite their lack of academic selectivity) to low-income families who wish to send their children to private schools. In several cases, these scholarships have been awarded through lotteries, allowing the effects of the programs to be evaluated as randomized field trials. A key advantage of the random allocation of students into lottery winners and losers is that it controls not only for observable differences in student and family characteristics but also for unobservable differences. Due to randomization, researchers can be fairly confident that scholarship winners and losers do not differ from one another on average in any respect other than their receipt (or not) of a scholarship.

Virtually all private scholarship programs have been located in urban areas, and their sizes have tended to be quite small (one or two thousand students is typical). Although the nationwide Children's Scholarship Fund provides financial aid to 40,000 pupils, these too are distributed in modest-sized groups, mostly in major cities, around the country.[137]

Private schools attended by scholarship students typically spend substantially less than public schools in the same neighborhoods. Since it can be argued that U.S. public schools undertake a wider range of activities than private schools, it has been suggested that public and private school expenditures are not directly comparable. To investigate this question, William Howell and Paul Peterson examined the programs of New York City in detail. They eliminated from their budgetary comparison all public school costs items that are absent (or at least noticeably lower) among most private schools (including transportation, special education, school lunches, and other ancillary services). They also excluded the "very substantial costs of the educational bureaucracy that manages the operations of the public schools at the city, borough, and district level." According to Howell and Peterson, even after "expenditures for all of these items are subtracted, public schools still spent more than $5,000 per pupil each year, more than twice the $2,400 per pupil spent by Catholic schools, fully 72 percent of which comes from tuition."[138]

Outcomes

In their book *The Education Gap*, Howell and Peterson studied academic effects of three private scholarship programs (in Dayton, New York City, and Washington, D.C.). They also compiled evidence on parental satisfaction levels in these three cities as well as among CSF participants around the country.

Effects of participation in the program varied starkly by race. White and Hispanic students saw no significant change in their academic achievement while African-American students gained .18 standard deviations after 1 year, .28 after two years, and .30 after 3 years of participation.[139] These averages, it should be noted, mask wide disparities from one city to another and from one year to another.

Scholarship programs also allowed recipients to attend schools with vastly lower rates of violence and classroom disruption, more frequent and deeper parent-school communication, and a greater availability of in-school tutoring and after-school services (despite their expenditures being roughly half those of comparable public school expenditures). It is not clear, however, if these private school characteristics would persist under a greatly expanded scholarship program.

Consistent with some of the international findings reported earlier, there was some evidence that achievement and class size were positively linked in private schools (i.e., larger classes were associated, weakly, with higher test scores).[140]

On all 16 measures of parental satisfaction gathered by the researchers, private school parents expressed more positive views. On 15 of those 16 measures, the percentages of parents "very satisfied" with particular school characteristics were two to four times higher than the corresponding public school parent percentages. The only measure for which the private school advantage was smaller was school location (in which private school parents were very satisfied 40 percent of the time versus 32.6 percent of the time for public school parents). To achieve an overall metric of parental satisfaction, Howell and Peterson aggregated parental answers to all the sub-questions, using all answers from "very dissatisfied" to "very satisfied," and then calculated an effect size of scholarship use in terms of standard deviations. The private school effect size for the three city voucher programs was .92 of a standard deviation. This was very similar to the .95 effect size found in the national CSF program, and both are very large effect sizes.[141]

It has been suggested that this difference could be due to a "reverse placebo effect" in which parents who participate in the voucher lottery but do not win vouchers become embittered toward the public schools in which they are forced to remain. This theory is contradicted by the evidence. In addition to the satisfaction data collected in the years after the lottery was held, data were also collected *before* the lottery was held. If the "reverse placebo" argument was right, satisfaction should have dropped when the control group parents learned that they had lost the lottery. Instead, there was a modest increase in their satisfaction with their public schools, though, as noted earlier, their satisfaction was dramatically lower than that of those who ended up in private schools.[142] Howell and Peterson also find that voucher applicants were not substantially more dissatisfied toward their public schools than the typical public school parent. As Howell and Peterson report for the cities they studied, and as RAND researchers conclude for the nation as a whole: "Those who used vouchers expressed an enthusiasm for their new private school unmatched by the typical public school parent."[143]

U.S. Publicly Funded Voucher Programs

Conditions

In addition to the privately funded scholarship programs just discussed, the United States also has publicly funded voucher programs in Cleveland, Milwaukee, and Florida. The Cleveland and Milwaukee programs offer vouchers to a small subset of low-income families living in those cities, while the Florida program offers vouchers to children statewide who are currently enrolled in public schools categorized as "low performing." The oldest of the programs is Milwaukee's, which enrolled roughly 11,000 children from across the metropolitan area in 2001–2002. It is limited to 15 percent of the enrollment in the Milwaukee Public School district. Cleveland's program had approximately 4,500 students in 2001–2002, while the Florida program had 47.[144]

Outcomes

Because vouchers were distributed by random lottery, Milwaukee's program could be evaluated as a randomized field trial (RFT), obviating the need to control for student characteristics or selection bias. Two randomized field trial analyses were performed using Milwaukee data from the mid-1990s when the program was about half its current size. The first analysis, done in 1996 by Jay Greene, Paul Peterson, and Jiangtao Du, found statistically significant gains (of slight to moderate magnitude) among voucher users in both mathematics and reading.[145] Cecilia Elena Rouse of Princeton University concluded in her 1997 analysis that voucher students' gains in mathematics were significant but that there was no significant difference between the treatment and control groups in reading.[146]

Before the findings just cited, John Witte, the government-appointed researcher for the Milwaukee voucher program, compared the performance of voucher students with a subset of public school students (rather than to the natural control group of lottery participants who did not win a voucher). In his final non-RFT study, Witte found only negligible academic differences between voucher students and his public school comparison group.[147]

During the period in which data for all of those analyses were collected, 80 percent of voucher students were concentrated in just three Milwaukee private schools, the program served just a few hundred children, and voucher recipients were forbidden to enroll in religious schools.

With regard to the Cleveland program, there is some question as to whether or not vouchers have consistently been handed out on a random lottery basis, allowing for RFTs comparing lottery winners and losers. According to a researcher at Indiana University, whose Center for Evaluation has been hired to assess the program, vouchers are indeed distributed by random lottery.[148] According to Howell and Peterson, however, "an RFT never was possible" in Cleveland. "Although vouchers initially were awarded randomly," they write, "a variety of administrative problems precluded holding an effective lottery; in the end, vouchers were offered to all applicants."[149]

To date, ICE researchers have followed two cohorts of voucher students. The final report on the first cohort found that voucher students were "significantly more likely to be from families of low income, headed by a single mother, and African-American than their public school counterparts."[150] It also concluded that "after controlling for initial differences in academic achievement and a limited set of demographic and classroom factors, scholarship students achieved at significantly higher levels than their public school counterparts in language and science. However, this was true only for students who attended private schools that existed prior to the Scholarship Program and did not apply to students attending private schools established solely to serve scholarship students." This result is, of course, similar to that observed in the Chilean subsidy program, wherein newly created private schools performed less well in their initial years than did preexisting private schools. Data from the Chilean case indicate that this disparity was gradually reduced to zero over time, but such long-term data are as yet unavailable from the Cleveland program. The ICE team has ceased to evaluate the ongoing performance of this cohort.

ICE's study of a second cohort in the Cleveland program found no statistically significant difference in student achievement at the end of grade two among any of four groups (those who had used vouchers since kindergarten, those who had used them only since the first grade, those who applied for but did not win vouchers, and those who did not apply for a voucher). The ICE team also noted that rejected voucher applicants began first grade at a disadvantage in language compared with voucher students who had attended private kindergarten, but that the rejected voucher applicants managed to mostly close this deficit during the first grade.

All researchers who have studied parental satisfaction among voucher recipients in Cleveland and Milwaukee have found voucher families to be significantly more satisfied with their schools than either applicants who did not win vouchers or public school parents who did not apply for vouchers.

Assessing the Five Feature Theory in Light of the Empirical Evidence

Table 13-3 provides a broad summary of the findings reported in the previous section.

Although this table is useful in revealing an overall pattern in the conditions and outcomes of private versus public schools, it glosses over important variations within sectors, and fails to identify the determinants of those variations. A series of separate analyses identifying these determinants and the variations they cause is presented below. The conclusions of those analyses will then be used to evaluate the relevance and accuracy of the theoretical predictions laid out at the beginning of this chapter.

The Impact of Parental vs. State Funding

With few exceptions, schools that are funded chiefly or entirely through tuition outperform schools that are funded chiefly or entirely by government agencies. Holding other factors constant,

Table 13-3
NUMBER OF FINDINGS ON SECTORAL DIFFERENCES IN
EDUCATIONAL CONDITIONS AND OUTCOMES

	Private Advantage	No Sig. Difference	Public Advantage
Achievement	20[1]	5[2]	2[3]
Efficiency	10[4]	—	1[5]
Parental Satisfaction	4[6]	—	—
Order/Discipline	3[7]	—	—
Graduates' Earnings	2[8]	1[9]	—
Condition of Facilities	2[10]	—	—

[1]Studies include Kingdon (India, aided private vs. public); Bashir (India, unaided private vs. public); Alderman et al. (India, aided private vs. public); James et al. (Pakistan); Jimenez and Lockheed (Indonesia); Jimenez and Lockheed (Philippines); Jimenez and Lockheed (Thailand); Jimenez and Lockheed (Tanzania); Angrist et al. (Colombia, PACES voucher program); Jimenez and Lockheed (Columbia); McEwan, 2000 (Dominican Republic, PP); McEwan, 2002 (Chile, PS and Catholic); Vegas (Chile, PS and Catholic); Contreras (Chile, PS); Sapelli and Vial, 2002 (Chile, PS); Sapelli and Vial, 2001 (Chile, PS and PP); Rouse (U.S., voucher); Howell and Peterson (U.S., private scholarships); Greene et al. (U.S., voucher); Metcalf et al., 1999 (U.S., voucher, preexisting private schools).

[2]Studies include McEwan, 2002 (Chile, PP); McEwan, 2002 (Chile, secular PS); Vegas (Chile, secular PS); Metcalf et al., 2001 (U.S., voucher, two newly created schools); Witte et al. (U.S., voucher).

[3]Studies include Lasibille et al. (Tanzania); Metcalf et al., 1999 (U.S., voucher, public schools vs. two newly created private schools).

[4]Studies include Kingdon (India, aided private vs. public); Kingdon (India, unaided private vs. public); Bashir (India, aided private versus public); Alderman et al. (Pakistan); James et al. (Indonesia); Jimenez and Lockheed (Philippines); Jimenez and Lockheed (Thailand); Lasibille et al. (Tanzania); Jimenez and Lockheed (Dominican Republic); Howell and Peterson (U.S., private scholarships).

[5]Studies include Bashir (India, public vs. unaided private schools).

[6]Studies include PROBE (India); Howell and Peterson (U.S., private scholarships); Greene et al. (U.S., voucher); Metcalf et al. (U.S., voucher).

[7]Studies include PROBE (India); Jimenez and Lockheed (Thailand); Howell and Peterson (U.S., private scholarships).

[8]Studies include Bedi and Garg (Indonesia); Glewwe and Patrinos (Vietnam).

[9]Studies include Yamauchi et al. (Philippines).

[10]Studies include PROBE (India); Sandra Cusato and Juan Carlos Palafox (Chile, high-performing PS vs. MUN schools).

every increase in the share of school budgets that is raised through tuition and fees contributes to increased achievement. There is, however, a diminishing return as the total share of the budget accounted for by parental contributions rises. Requiring a modest parental co-payment where none was previously required is thus apt to be of greater benefit than raising tuition from 80 percent to 100 percent of total school income.

The one notable exception to this overall pattern comes from Bashir's study of Tamil Nadu (where the government had imposed barriers to the creation of unaided schools), but those results appear not to be representative of Indian unaided schools as a whole, or even of unaided schools in Tamil Nadu itself (if, as seems to have been the case, less expensive unrecognized unaided schools were not considered).

Another indication that direct parental funding is associated with improved outcomes can be seen in the distribution of spending/ achievement correlations. The association between higher spending and higher achievement is very common among private unaided schools, less common among aided private schools, and rare among government schools.

The Impact of Private vs. Government Management

Holding constant the level of direct parental financing, private schools are generally more effective than public schools, implying a separate effect because of management structure and incentives.

Private schools, particularly those charging tuition, tend to have lower average per-pupil expenditures than public schools, often a great deal lower. They also allocate their funds differently. When not forbidden from doing so by law, private schools are much less likely to hire government-certified teachers. They also pay lower salaries, and they spend a smaller percentage of their budgets on salaries (placing greater importance, for example, on textbooks and teaching materials). Private schools seem to make wiser choices, and to get value for their money. The percentage of credentialed teachers in a school is not generally correlated with student achievement, and teachers' salaries appear to be positively and strongly correlated with student achievement in private schools but negatively (though negligibly) so related in government schools.

In most cases, private schools are more effective than government schools, and more efficient as well, given their lower expenditures. Academic achievement is usually significantly higher in private schools, holding student characteristics constant, and these gains are most often robust to controls for peer group effects when these are included. The earnings of private school graduates may be significantly higher as well, though the weight of evidence on this point is more limited.

Privately managed schools tend to have better-maintained facilities and more orderly classrooms than government schools. This is true whether the private schools are government subsidized or not, but the difference appears to be largest between unsubsidized private schools and government schools.

Private schools also seem more responsive to parental wishes in their course offerings and attention to individual students. In many countries, government schools shun the teaching of foreign languages despite the parental demand for such instruction. Private schools respond to this demand much more readily. Commenting on the greater frequency with which English is taught in private schools, one teacher in rural India asked a PROBE researcher, "Why should they pay us . . . if we don't give them something special?"[151] Parents also complained to PROBE researchers that public school teachers often ignored first-graders and children of lower castes, and the researchers noted that such complaints were much less common among parents of private school students.[152]

Summing up the generally more professional atmosphere found in rural private schools, the PROBE report noted "the key role of accountability" in private versus government schooling, stating that—

> In a private school, the teachers are accountable to the manager (who can fire them), and, through him or her, to the parents (who can withdraw their children). In a government school, the chain of accountability is much weaker, as teachers have a permanent job with salaries and promotions unrelated to performance. This contrast is perceived with crystal clarity by the vast majority of parents.[153]

The Impact of Competition

Increased competition sometimes leads to improved performance by public schools, but the relationship is both stronger and more consistent in the private sector. Chilean public schools were found to respond positively (though modestly) to heavier competition, but the response by private schools was greater. In some urban areas of Pakistan and India, even the poorest families are more likely to pay for unsubsidized private schooling than to send their children to free public schools, indicating that public schools have been failing to improve in response to competition. Because of their higher population densities, urban areas have consistently higher levels of competition and hence are more likely than rural areas to enjoy the benefits associated with competition.

There are several possible explanations for public schools' lower responsiveness to the presence of competitors. First, their services are usually free or at least substantially less expensive than those of private schools, and hence they may not need to provide superior or even comparable service quality to attract clients. This would partially explain the lower student achievement and inferior facilities maintenance at public schools. Public schools are also unlikely to be closed down by the government bodies overseeing them even if they fail to attract a significant student body. This pattern has, in fact, been observed by some of the researchers studying the Chilean subsidy system. In the most extreme cases (e.g., in Pakistan and India), state funding sometimes flows to district education bureaucrats or putative school managers even when they have neglected to open schools. There is no equivalent of these abuses in the private sector because parents do not pay tuition to nonexistent private schools.

The Quality of Parental Decisionmaking

Parents do appear to make wise decisions regarding their children's education. Evidence from Pakistan and Tanzania, for instance, suggests that parents not only could distinguish between different levels of academic quality but also chose their schools in part on the basis of those distinctions.

The interesting pattern in class-size effects between sectors is also suggestive. Readers will recall that class size was often found to be positively related to academic achievement in private schools (i.e., bigger classes have better scores) but unrelated or negatively related in public schools (i.e., bigger classes have worse scores). One plausible explanation for this finding suggested by Alderman et al. is that

309

the better private schools attract more students and, hence, have larger classes. This logic would be consistent with the fact that most of the private schools discussed in this chapter are located in less developed countries and are often serving low-income families within those countries, implying that the costs of expansion (in facilities and staff) might be a comparatively high hurdle for them to overcome. This circumstance would tend to drive up class sizes within popular schools.

The fact that academically superior private schools attract large numbers of students despite their higher out-of-pocket costs to families suggests that parents do indeed make better decisions regarding their own children's education than do the bureaucrats who are operating public schools make on their behalf. That point of view finds further support in the prevalence of government requirements for official teacher certification despite the irrelevance of such certification to academic achievement.

The Impact of Regulation on Private Schools

Private schools that are funded chiefly or entirely by the state, and that are heavily regulated by the state, tend to behave similarly to government schools, and to be less efficient and effective than unaided schools (except in those situations in which the creation of unaided schools has been constrained by the government). In Uttar Pradesh, for example, private aided schools spend only slightly less than government schools and are only slightly more efficient than government schools. More autonomous private unaided schools, by contrast, are significantly more efficient than either government or private aided schools. In Tamil Nadu, where regulation of aided schools is looser, aided schools are significantly more efficient than government schools.

Tamil Nadu's regulatory hurdles to the creation of unaided schools, which were only eased during the mid-1990s, seem to have drastically limited the number of such schools created in that state and may have contributed to their higher costs (as compared with unaided schools elsewhere in India).

The Supply of Private Schools

Private schools exist wherever there is sufficient demand to sustain their operations, even in regions of extreme poverty. The notions

310

that private schools serve only the wealthy or that they are mostly selective and elitist institutions are emphatically contradicted by the evidence.

The supply of private schools has grown substantially when the out-of-pocket cost advantage of government schools has been reduced (as in Chile), and even when it has not (as in Pakistan and India). In Chile, where subsidies for private schools were introduced nationwide in the early 1980s, the private-sector share of total enrollments more than doubled over the ensuing 15 years, and continues to grow today. These findings contradict claims that private school supply would not expand in response to large-scale voucher or tax credit programs in the United States.

A cautionary note is advisable, however: Newly created schools seem to perform less well than established schools. This is true whether or not the new schools are established in response to the introduction of a government subsidy program. The experiences of Chile and Tanzania suggest that this inferiority diminishes over time, with the longer term Chilean data indicating that the difference eventually disappears entirely.

Assessing the Predictions

This section reviews the five predictions of the Five Feature Theory and tests their validity against the findings presented earlier.

1. When parents lack choice and control over their children's education, they are likely to have greater difficulty obtaining the kind and quality of educational services they seek. To the extent that an official curriculum is imposed by the state (thus greatly limiting parental choice and control), it is expected to precipitate social conflict (at least in pluralistic societies).

The first prediction of FFT was that reductions in parental choice would make it difficult for parents to secure the kind and quality of educational services they seek. Parental choice is indeed limited in most of the nations discussed previously, given that government schooling is usually offered either for free or at a substantially lower fee than private schooling. Under these circumstances, parents are under substantial financial pressure to send their children to government schools regardless of their educational preferences. PROBE researchers noted, for example, that the majority of parents they surveyed would opt for private schools if it were not for their higher out-of-pocket cost. Some portion of government school attendance thus seems to result from financial expediency rather than from a free choice between two equally costly educational options.

Under FFT, government schools should therefore tend to provide lower levels of educational effectiveness and efficiency than private schools, and this does indeed appear to be the case. Several of the studies also reported that private schools were more responsive to the curricular demands of parents, particularly in the area of foreign language instruction (usually English). This too is in line with the first FFT prediction. Though state-mandated curricula were imposed in some of the nations or regions studied, no data were collected on the social effects associated with these curricula, and so this portion of the first FFT prediction cannot be addressed here.

2. Lack of competition between schools is expected to increase costs and decrease quality and efficiency, while also lessening the likelihood that schools will try to do their best with each and every child. It is also expected to be associated with inferior facilities maintenance and with parents having reduced access to concrete information on their children's performance.

Only one study (Gallego) specifically attempted to isolate the effects of competition, and it found that increased competition is associated with improved academic quality. A great deal of indirect evidence can also be brought into play, however, because it has already been noted that government schools are generally much less exposed to competitive pressures than are private schools. We should therefore expect that government schools will on the whole suffer from the effects of reduced competition. This indeed is the case, as government schools typically had higher costs, inferior achievement, and lower efficiency.

The prediction that lack of competition would be associated with poor facilities maintenance also finds corroboration in the experiences of several nations, though relevant data were not collected in many cases.

Findings from the PROBE report offer some support for the prediction that government schools, insulated as they are from the full effects of competition, fail to do their best with every child they enroll. This is too meager a basis, to be sure, to reach a solid conclusion on this point. There is also insufficient evidence on which to base any conclusion regarding the relative availability of information on student performance in more competitive versus less competitive environments.

3. Government restrictions on the creation and autonomy of schools are predicted to abbreviate the range of educational services available to families, preventing schools from offering the services desired by their specific clienteles. Caps on school fees and the imposition of government budgeting rules are expected to stifle innovation and expansion by making it difficult for schools to raise and allocate the funds necessary to pay for these activities. Lack of school autonomy, particularly in combination with lack of parental choice, may also result in a less communal and more disruptive school and classroom atmosphere.

Few studies explicitly collected data assessing the relationship between school autonomy and the diversity and responsiveness of schools, though some inferences can be made. Barriers to the creation of private unaided schools in Tamil Nadu may have contributed to the unusually small share of the market held by unaided schools in that state—thus all but eliminating that educational option for most families. It is also true that government school systems, with their officially determined curricula, are less responsive to many parents' demand for foreign language instruction.

Neither levels of innovation nor the expansion of successful schools were explicitly documented in the research covered in this study, so it is not possible to draw a link between these phenomena and budgetary autonomy. Given that Chile's private subsidy program forbade the private schools to charge tuition during its first decade, but then began allowing tuition fees after 1993, it might provide a good test bed for this question in future research.

According to anecdotal testimony related by Gulosino and Tooley, government rules concerning private school budgets appear to pose a range of operational difficulties for schools, including making it difficult for them to finance the upgrading of their facilities. That was not predicted by the FFT.

In India, Thailand, and the United States, classrooms were more orderly in relatively autonomous tuition-charging private schools than in other school sectors, just as predicted by the FFT.

A particularly widespread effect not predicted by the FFT is that government constraints on the creation and operation of private schools has led to the proliferation of unrecognized, unsanctioned private schools in several nations. Government attempts at controlling the characteristics of private schools have thus often led to the opposite of the intended outcome: a profusion of informal and unregulated "underground" schools.

There is also evidence from India that more extreme levels of government regulation of private schools are associated with lower academic achievement and/or efficiency. In Uttar Pradesh, autonomous unaided private schools significantly outperform tightly regulated aided schools. The aided schools of Tamil Nadu seem to perform substantially better under their lighter regulatory burden. This was not specifically expected under the FFT.

4. Reducing or eliminating direct payment of tuition by parents is predicted to erode parental control and choice (leading to the problems associated with low parental choice), and increase corruption and fraud. Since state education funding is generally associated with comprehensive state regulation, it is also likely to decrease the level of meaningful competition among schools by homogenizing the services they offer. The extent of the damage caused is suggested to be proportional to the reduction in parental fees.

Many of these negative outcomes appear to be borne out by the empirical evidence. The Indonesian findings by James et al. show that direct financial responsibility is positively and significantly correlated with school efficiency. This finding is consistent with the FFT prediction to the extent that lower levels of direct parental funding insulate schools from competitive pressures, lessening their incentive to operate efficiently.

The cases of India and Pakistan reveal a stark contrast between government-funded schools and tuition-charging private schools. Pakistan's government schools are generally viewed as being in widespread disarray, appear to be academically inferior to private fee-charging schools, and are shunned by most of the poor in urban areas, who instead opt for fee-charging schools.

Kingdon finds tuition-charging private schools to be significantly more effective and efficient than government-funded private schools. The private schools found by PROBE researchers to be much better maintained and more actively engaged in teaching than their government counterparts were virtually all unaided schools.[154] Only Bashir's findings on Tamil Nadu cloud this picture, and these, as discussed earlier, are not representative of unaided schools in India as a whole or perhaps even in Tamil Nadu itself.

Government funding intended for public schools in these countries appears to be misspent, squandered, or embezzled with alarming frequency—a problem not commonly observed in schools that parents pay directly for their children's education.

The predicted positive relationship between government funding and government regulation is also evident in most of the nations covered in this study. In India, for example, aided schools are pervasively controlled by the government, though there is some variation from state to state. This regulation appears to impede the effectiveness and efficiency of aided schools in proportion to its breadth and depth (with less intrusively regulated schools in Tamil Nadu doing better than aided schools in other states). Thailand's offer of government funding to "elite" private schools was also accompanied by a heavy regulatory burden, and the Chilean Subsidy program initially forbade tuition-charging at subsidized private schools.

5. Lack of the profit motive is expected to stifle innovation and impede the process by which more effective schools would expand and either take over or crowd out their less effective competitors. It is also argued to dull the incentive for cost-cutting and efficiency, discourage entrepreneurs from entering the profession, and discourage the most ambitious and proficient educators from remaining in the profession in the long term.

Conclusions on this prediction are difficult to reach with any certainty given the lack of explicit comparisons of for-profit with nonprofit schools, the prevalence of regulations affecting private school budgets and fees, and the contradictory nature of the few suggestive findings available. In Chile, for instance, nonprofit Catholic schools are generally found to outperform secular private schools, and McEwan has stated that "many" secular private schools are operated for profit. Neither McEwan nor any of the other researchers to publish on Chilean education appear to have actual figures on the total percentage of private schools that are operated for profit, however, or on the relative performance of for-profit versus nonprofit schools. Neither has any effort been made to compare total per-pupil expenditures between Catholic and secular subsidized schools in Chile. Finally, subsidized schools had no control over their per-pupil income for the first 11 years of the program, being forbidden to charge fees, and this substantially alters the context in which profit-maximizing behavior would be expected to take place.

In the Dominican Republic, Jimenez and Lockheed found that nonprofit religious schools are far less efficient than secular private schools, and that secular private schools are "often" operated for profit. Again, no actual breakdown is provided on the proportion of secular schools operated for profit.

Theory, Evidence, and Education Tax Credits

The Five Factor Theory appears to be substantially corroborated by the pattern of empirical findings discussed here. Several predictions are not fully addressed by the available evidence, but contradictory findings are few and supportive ones are numerous.

Knowing that the Five Factors do seem associated with superior educational conditions and outcomes, we are left with the question of how best to reintroduce them in nations where they are hobbled or absent. In my book, *Market Education: The Unknown History,* I argued that a two-part state tax credit program was the best approach. The first part of the program would allow individuals and businesses to take dollar-for-dollar tax credits against donations to private scholarship organizations, much like the ones studied by Howell and Peterson. Low-income parents would then receive scholarships from these organizations to cover most (or all, in the case of the very poor) of the cost of their children's education. For parents who could afford it, a sliding co-payment, based on ability to pay, could be required. The second part of the program would allow any parent not enrolling their child in a government school to take a nonrefundable tax credit to help them cover the cost of their child's education.[155]

My chief reason for advocating these tax credits over a voucher program was that they could preserve a higher level of direct financial responsibility for parents. Some analysts have dismissed this argument, asserting that it does not matter *whose* money is paying for a child's schooling so long as parents control *where* the money is spent.[156] The facts examined in this study call that dismissal into question. Schools to which parents pay some or all of the costs from their own pockets *do* appear to offer superior conditions and outcomes to schools to which the state pays most or all of the costs, even when parents have a choice of state-subsidized schools. Moreover, schools that are mostly or fully funded by the state tend to be much more heavily regulated than parent-funded schools—and extensive government regulation of schools seems to have a negative effect on educational outcomes. This tendency has proved to be true whether or not funding follows the students.

On the issue of regulatory encroachment, it has been asserted that tax credit programs would attract just as much regulation as vouchers. To date, there is insufficient empirical evidence to determine the merit of that assertion. Even if the assertion is true, however, it does not address the fact that direct parental financial responsibility is also associated with improved educational conditions and outcomes. On the whole, therefore, the findings of this study seem to lend additional support to the arguments I have previously presented favoring nonrefundable tax credits over vouchers.

Rather than rehashing those arguments more extensively here, I would direct readers to my book, *Market Education: The Unknown History* as well as to the Fall 2002 issue of *The Independent Review*, in which I present the case for tax credits over vouchers. In the same issue, Joseph Bast presents the case for vouchers over tax credits.[157]

The constituency that seems poised to benefit most substantially from the introduction of an education tax credit program is the population of large cities. Those densely populated areas offer the greatest prospects for a wide range of educational choices and vigorous competition among schools, making them the ideal starting point for an incremental phase-in of tax credits. Another paper, published in the *Oklahoma Policy Blueprint* outlines just such an "urban-first" phase-in of education tax credits, pointing out that it would also help to ensure revenue neutrality.[158]

Notes

1. See Andrew J. Coulson, *Market Education: The Unknown History* (New Brunswick, N.J.: Transaction, 1999).

2. For example, see Andrew J. Coulson, "Toward Market Education: Are Vouchers or Tax Credits the Better Path," Cato Policy Analysis no. 392, February 23, 2001. Available online at http://www.cato.org/pubs/pas/pa392.pdf.

3. Two exceptions to the novelty of the data used in this chapter are the studies of the Cleveland and Milwaukee voucher plans, which were considered peripherally in my earlier work, and are again discussed here because of their high profile in the U.S. education policy debate.

4. Coulson, 1999, pp. 294–297.

5. Ibid., pp. 297–299.

6. Ibid., 1999, pp. 269–272.

7. Ibid., 1999, p. 274.

8. For a more elaborate discussion, see Ibid., Chapters 9 and 10.

9. Ibid., pp. 294–297.

10. Ibid., pp. 301–302.

11. Ibid., pp. 299–301 and 343–345.

12. Ibid., pp. 268–269.

13. Ibid., pp. 297–299.

14. Ibid., pp. 304–306.

15. Geeta Gandhi Kingdon, "Private Schooling in India: Size, Nature, and Equity-Effects," *Economic and Political Weekly* 31, no. 51 (1996): 3306–3314. Available online at http://www.econ.ox.ac.uk/Members/geeta.kingdon/PublishedPapers/private-schoolinginindia.pdf. See p. 8 of online version.

16. Ibid., p. 24 of online version.

17. Students at unrecognized schools can pay a fee to take official exams at recognized schools and thereby earn officially recognized degrees, though the cost of doing so is substantial for poor parents.

18. James Tooley, "Serving the Needs of the Poor: The Private Education Sector in Developing Countries," in *Can the Market Save Our Schools*, ed. Claudia R. Hepburn (Vancouver, B.C.: The Fraser Institute, 2001).

19. The five states are Bihar, Madhya Pradesh, Rajasthan, Uttar Pradesh, and Himachal Pradesh.

20. Anuradha De, Jean Drèze, Shiva Kumar, Claire Noronha, Pushpendra, Anita Rampal, Meera Samsom, and Amarjeet Sinha, *The PROBE Report: Public Report on Basic Education in India* (New Delhi: Oxford University Press, 1999).

21. The PROBE team indicated that unrecognized schools had probably been under-counted. See De et al., p. 103.

22. Ibid., p. 104.

23. Ibid., pp. 40–41.

24. Ibid., p. 43.

25. Ibid.

26. Ibid., p. 104.

27. Ibid., pp. 103–104.

28. Ibid., p. 103.

29. Kingdon, "Private Schooling in India," p. 25.

30. De et al., p. 104.

31. Headteacher is the Indian (and British) term for school principal. In very small schools, it is more accurate to think of a headteacher as a teacher with administrative duties than as an administrator with teaching duties.

32. De et al., p. 47.

33. Ibid., p. 63.

34. Lydie Ehouman, Sandra Fried, Theresa Mann, Haroon Ullah, "Tamil Nadu: The Path to Becoming India's Leading State," a study conducted for the government of Tamil Nadu by the Center for International Development, Kennedy School of Government, Harvard University, 2002, p. 45. Available online at http://www.cid.harvard.edu/india/docs/KSG percent20student's percent20paper.pdf.

35. Ibid., p. 64.

36. Ibid., p. 102.

37. Ibid., p. 104.

38. Ibid., p. 102.

39. Ibid., p. 104.

40. Geeta Gandhi Kingdon, "The Quality and Efficiency of Private and Public Education: A Case Study of Urban India," *Oxford Bulletin of Economics and Statistics* 58, no. 1 (1996): 55–80. Note that Kingdon did not compare parents' total nontuition expenses (e.g., clothing/uniforms, transportation, textbooks, students' school supplies), which do tend to differ from one sector to another, and can be substantially higher among students attending private unaided schools. It is difficult to determine how these figures should be compared. However, some parents may choose to spend more than others on items such as clothing and school supplies, but such variations have little or nothing to do with the efficiency of the schools their children attend. A rough attempt at controlling for these cost variations is nevertheless attempted below, using data from De et al. and Sajitha Bashir, "The Cost Effectiveness of Public and Private Schools: Knowledge Gaps, New Research Methodologies, and an Application in India," in *Marketizing Education and Health in Developing Countries: Miracle or Mirage?*, ed. Christopher Colclough (Oxford: IDS Development/Clarendon Press, 1997).

41. Geeta Gandhi Kingdon, "Efficiency of Private Education," pp. 55–80. To isolate and accurately determine the effects that school type has on student achievement, we need to either eliminate or compensate for any nonrandom selection of children into different school types on the basis of unobserved characteristics that may affect achievement. In other words, we need to either ensure that students are randomly assigned to the different school types (impossible in the current scenario) or we need to mathematically compensate for the nonrandom nature of student selection into particular school types. Failing to do this will result in selection bias, by which unobserved factors may affect both the type of school a given child attends and that child's achievement.

42. Geeta Gandhi Kingdon, "Efficiency of Private Education," p. 26.

43. Sajitha Bashir, "The Cost Effectiveness of Public and Private Schools: Knowledge Gaps, New Research Methodologies, and an Application in India" in *Marketizing Education and Health in Developing Countries: Miracle or Mirage?*, ed. Christopher Colclough (Oxford: IDS Development/Clarendon Press, 1997).

44. This expenditure included not only tuition but also the cost of clothing, transportation, and other items. It is a total out-of-pocket cost estimate derived from parental surveys.

45. Bashir states that "Government regulation [of unaided schools] is confined to ensuring that prescribed standards for physical infrastructure [e.g., large school grounds] and initial endowments [a cash bond] are adhered to." See Bashir, "Cost Effectiveness", p. 139. Unrecognized schools do not adhere to these requirements because of their high cost, as noted in the *Conditions* section. The PROBE team also pointed out that unrecognized schools can be hard for researchers to locate because they do not appear on government lists and do not maintain a conspicuous presence. Bashir also indicates that all of the unaided schools in her sample were "matriculation schools," which are necessarily government-recognized. See P. Duraisamy, Estelle James, Julia Lane, and Jee-Peng Tan, "Is There a Quantity-Quality Trade-Off As Enrollments Increase? Evidence from Tamil Nadu, India," World Bank Research Report, 1997, pp. 12–13. Available online at www.worldbank.org/html/dec/Publications/Workpapers/WPS1700series/wps1768/wps1768.pdf.

46. P. Duraisamy et al., "Is There a Quantity-Quality Trade-Off," p. 30.

47. Geeta Gandhi Kingdon, "Private Schooling in India: Size, Nature, and Equity-Effects."

48. Duraisamy et al., "Is There a Quantity-Quality Trade-Off," p. 6.

49. In Tanzania, teachers' salaries are positively and strongly correlated with higher achievement in the private sector but not in the public sector (where the correlation was actually reversed, though negligible in magnitude). See the section below on Tanzania for details.

50. See, for example, Coulson, 1999, p. 269.

51. Jason Burke, "Where State Fails, Others Give Poor a Chance: Official Corruption and Indifference Have Wrecked the Education System, So People Are Turning to a Range of Private Schools," *The Guardian*, February 28, 2000. Available online at http://education.guardian.co.uk/Print/0,3858,3968295,00.html.

52. Burke, "Where State Fails."

53. World Bank, "Assistance to Private Schools Serving Poor Children: Pakistan." Available online at www.worldbank.org/education/economicsed/finance/demand/demfin/assistance_to_private_schools_pk.htm

54. Masooma Habib, "Education in Pakistan: All Demand and Little Supply," paper presented at the Pakistan Economic and Social Development Conference, March 7, 1998, MIT Sloan School of Management. Available online at www.care.org.pk/About_care/press/Masooma_Habib.htm.

55. Harold Alderman, Peter F. Orazem, and Elizabeth M. Paterno, "School Quality, School Cost, and the Public/Private School Choices of Low-Income Households in Pakistan," *Journal of Human Resources* 36, no. 2 (2001): 304–326.

56. World Bank, "Poverty in Pakistan: Vulnerabilities, Social Gaps and Rural Dynamics," conference presentation, Islamabad, January 8, 2003. Available online at http://lnweb18.worldbank.org/sar/sa.nsf/Attachments/Presentation-Poverty/$File/Presentation-Poverty.pdf.

57. Fifteen percent of children in the rural areas of Punjab are enrolled in private schools, while 40 percent of urban children are enrolled in private schools. Note that this does not imply that all of the other children were enrolled in public schools but rather that they were either not in school at all *or* they were enrolled in public schools. See Burke, "Where State Fails."

58. Alderman, Orazem, and Paterno, "School Quality, School Cost," pp. 5–6.

59. Ibid., p. 19.

60. Arjun S. Bedi and Ashish Garg, "The Effectiveness of Private Versus Public Schools: The Case of Indonesia," *Journal of Development Economics* 61 (2000): 463–494.

61. Estelle James, Elizabeth M. King, and Ace Suryadi, "Finance, Management, and Costs of Public and Private Schools in Indonesia," *Economics of Education Review* 15, no. 4 (1996): 387–398.

62. Ibid.

63. James, King, and Suryadi, p. 393.

64. Ibid., p. 395.

65. Arjun S. Bedi and Ashish Garg, "The Effectiveness of Private Versus Public Schools: The Case of Indonesia," *Journal of Development Economics* 61 (2000): 469.

66. Ibid., pp. 480–481.

67. Ibid., p. 482. Emphasis in the original.

68. Ibid., p. 483.

69. Emmanuel Jimenez and Marlaine E. Lockheed, "Public and Private Secondary Education in Developing Countries, a Comparative Study," World Bank Discussion Paper no. 309, December 1995, p. 47.

70. Charisse Gulosino and James Tooley, "The Private Sector Serving the Educational Needs of the Poor: A Case Study from the Philippines," Working Paper, E. G. West Centre, School of Education, University of Newcastle, August 2002, pp. 2–4.

71. Jonathan Ablett and Ivar-André Slengesol, *Education in Crisis: The Impact and Lessons of the East Asian Financial Shock, 1997–99* (Paris: UNESCO, 2000), p. 23. Available online at http://unesdoc.unesco.org/images/0012/001233/123331e.pdf.

72. Jimenez and Lockheed.

73. Ibid., p. 56.

74. Ibid., p. 57.

75. See Futoshi Yamauchi, Kenn Ariga, Nipon Poapongsakorn, Joy Abrenica, Kiratipong, Tosmai, Sake, and Vanessa, "Why Do Schooling Returns Differ So Much? Observations and Puzzles from Thailand and the Philippines," Conference paper, October 2002. Available on-line at http://www.kier.kyoto-u.ac.jp/~ariga/download/ADBI2002/education3.pdf. See also Futoshi Yamauchi and Joy Abrenica, "Is Private School Premium Spurious? The Role of Private Schools in the Philippines," Conference paper, October 2002. Available online at http://www.kier.kyoto-u.ac.jp/~ariga/download/ADBI2002/education2.pdf.

76. Jimenez and Lockheed, p. 67.

77. Ibid.

78. Paul Glewwe and Harry Anthony Patrinos, "The Role of the Private Sector in Education in Vietnam. Evidence from the Vietnam Living Standards Survey," World Bank LSMS Working Paper no. 132, 1999.

79. Glewwe and Patrinos, "The Role of the Private Sector," p. 11.

80. Ibid., p. 22.

81. Gérard Lassibille, Jee-Peng Tan, and Suleman Sumra, "Expansion of Private Secondary Education: Experience and Prospects in Tanzania," World Bank Working Paper no. 12, revised draft of July 1999. Available online at www.worldbank.org/education/economicsed/finance/demand/related/Africa/Private.doc.

82. Jimenez and Lockheed, p. 37.

83. Ibid., pp. 35, 37.

84. Lassibille, Tan, and Sumra, "Expansion of Private Secondary Education," p. 6.

85. Ibid., p. 5.

86. Ibid., pp. 10–11.

87. Ibid., p. 44.

88. Jimenez and Lockheed, p. 40.

89. Another study using data from the early 1980s apparently corroborated the sectoral effects on academic outcomes found by Jimenez and Lockheed, but a copy of that study was not available at the time of this writing, and hence it is not reviewed here. See George Psacharopoulos, "Public Versus Private Schools in Developing Countries: Evidence from Colombia and Tanzania," *International Journal of Educational Development* 7, no. 1 (1987): 59–67.

90. Jimenez and Lockheed, p. 36.

91. Ibid., p. 40.

92. Ibid., p. 41.

93. Lassibille, Tan, and Sumra, 1999, p. 11.

94. Ibid., p. 45.

95. Ibid., pp. 22–23.

96. Jimenez and Lockheed, p. 28.

97. Joshua D. Angrist, Eric Bettinger, Erik Bloom, Elizabeth King, and Michael Kremer, "Vouchers for Private Schooling in Colombia: Evidence from a Randomized Natural Experiment," World Bank Working Paper, 2002, p. 4. Available online at http://www.nber.org/~confer/2002/si2002/angrist.pdf.

98. Jimenez and Lockheed, p. 30 and preceding pages.

99. Ibid., p. 22.

100. Angrist et al., p. 14.

101. Ibid., pp. 1–2.

102. Ibid., pp. 26–27.

103. Jimenez and Lockheed, p. 85.

104. Ibid. and World Bank, "Dominican Republic Assistance to Private Schools Serving Poor Children," Dominican Republic, Second Education Project, undated. Available online at http://www.worldbank.org/education/economicsed/private/case/dominican.htm.

105. Jimenez and Lockheed, p. 100 and subsequent pages.

106. Ibid., p. 101.

107. Claudio Sapelli and Bernardita Vial, "Evaluating the Chilean Education Voucher System," Instituto de Economia Pontificia Universidad Catolica de Chile, Working Paper, April 2002, p. 3. Available online at http://www.msu.edu/~herrer20/documents/ec823/papers/paper4.pdf.

108. Chang-Tai Hsieh and Miguel Urquiola, "When Schools Compete, How Do They Compete? An Assessment of Chile's Nationwide School Voucher Program," Working Paper, January 2002, p. 6. Available online at http://www.wws.princeton.edu/~chsieh/vouchers.pdf.

109. Sapelli and Vial, "Evaluating Chilean Voucher System," 2002, p. 4.

110. Sapelli and Vial, "Evaluating the Chilean Education Voucher System," Instituto de Economia Pontificia Universidad Catolica de Chile, Working Paper, second draft, June 2001.

111. Sandra Cusato and Juan Carlos Palafox, "Qualitative Study of Schools with Outstanding Results in Seven Latin American Countries," Research Report, UNESCO-Santiago, Regional Bureau of Education for Latin America and the Caribbean, 2002, p. 86. Available online at www.unesco.cl/pdf/laboratorio/study.pdf.

112. Ibid., p. 58.

113. Emiliana Vegas, "School Choice, Student Performance, and Teacher and School Characteristics: The Chilean Case," Research Report, Development Research Group, World Bank, Washington, D.C., 2001, p. 4. Available online at http://www.worldbank.org/wbi/B-SPAN/docs/school_chile_doc.pdf.

114. Ibid.

115. Patrick J. McEwan, "Public Subsidies for Private Schooling: A Comparative Analysis of Argentina and Chile," *Journal of Comparative Policy Analysis: Research and Practice* 4 (2002): 189–216.

116. Ibid.

117. Emiliana Vegas, "School Choice."

118. Dante Contreras, "Vouchers, School Choice, and the Access to Higher Education," Yale University Economic Growth Center, Discussion Paper no. 845, June 2002, p. 3.

119. Sapelli and Vial, "Evaluating Chilean Voucher System," 2002.

120. One of these studies is the James, King, and Suryadi "Schools in Indonesia," paper cited earlier. See p. 395.

121. Personal communication with Claudio Sapelli, March 18, 2003.

122. Sapelli and Vial, "Evaluating Chilean Voucher System," 2001, pp. 16–17.

123. Ibid., p. 17.

124. Hsieh and Urquiola, "When Schools Compete," p. 33.

125. Ibid., pp. 19 and 22.

126. Ibid., p. 21.

127. Ibid., p. 23.

128. Ibid., p. 33.

129. Ibid., p. 23.

130. Ibid., p. 25.

131. Ibid., p. 26.

132. Sapelli and Vial, "Evaluating Chilean Voucher System," 2002, p. 2.

133. Francisco A. Gallego, "Competencia y Resultados Educativos: Teoría y Evidencia para Chile," Central Bank of Chile, Working Paper no. 150, April 2002.

134. Sapelli and Vial, "Evaluating Chilean Voucher System," 2002, p. 6.

135. Hsieh and Urquiola, "When Schools Compete," pp. 24–25.

136. Gallego, "Competencia," p. 44.

137. See, for instance, William G. Howell and Paul E. Peterson, *The Education Gap. Vouchers and Urban Public Schools* (Washington: Brookings Institution, 2002), p. 29.

138. Ibid., p. 92.

139. Ibid., p. 151.

140. Ibid., p. 161.

141. Ibid., p. 175.

142. Ibid., p. 178.

143. Ibid., p. 184.

144. See http://www.SchoolChoiceInfo.org.

145. Jay P. Green, Paul E. Peterson, and Jiangtao Du, with Leesa Boeger and Curtis L. Frazier, "The Effectiveness of School Choice in Milwaukee: A Secondary Analysis of Data from the Program's Evaluation," Harvard University Occasional Paper no. 96-3, 1996.

146. Cecilia Elena Rouse, "Private School Vouchers and Student Achievement: An Evaluation of the Milwaukee Parental Choice Program," Working Paper, May 1997.

147. John F. Witte, Troy D. Sterr, and Christopher A. Thorn, "Fifth-Year Report: Milwaukee Parental Choice Program," Department of Political Science and the Robert M. La Follette Institute of Public Affairs, University of Wisconsin-Madison, December 1995. Available online at http://dpls.dacc.wisc.edu/choice/choice_rep95.html.

148. Personal communication with Natalie A. Legan, Research Associate, Indiana Center for Evaluation, March 10, 2003.

149. Howell and Peterson, 2002, p. 42.

150. Kim Metcalf, "Cleveland Scholarship Program Evaluation: 1998–2000," Technical Report, Bloomington, Ind., Indiana Center for Evaluation, 2001.

151. De et al., p. 104.

152. Ibid., p. 51.

153. Ibid., p. 64.

154. Fewer than five percent of the private schools found to be serving the rural poor by PROBE researchers were aided schools. See De et al., 1999, p. 103.

155. A tax credit is nonrefundable if it allows taxpayers to keep more of the money they earn, but it cannot result in a positive outlay from the government treasury to the taxpayer. All taxpayers, by contrast, can claim refundable tax credits, and if their tax liability is less than the value of the credit, they receive a payment ("refund") from the government treasury in the amount of the difference (up to the full value of the refundable credit). Refundable credits are, for all intents and purposes, equivalent to vouchers. For a further discussion of this issue, see Coulson, 1999, pp. 333, 373–374.

156. For example, see John Humphreys, "Funding School Choice: Vouchers or Tax Credits. A Response to Buckingham," *Policy* 18, no. 1 (Autumn 2002): 15–18. Available online at http://www.cis.org.au/Policy/aut2002/polaut02-3.pdf.

157. See Andrew J. Coulson, *Market Education: The Unknown History* (Brunswick, N.J.: Transaction, 1999); and "Giving Credit Where It's Due: Why Tax Credits Are Better Than Vouchers," *The Independent Review* 7, no. 2 (2002): 277–287. See also Joseph L. Bast, "Why Conservatives and Libertarians Should Support School Vouchers," *The Independent Review* 7, no. 2 (2002): 265–276.

158. Andrew Coulson, "Fulfilling a Promise: A Plan for Bringing Educational Freedom to All Oklahomans" in *Oklahoma Policy Blueprint*, ed. Brandon Dutcher (Oklahoma City: Oklahoma Council for Public Affairs, 2002). See particularly the final section.

Contributors

David A. Bositis is a senior political analyst at the Joint Center for Political and Economic Studies. Before joining the Joint Center in 1990, Bositis taught political science at George Washington University and SUNY-Potsdam. He has an M.A. and Ph.D. from Southern Illinois University.

Andrew J. Coulson is the Mackinac Center's senior fellow in education and a member of the Advisory Council of the E. G. West Centre for Market Solutions in Education at the University of Newcastle, United Kingdom. He is the author of *Market Education: The Unknown History* and has contributed chapters to books published by the Hoover Institution and the Fraser Institute, among others. Coulson has a B.Sc. in mathematics and computer science from McGill University.

Floyd Flake is the senior pastor of the Greater Allen A.M.E. Cathedral in Jamaica, Queens, and president of Wilberforce University in Ohio. He is also a senior fellow in social and economic policy at the Manhattan Institute as well as an adjunct fellow for the Brookings Institution Center on Urban and Metropolitan Policy. Flake served in Congress from 1986 to 1997. He founded Allen Christian School in Jamaica in 1982. He has a D.Min. from the United Theological Seminary in Dayton, Ohio.

Howard Fuller is the founder and director of the Institute for the Transformation of Learning as well as a distinguished professor of education at Marquette University in Milwaukee. He chairs the boards of the Black Alliance for Educational Options and the National Charter School Alliance. Fuller was the superintendent of Milwaukee Public Schools from 1991 to 1995. He has a Ph.D. in sociological foundations of education from Marquette University.

Frederick M. Hess is a resident scholar at the American Enterprise Institute and executive editor of *Education Next*. His books include

Revolution at the Margins, School Choice in the Real World, Spinning Wheels, and *Bringing the Social Sciences Alive.* A former high school social studies teacher, Hess has an M.Ed. in education and an M.A. and Ph.D. in government from Harvard.

Tracey Johnson is the former executive director of the Washington Scholarship Fund. During her five years at the Fund, she did extensive development work and established the scholarship movement's first parent resource center. She has also helped other scholarship organizations implement scholarship distribution programs. Johnson has a B.A. in government from American University.

Chaim Karczag is a research associate at the National Council on Teacher Quality. He has an M.A. in political science from Lehigh University.

Casey Lartigue Jr. is a senior partner with the D.C. K-12 Education Initiative, a project of the philanthropic organization Fight for Children. He is a former policy analyst with the Cato Institute's Center for Educational Freedom in Washington, D.C. The author of two widely quoted studies on education in the nation's capital, Lartigue is a much sought-after speaker about school choice and minority education issues.

Paul E. Peterson is the Henry Lee Shattuck professor of government and director of the Program on Education Policy and Governance at Harvard, a senior fellow at the Hoover Institution, and editor-in-chief of *Education Next.* Formerly, he directed the Center for American Political Studies at Harvard and the Governmental Studies Program at the Brookings Institution. He has written or edited more than 100 articles and 20 books. Peterson received his Ph.D. from the University of Chicago where he was a professor for many years.

Gerard Robinson is a doctoral candidate in policy studies at the University of Virginia where he serves as a graduate instructor for the Curry School of Education Forum on Educational Issues. He served as a legislative liaison for the D.C. Public Schools District from 1999 to 2000. Robinson has a graduate degree in education from Harvard.

Irasema Salcido is principal and founder of Cesar Chavez Public Charter High School for Public Policy in Washington, D.C. Before its founding, she worked for nine years in the D.C. public school system. She has an M.A. in education, administration, and social planning from Harvard.

David Salisbury is director of Cato's Center for Educational Freedom. Before joining Cato, he was president of the Sutherland Institute, a free-market think tank in Salt Lake City, Utah, and executive director of Children First Utah, a nonprofit group that provides scholarship funds for children to attend private school. He was on the graduate faculty of the College of Education at Florida State University for 13 years. Salisbury has a B.A. and Ph.D. from Brigham Young University.

Eric Wearne is a research assistant at the Georgia Public Policy Foundation and a doctoral student in Educational Studies at Emory University. A former public school teacher, he holds an M.A. in English Education from the University of Georgia.

Index